THE DOG MERCHANTS

Inside the Big Business of Breeders, Pet Stores, and Rescuers

KIM KAVIN

PEGASUS BOOKS
NEW YORK LONDON

THE DOG MERCHANTS

Pegasus Books Ltd.
80 Broad Street, 5th Floor
New York, NY 10004

Copyright © 2016 Imagine Media LLC

First Pegasus Books cloth edition May 2016

Interior design by Maria Fernandez

ISBN: 978-1-68177-140-3

10 9 8 7 6 5 4 3 2 1

Printed in the United States of America

Distributed by W. W. Norton & Company, Inc.

For all the ones who can still be saved

CONTENTS

LIST OF ABBREVIATIONS

America's Pet Registry, Inc. (APRI)

American Canine Association (ACA)

American Kennel Club (AKC)

American Society for the Prevention of Cruelty to Animals (ASPCA)

Fédération Cynologique Internationale (FCI)

Humane Society of the United States (HSUS)

Monmouth County Society for the Prevention of Cruelty to Animals (MCSPCA)

People for the Ethical Treatment of Animals (PETA)

Royal Society for the Prevention of Cruelty to Animals (RSPCA)

Society for the Prevention of Cruelty to Animals (SPCA)

US Department of Agriculture (USDA)

"Money will buy a pretty good dog, but it won't buy the wag of his tail."

—*Josh Billings*

INTRODUCTION

B uffalo steaks. That's what put me over the edge.

I was standing in the meat department at the grocery store, a package of ground turkey in one hand and my smartphone's Google app in the other, struggling to determine whether the free-range, nobody-was-cruel-in-the-making-of-this-food-product label was actually a cover-up to get my money into the coffers of some multinational factory farm, when I glanced up and saw buffalo steaks. They were a new offering, and they seemed as exotic as wildebeest next to the chicken breasts and sausage patties. The buffalo label screamed "all natural," too, right above a photograph of a big, open, grassy plain full of sunshine and fresh air, where the buffalo ostensibly roamed while the deer and the antelope played.

Yeah, right, I thought. *Maybe back in 1875.*

When I looked down the aisle again, it seemed different, almost as if I were viewing it through a fisheye lens. The moment felt a bit like vertigo, or as if I'd been sucked into *The Matrix*. Endless packages of chops and ribs and wings and thighs—all of it suddenly appeared to me not as food, but instead as a flowing river of neatly packaged cash. Somehow, even through my super-fandom of books including *Fast Food Nation* and *The Omnivore's Dilemma*, it was only in that moment that I truly understood the supermarket meat aisle is based not on food but instead on the smartly marketed products of a global food-producing industry.

Not long after that day, I found myself sitting at the top of the bleachers inside a barn where America's biggest legal dog auction is regularly held. I watched hundreds of Retrievers and Terriers and Hounds get sold to the highest bidders, many of them owners of large-scale commercial breeding farms (or, to use the more commonly applied term, puppy mills). The auction, at least for the people, was an upbeat and welcoming affair, with men, women, and children alike smiling and laughing, buying snacks and nachos from the concession room, and doing the math on whether any given dog could produce enough sellable puppies to justify owning and feeding her. To someone like me, who thinks of her own dogs as family, it was kind of like watching orphaned children being auctioned based on their looks. Need a blonde? Finding wiry hair easier to manage these days? Freckled complexion, coming up next at a cut-rate price!

As the hours upon hours of auctioneering went on, I at first felt frustrated by the sight of the dogs being sold to the highest bidder, then disturbed by the fact that my own dogs (a couple of wonderful mutts) would be considered worthless in this room, and then, finally, resigned to the fact that dogs, like that big case of meat in the supermarket, are ultimately a product—a smartly packaged, endlessly varied product that is legally for sale all around the planet. As with food, though, most of us don't think of the dogs that way. It simply doesn't occur to us that so much effort goes into establishing and controlling the marketplace, or that so much time goes into packaging and promoting the end product for sale. We love dogs, we coo over puppies, and our thought process pretty much stops there. It takes a sight like a dog auction to drive home the point that dogs are in fact a big business, and to open our minds about the sheer scope of the industry that we buy into with every beautiful pooch we bring home.

Like many people, I'm trying more and more these days to be a conscious consumer. Beyond reading grocery store labels, I'm carrying canvas grocery bags and eschewing plastic as if it's dripping in Iraqi oil. I'm seeking out farmers markets and family-owned shops instead of running my credit card through the machines that hackers love to target at big-box stores. I'm buying fuel-efficient cars and Energy Star–rated home appliances. I'm trying to find affordable clothes that aren't sewn by twelve-year-old girls in Bangladesh earning fifty cents a day. I'm tiptoeing daily through the minefield of meanings behind everything from "cage-free" to "humanely raised."

And now, after considering what I've seen during several years of researching this book, I am seeking new and better ways to think about dogs as a product before I hand over another cent to anybody who is selling them, breeders and rescuers alike. I am applying my role as a conscious consumer to the dog industry because, given what I have learned, I believe that no matter how much all of us love our pups, thinking of them as products—just like so many of the sellers do—is the only way we can truly change the dog industry for the better.

Most of us dog lovers, even if we've had pups all our lives, don't realize the truly staggering scope of the global market we enter with every purebred or mutt we welcome into our families. The American sector is the most saturated, with about half the households owning a dog. Continental Europe and the United Kingdom are still growing as markets, with about a quarter of the households owning a dog. A reasonable estimate is that some thirty million pet dogs are brought home around the world every year. Dog lovers could give a home to every single dog who has been abandoned in every single shelter, and millions more pups would be needed annually to satisfy consumer demand. The money spent buying dogs as pets represents income to small- and large-scale breeders, pet stores, public shelters, and private rescue groups of somewhere in the vicinity of $11 billion each year around the globe.

Now, those numbers are admittedly fuzzy; *all* numbers involving the buying and selling of dogs are estimates because no central databases exist (that's one reason, perhaps, that no book like this has ever been written, because it is so hard to pin down exactly what is going on in terms of cash flow in the dog business). Still, given the statistics available, it's reasonable to assume that the business of selling dogs has about the same value as the global IKEA brand. The sale of dogs generates the kind of money that all of Nevada, including Las Vegas, brought in on gaming revenues in 2013. Dog lovers spend as much to acquire pooches every year as Burger King paid in 2014 to buy Tim Hortons, creating the world's third-largest fast-food conglomerate. It's cash flow that people who own the action will battle to control, cash flow that leads to unscrupulous people starting cheap production facilities and smuggling operations everywhere from Missouri to Mexico to Poland, cash flow that leads to powerful marketing campaigns designed to sway our decisions as consumers. This is business income that entrenched breeding interests at the top of the dog market will fight to protect, and it is piles and piles of dough that nonprofit groups—raking in hundreds of millions of dollars a year in donations—want to keep collecting.

In any business where such big money is involved, problems from capitalist greed to outright corruption always will surface, and those of us trying to be conscious consumers can feel overwhelmed about trying to make a difference. The reality is that an individual purchase usually won't make the slightest dent in problems on a global industry scale. Take factory farms, for instance, and the conscious consumer's search for beef and chicken produced by farmers who meet a higher standard of animal care. The scope of multinational corporate control over the meat supply can be paralyzing, so much so that it leads to Googling until one gets vertigo in the meat aisle. Trying to support the "good guys" who raise animals on small, open farms instead of in disgusting, cramped conditions can seem almost impossible in the stores where most of us regularly shop. The "bad guys" have already bought up and relabeled the more wholesome brands of meat in an effort to keep taking our money without us realizing where it is going.

Here's the good news that I've discovered: When it comes to dogs, the endgame is not so clear. What each of us does when it comes time to buy a dog really can make a difference. So many of the worst offenders are such small players in this big global web that if conscious consumers can learn how to spot them, we can end them—by voting with our wallets to buy mutts and purebreds alike from people who treat *all* dogs well.

We buyers are an estimated $11 billion global force that is many, *many* times larger than any breeding operation or rescue organization anywhere on the planet. We conscious consumers are still far more powerful than every last one of the bad guys in this particular marketplace. We buyers can close the substandard puppy farms and empty even the highest-kill-rate shelters by giving money to responsible sellers of dogs. It can be done today if the majority of dog lovers become educated about the industry and spend our money accordingly.

In the following pages, all kinds of people who are involved in the production, marketing, and sale of dogs are portrayed: small-scale breeders, large-scale breeders, show dog promoters, dog auctioneers, puppy distributors, public shelter workers, private rescue volunteers, animal law experts, dog-savvy marketers, and more. There's reporting on a company that, at its peak, was selling as many as ninety thousand puppies a year. There's an in-depth look at the life of a man who once auctioned a single dog for $12,600. There's a deep-research tour of a shelter that went from high-kill to no-kill and now operates out of a $6 million facility. And there's the discovery of precisely how much some groups are willing to spend to buy our votes when it comes to dog-related legislation.

Each of these people, and many more in the following pages, offers another layer of understanding about the industry that generated the beloved dogs sleeping soundly in our living rooms. I've knit their stories together to create new understanding of the big picture of dog sales worldwide—where sometimes, unbeknownst to most of us, breeders and rescuers operate out of the very same room. Taken together, the stories in this book make clear that dog lovers, whether we care about purebreds or mutts or both, often have far more in common than we are led to believe by those doing the marketing, and we have a great deal more power than we ever imagined to mold the business however we'd like, for the good of dogs everywhere.

I don't know about anybody else, but I'm tired of feeling dizzy and manipulated while trying to shop responsibly. I'm beyond the naïve belief that one side of an argument is grand while any other viewpoint is inherently evil. With this book, I am trying to move the conversation forward so that all dog lovers can understand exactly what we are buying into, no matter which dog we choose as our own. I'm not on the side of the breeders, and I'm not on the side of the rescuers. I'm on the side of the dogs.

If you, like me, are interested in applying the rationale of a conscious consumer the next time you add a dog to your family, then please, read on. Together, we really can change the world. Dogs are an industry where, thank heavens, smart shopping still can make a major difference.

CHAPTER ONE

SETTING THE BASE PRICE

"The entrepreneur always searches for change,
responds to it, and exploits it as an opportunity."
—*Peter Drucker*

T wo signs, one on each side of the road, greet everybody who
drives southbound into Wheaton, Missouri. The first one, to
the right, is the official green rectangle marking the municipal
border along state Highway 86. It announces the population of this
place as 696 souls. The second sign, on the left, proudly proclaims
the half-square-mile city as the home of the 1996 state championship high school softball team, the Bulldogs. It most likely was
erected without the slightest hint of irony.

There was hardly a car in sight driving past these signs just
before ten o'clock on the morning of Saturday, October 5, 2013.
That could've been because of the gray storm clouds fast closing
in, or maybe the highway is pretty much empty for miles on most

days of the week, what with the nearest city of any real size being more than an hour or two away to the northeast, up in Springfield, or to the west, out in Tulsa, Oklahoma. And odds are this stretch of road was a lot more popular a couple of hours earlier, especially the mile or so of it that led to a third sign on that morning. This one was temporary and small, the kind of sign Realtors use to announce an open house on a street corner. It stated, simply, that there was an auction that day. If drivers didn't already know it, then they would have had no idea this sign had anything to do with dogs—or that they were driving into the heart of one of the biggest dog-breeding regions in the largest dog-buying nation on Earth—but it's the sign that everybody who had gotten up before dawn that morning had been watching for since they'd driven away from their homes with a hot cup of coffee and the hopes of making a little money or of scoring some good deals.

The arrow on that small sign pointed right, directing drivers to three side-by-side green barns past the intersection with Highway 76. That's where all the vehicles were on this chilly, rainy morning, in what otherwise seemed like the middle of somewhere that was about as close to nowhere as a person can get in the United States of America. A mess of sedans and pickups and SUVs and trucks towing trailers was parked scattershot all along the dirt driveway and grass leading up to the barns, much as they'd be if their drivers had arrived excitedly and wanted to be first through the gate to enjoy a day at a town fair. The license plates were from Missouri and Kansas and Oklahoma and Arkansas and Iowa. Some of the drivers, given the distance, had probably driven the night before and booked a room for about $50 at the Booneslick Lodge in Neosho, the nearest place with motels, about a half hour away.

Just before ten o'clock, a few stragglers hustled over the mud puddles and held the middle barn's door open for one another, as polite strangers do. Inside, the lights were bright and the mood was bubbly, sort of like the atmosphere before the opening notes are strummed at a concert. Four sets of metal bleachers surrounded a fenced-off area to the right, where a folding table, the kind you'd see at a bake sale, was beneath a podium branded with the Southwest Auction Service logo. In the space close to that fenced-off area, closer than the bleachers allowed, a good number of people had opened their own lawn chairs and settled in to ensure an unobstructed view. One might say they'd scored the best floor seats. There were families, some with kids in tow, as well as a number of couples. Most wore jeans, sweatshirts, and flannel. One or two of the men had on overalls, and nearly every face in the building was white. A few of the men draped their arms over the shoulders of the women sitting next to them, as comfortable as they might be on one of the countless Baptist or Methodist church pews in the area. Maybe a half dozen of the men in the bleachers, a minority sitting clustered together, wore button-down shirts, suspenders, hats, and beards suggesting that they might be Amish.

Green paw prints painted on the gray concrete floor led attendees from the doorway past the bleachers to the left, where six or seven people waited in line at the registration counter. Women behind the counter took their information: the person's name, address, and driver's license number or, if he had one, his USDA license number. The women did all of the paperwork with a smile and, when they could, used the first names of returning customers for a personal touch.

A stack of programs sat atop the counter for the taking. Each thirteen-page copy, stapled in the corner, had a bright orange cover and white pages printed on both sides with descriptions of the nearly three hundred dogs scheduled to be auctioned that day. Some people sat at nearby tables, drinking sodas purchased from the concession room and poring over each dog's listing the way quarter horse bettors scrutinize race cards at the track. Others simply handed over their information, got their numbered bidding card, and moved on, walking past the framed poster that so many dog lovers know from veterinarians' offices back home, the one that shows all of the recognized dog breeds in neatly ordered rows.

Some people stopped to chat and browse at the two folding tables near the bathrooms, tables staffed by APRI, and a dog supply company offering everything from ear cleaner to syringes. Most of the attendees, though, found their seats without delay. A girl in a pink sweatshirt and sparkly matching headband climbed up the bleachers to sit next to her parents, munching on nachos and looking appropriately put-upon for her teenage years, no doubt wishing she could instead be out somewhere with her friends. A woman nearby carefully laid down her seat cushion, the kind that are common at college football games, obviously anticipating a long day of trying to stay comfortable on the metal bleacher seats. Some sixty or seventy people were inside the barn as the auction was about to start, and the crowd would keep growing all day, sometimes to the point of creating a standing-room-only section. Everybody who had arrived early and staked out a good spot needed to mark their territory.

Down at the podium by the folding table, Bob Hughes, the owner of Southwest Auction Service, cleared his throat and took the microphone. His voice reverberated through the big speakers hanging from the barn's roof, bouncing off the walls and drowning out most of the barking that was coming from behind the closed door to an adjacent room. The crowd instinctively hushed, with some folks sitting up a little straighter and leaning forward to listen. Hughes seemed happy and calm, welcoming his customers with a smile just as he always has since starting out as an auctioneer back in 1988.

There was no way to know whether this day's auction would top his best sale to date, which, according to his marketing materials, brought in $514,371, or whether any of the dogs waiting in cages in the back would go for a better price than the most expensive dog he ever sold, an English Bulldog who went for $12,600. But the crowd seemed good, he recognized many of the faces, and he knew there was probably a fair bit of money in the room, so he got right down to business.

Several men helping out that day brought items to the table for display one by one, then acted as spotters, scanning the crowd for anyone who held up an auction number to bid on the prices Hughes called out in staccato succession: *Two hundred . . . two hundred . . . two hundred . . . do I hear two hundred . . . now two-fifty, two-fifty, over there for two-fifty. . . .* Among the spotters was Hughes's adult son, Chadd, wearing a pink, long-sleeved Oxford shirt with SOUTHWEST AUCTION SERVICE embroidered along one sleeve. He was a bit more stylish than his dad, having adorned his blue jeans with a belt covered in bling. "Ho!" Chadd shouted and pointed when he saw an auction card raised into the air. "Yah!" other spotters hollered and pointed as more bidders joined in, raising the prices as they competed from around the room to win the best deals.

The first items that went up for bid could've been at any garage sale or flea market. Plastic dog bowls, stacks and stacks of them, were fifty cents apiece. Brand-new nail trimmers went for two-fifty a package, pet carriers for ten bucks, and space heaters for six dollars. Sellers offered up everything from wire-coated panels—"They're great for building playpens," Hughes told the crowd—to boxes of HomeAgain microchips. Rubber-backed carpet squares, used feed boxes, and bags of almost-expired Greenies treats came and went from the folding table. A few random piles of stuff seemed to have been hauled straight out of basements or attics, like a box of Easter decorations and stuffed animals. Hughes found buyers for all of it, at whatever price the market inside the barn would bear.

After about an hour, more helpers emerged from the door to the adjacent room, the one that contained all the dogs. The barking echoed louder throughout the barn as the helpers swung the door open, revealing rows of stacked cages, then was muffled again when they shut the door behind them, so the dogs could no longer be seen. Some of the helpers were women, some were men; some were middle-aged, others were teenagers. They wore clothes they didn't seem to mind getting dirty, everything from a football jersey to a green sleeveless T-shirt printed with the British-inspired catchphrase "Stay Calm and Graduate from College." They lined up folding chairs, seven of them in all, along the inside of the fenced area. Then they went back through the door and reemerged a few minutes later, each holding one dog in his or her arms. There was an American Eskimo—dog number 1 in the day's program—along with a Beagle and five Chihuahuas, all brought out in alphabetical breed order. All of the handlers petted the dogs they held, trying to maintain quiet and calm.

Hughes had the crowd going pretty good when he saw the first of the dogs come out, spotting them from the corner of his eye and then turning his head and shoulders with acknowledgment. He had been sitting behind the podium, comfortably leaning forward on his elbows to call prices into the microphone while the bid spotters paced the floor in front of him, but now he held the mike in his hand and stood fully upright, making his presence known.

"Okay, everybody," he said, slowing his pace of speech from the rapid fire of an auctioneer to the distinct clarity of a schoolteacher. The crowd, abuzz from the action, settled down to listen. "We're about to start with the dogs," Hughes said, "so let's go over some rules."

A sign on the wall behind him, clearly posted, stated that no cameras or recording devices were allowed. It's the same warning that is printed on the promotional fliers Hughes sends out before auctions, only on the fliers it's in all caps and comes with an added warning:

PRIVATE PROPERTY!! ABSOLUTELY NO CAMERAS, VIDEO CAMERAS, CELL PHONE RECORDING OR ANY OTHER TYPE OF PHOTOGRAPHIC DEVICES ALLOWED WITHOUT THE PROPERTY OWNER'S WRITTEN CONSENT! VIOLATORS WILL BE PROSECUTED FOR TRESPASSING AND DAMAGES FOR SLANDEROUS INTENT!

Hughes now wanted to make sure those notices had been brought to everyone's attention and explicitly explained. He held his own iPhone to his ear and said, "If we see you talking like this, that's okay." Then he pointed it to the ground, as one might when typing a text message. That was all right with him, too. Then he held the phone out in front of him, as if searching for a signal—or surreptitiously aiming a camera. Anybody doing that, he said, would get a visit from a Southwest Auction Service employee, who would look through the photographs stored in the phone. If any of the photos made management uneasy, he said, the phone would be deposited with local law enforcement. He added that he attended the officers' charity events each year, as any well-respected, well-connected local businessman might.

When the crowd was sufficiently forewarned, Hughes held out his empty hand, palm facing down, as if to calm anyone who might be feeling threatened. "Listen," he said. "We welcome everybody here—buyers, sellers, rescues, vets, whoever. This is the United States of America. You're entitled to have your own agenda. But you are on private property, and these are our rules."

Hughes then motioned for dog number 1, the American Eskimo, to be carried to the auction table. The fluffy white female was listed in the program as being four years old and a good mom when bred in the past, with official purebred papers from APRI. Her name was Alice, but it wasn't used; all of the dogs that day would be called by number, not by name. She was listed as being part of a "breed sellout," meaning her owner was no longer breeding American Eskimos and had no further use for her.

As the bidding started, the handler petted dog number 1 continuously, keeping her calm enough to stand on the table in plain view while Hughes called out bids from the crowd over the microphone. The spotters kept pacing the concrete floor and scanning the bleachers for buyers, just the same as when the nail clippers and Easter decorations had been the items up for auction. Dog number 1 didn't seem particularly happy on the table, nor particularly bothered; bewildered is probably a fair word. She didn't squirm, she didn't shake, and she didn't bare her teeth or growl. She didn't let out a bark or so much as a whimper. She didn't piddle on the table in fear, the way some of the other dogs would later that day, nor did she try to play the way some of the puppies coming out that afternoon would. Dog number 1 just stood there, rather nonchalantly, allowing the handler to pet her as bidding on her life continued all around.

Nobody holding up a card to raise the price on dog number 1 got up from his seat in the bleachers. Nobody asked about her temperament or health, although as the day went on, Hughes would start mentioning up front which dogs were missing some or all of their teeth. Some of the attendees may have inspected the dogs in the back room before the auction started, but now that bidding had commenced, nobody walked up front to give dog number 1 a close look or to touch her, or to assess her in any way beyond her looks from a distance. Next to her description in the program was the name of her seller—a commercial breeder who, during a USDA inspection in 2011, was said to have had an American Eskimo dog living in conditions that did not meet federal standards, such as having a wooden post at the edge of the dog's pen chewed so badly that screws were sticking out—but nobody asked whether that dog might have been this one. The sale of dog number 1 was a pure business transaction, one based on her status as breeding stock. Ultimately, she went for $60, and then she was carried back to the room where she'd started out, and where she would stay in a cage until her new owner was ready to collect her at the end of the day.

Now the auction table was open for dog number 2 in the program, a two-year-old Beagle who had recently birthed eight puppies. She was put in the American Eskimo's place and, in the same way, constantly petted by a handler to keep her calm. Bidding began immediately, with maybe a ten-second pause during the switch, just enough time for Hughes to take a breath and start again in his fast-paced auctioneer patter. There were, after all, some three hundred dogs to work through before sundown. It was going to be a full day's effort to get them all sold.

Most of the people in the room paid no attention as the American Eskimo left and the Beagle was brought out. They had come that day for other dogs, and they would wait patiently or chat among themselves as the well-organized program made its way through the Bull Mastiffs and the Dachshunds and the English Sheepdogs and the Pomeranians and the Retrievers and the Soft-Coated Wheatens and all the rest of the breeds in the back room. The teenage girl sitting in the bleachers wearing the pink sweatshirt and sparkly matching headband kept munching on her nachos, not even bothering to look up. She was no doubt upset that her parents had dragged her to yet another auction on a perfectly good Saturday. These long days in the barn were always the same, so routine that they had become downright boring.

Southwest Auction Service sells many things, from farm equipment to firearms, but it is also home to the largest, most successful USDA-licensed dog auction in the United States, whose citizens buy more dogs each year than any other nation's in the world. And Bob Hughes, who may look to newcomers like the auction's franchise-building star player, is actually the continuation of a dynasty. He'll tell anyone who asks, with a modest amount of humility, that the Hugheses are regarded in these parts as the first family of the pet industry. To know him, and to understand how he came to be calling out prices by the hundreds and thousands of dollars at that podium, one first has to know his parents.

Jim Hughes was a middling college student who earned Cs before graduating. He served six months of active duty in the US Army, where he apparently figured out just as fast as his commanding officer that he wasn't the type to take orders from others. After that, he moved to Ohio and worked as a chemist for the state's Department of Agriculture. In the late 1950s, he married a woman named Sue and the couple spent five years living in California, where Jim worked as a chemist for San Bernardino County. It wasn't the life they wanted, though, so he and Sue bought a four-hundred-acre farm just outside of Wheaton in the early 1960s, and he promptly began raising cows and crops just like lots of other farmers in the southwest corner of Missouri.

"What happened was that sometime in the early sixties, Mom wanted a color TV," as Bob Hughes tells the story he has heard since he was a child. "They were barely making it with the farm, so Dad said, 'You want a color TV? You earn it!' Well, Mom bought a couple of Poodles. She'd ship the puppies to my grandmother out in Columbus, Ohio, where she could sell them out of the newspaper to the big city market. She got a hundred ten, a hundred twenty dollars apiece for those puppies. That was big money back then."

Jim, meanwhile, was doing everything he could to keep the farm going, but "we promptly began to starve to death," as he put it in an article about his early business life. Jim had started out with thirty-two cows and then added pigs to increase his income, along with his workload. He ultimately built up the farm to one hundred and forty-eight cows and twenty-seven sows, which had him doing backbreaking chores for eighteen to twenty hours a day. As he remembers things, Sue didn't bring in Poodles at that time; they were Schnauzers and Pekingese—and the market for what they produced was beating the heck out of the market for what his cows and pigs were generating. And truth be told, the initial breeds weren't of much consequence as more and more of them arrived, diversifying Sue's stock. Her handful of dogs soon grew to more than 320 on the Hughes farm, and Jim ultimately decided they were a better bet in terms of a cash crop. He was killing himself and barely breaking even, and his wife was earning enough to have to pay income taxes by playing around with puppies.

A lot of the other dairy farmers thought Jim Hughes was nuts, letting his place literally go to the dogs—as Bob Hughes tells it, "They'd come over and ask him, 'Hey Jim, how much milk does a Maltese give?'"—but the Hugheses didn't mind the needling because they were onto something big. In fact, they were among the first people to tap into what would ultimately become the biggest market for purebred dogs in the history of the world.

Just as Jim and Sue were becoming large-scale breeders, a post–World War II surge in middle-class income had Americans leaving the cities to embrace the suburban lifestyle of a house with a yard, a couple of kids, and a beloved dog. The United States, always a melting pot of people, had until then been a place where if there were a family pet at all, it was usually a garden-variety mutt. That changed in the middle of the twentieth century. The Westminster Kennel Club Dog Show started airing on television in 1948, three years before the premiere of *I Love Lucy*, and dogs like those fancy purebreds shown on TV—dogs previously owned only by the wealthy and famous—were showing up in the newspaper classifieds in places like Columbus, Ohio, at prices working people could afford if they saved a bit. The purebred dogs, as much as the suburban houses, became a middle-class lifestyle status symbol.

"It got to a point where my grandmother told Mom, 'I can't keep up with selling all of these puppies, but there's a pet store here in Columbus that wants them,'" Bob says. "Well, that was the first-ever Petland. They're now the biggest chain of pet stores in the USA."*

While Sue was selling puppies, other farmers' wives were selling eggs—but they saw that the size of the Hughes home had doubled and that the family had a new car, and they started asking her about the puppy business at church, as Bob tells the story. That's where Jim and Sue saw their next business opportunity, which was dealing dogs among their neighbors to help them start

---

* Petland, whose US stores regularly sell purebred and popular hybrid puppies such as Goldendoodles, also has stores today in Canada, Japan, South Africa, China, Mexico, Brazil, and El Salvador. In the United States, PetSmart and Petco have more locations than Petland, but they generally do not sell dogs from breeders. Some US PetSmart and Petco locations do allow rescue organizations to offer homeless dogs for sale inside their stores.

kennels, too, and then dealing those dogs' offspring among all the new kennels as owners tried to diversify their own breeding stock. The Hugheses opened a business called DoBoTri Kennels, a name that most folks thought stood for some kind of a three-colored Doberman Pinscher but actually referred to their three kids: Doug, Bob, and Tricia. DoBoTri allowed the family to buy all the color televisions they wanted for the next several decades, and Jim walked around telling people that he knew more about the dog industry than any other human being in the world. During the course of a half century, Jim bought a half million dogs as everyday business. "Barry County, where Wheaton is, had the largest volume of breeders in the United States because it all sprang from my dad's kennel," Bob says proudly today. It's a legacy that continues, too. Southwest Missouri is still considered the epicenter of large-scale breeding, with the state having one registered commercial kennel for every three thousand people. The next-closest state is Nebraska, which has only about a quarter as many.

DoBoTri Kennels is no more; Jim and Sue sold it to the Hunte Corporation, a nearby puppy distributor, in the early 2000s. (More on Hunte later.) But that was long after Bob had started following his dad out on business, learning the dog industry from the inside out. Bob worked for DoBoTri throughout most of the 1980s and into the 1990s, selling dogs among all the breeders in the region. He was acting as what is known in the dog business as a *broker*, which is a middleman or salesman who connects dog breeders with wholesale buyers, be they other breeders, research facilities, or pet stores.

From there, it was a pretty easy business jump for Bob to become an auctioneer: a person who gets all the sellers and buyers into a single room and takes a commission for brokering the best deal on each dog.

"I had always wanted to be an auctioneer," Bob recalls. "The people who succeed in life sell what they know, and I know about dogs. There was a guy in Versailles, Missouri, who had held a few auctions, but he was a real estate guy. So I went for it. My first auction was a lady with two hundred dogs going out of business. I got her three times the money she expected."

That was the beginning of Southwest Auction Service, which is the business Hughes is now teaching to his son, Chadd, while holding grandchildren on his lap—toddlers he refers to over the microphone in the barn as "the next generation." (As with any good dynasty, there are already heirs apparent.) Bob did breed dogs for a while, but he says he leaves that to Chadd now; in 2013, Chadd was offering one of his Bull Terriers, advertised as a grandson of the 2006 Westminster Kennel Club Dog Show best in show champion, for stud service. Chadd also sometimes takes the mike at the auctions, calling out the prices in a way that sounds eerily like Bob's own patter. Their teamwork has the auctions generating some good business, too. One held on February 11, 2012, when the world's economy was still lurching to recover postrecession, brought in nearly a quarter million dollars, according to *Kennel Spotlight*.

The auction house in the barn takes a commission off the top, just like the far more famous auctioneers do when selling artwork or jewelry at Christie's in London or New York City. And someday, Bob Hughes hopes to bring in the kind of money the bigger auctions make. He sees every other type of animal and its offspring being auctioned publicly, sometimes for hundreds of thousands of dollars apiece, just after each industry's big annual competition show. He thinks dogs should be no different.

"When I got $12,600 that one time, a guy came up to me and said, 'Wow, you sure got a lot of money out of that dog,'" Bob recalls. "I looked at him and said, 'Did I?' Because we'll only know what these dogs are really worth when the American Kennel Club lets me hold an auction just after Westminster one year, using the champion. They do it with horses. Some horses go for a quarter million dollars apiece. What if Tiger Woods's wife likes a certain kind of dog and wants to bid up the price to get the best one? We'll never know the truth on these prices until they let me do an auction of the champion dogs."

⋰⋱

Alas, the huge money wasn't pouring forth on October 5, 2013. As the clock ticked toward three o'clock and the program's fifteen English Bulldogs started arriving at the auction table, Hughes looked disappointed in the prices they were bringing. The females were going for $185 to $740 apiece, the males for $475 to $600, with the ranges dependent on everything from their ages to their looks to their history of producing puppies. Hughes probably wasn't expecting five figures, like he got for that standout English Bulldog a number of years earlier, but something closer to four figures, or even a bit more than that, would have been nice.

"They seem low," he said, leaning back from the microphone and appearing to puzzle over what was keeping the crowd from upping the ante. This was a good-looking group of dogs, ten females and five males ranging from a few months to about five years old. Every single one of them had AKC registration papers (nearly one out of three dogs in the auction that day were eligible), and a few of the older dogs had recently produced litters of five to eight puppies apiece. One had managed to turn out ten in a single birthing.

"The most expensive dog I ever sold was an English Bulldog," Bob told the crowd, leaning full-throated back into the auction and nudging the sales harder than he had all day. "I know they're not as popular right now, but give it two or three years. They'll come back."

Chadd then took the mike, holding it with a little flair, and tipped it bottom side upward the way Jay-Z might. Chadd called out some prices before adding his own perspective, trying to raise the bids on the English Bulldogs to where the Hugheses thought they should be. "Anybody in the dog business knows that if you have *the dog* when the trend hits, that's when you make your money," Chadd told the crowd. Bidders shouldn't shun a breed because it was a slow seller today, he implied; buying at a cut-rate price now could set up a gold mine of product to sell later.

Jane Rosenthal, watching from front and center in the audience, shifted a bit in her lawn chair and tried to figure out how much money she had left to spend. Her mind was likely spinning with figures, not just those of the English Bulldogs, but of what she thought might be the prices on the breeds yet to come out. Given her experience at previous auctions, she probably knew it was going to be hard to get in on the Soft-Coated Wheatens, which were popular and would ultimately be the top sellers that day at an average of $1,485 apiece. She also likely knew she had little chance of horning in on the action for a French Bulldog, since that breed would be a close second at an average of $1,452 per dog. A couple of Cavalier King Charles Spaniels were yet to be auctioned, plus a slew of Yorkshire Terriers—enough Yorkies, actually, to fill five full pages in the program—and she might be able to offer the winning bid on some of those with the cash she still had on hand.

Rosenthal is from northwestern Iowa, and she used to be a breeder. Not a commercial breeder, like what Hughes estimates as a good two-thirds of the people in the bleachers that day. She was a show breeder, turning out a far smaller quantity of Japanese Chin puppies with the potential to win at conformation dog shows (like the Westminster Kennel Club Dog Show, where dogs are judged by how well they conform, in terms of looks, to breed standards).

She was an eager show participant until cancer struck her in 2007 and the chemotherapy drained what used to be her passion in life. "I just wasn't interested in going to dog shows anymore," she says. "I'd heard about the dog auctions and I got curious. I went to my first one in 2008. It was mind-blowing. Your brain is totally scrambled. I've been to the big shows like Westminster at Madison Square Garden, but I never saw so many dogs like this."

At that first auction, Rosenthal saw another woman who was buying dogs for a rescue group. She was outbidding the breeders to move the dogs from the commercial life into homes as pets. The rescuer would walk into the auction, hand over her driver's license at the registration table, and then raise her bidding card just like everybody else in the room. Rosenthal soon had her own group, Luv A Chin Rescue, and before she knew it, she was helping other rescuers buy all kinds of breeds out of the auction. Rescuers who had homes lined up and waiting would call Rosenthal from all across America, telling her which dogs they could place with families if she could win their bids. "Lately, there haven't been a lot of Chins," she says, "but we have over twelve hundred in our database that we've gotten out since 2008."

A Chin that Rosenthal bought at the auction in 2008 gave birth to six puppies just four days later. The dog had previously been bred twice and had produced fifteen puppies by the time she was two years old—the age at which a show breeder might just be starting to think about breeding a Chin for the first time.

"So over the life of the dog, it's a huge difference," Rosenthal says. "If she'd gone to a commercial breeder instead of to me, think of how many puppies she'd crank out over the years. If you figure ten puppies a year for a good seven years, that's seventy puppies, not the ten or maybe fifteen, tops, that she'd produce with a show breeder."

In other words, Rosenthal felt she hadn't just saved that one dog by outbidding the breeders in the room. She believed she had potentially saved lots more dogs from similar lives.

Penny Reames, a rescuer from Kansas, feels the same way. She wasn't at the October auction in Wheaton, but she has been there before, trying to outbid the breeders for the Scottish, Cairn, and West Highland White Terriers, which she then sends to a rescue group some 1,300 miles away in New Hampshire, where demand for their breeds is high. Reames tries especially hard to make it to the auctions in the fall, she says, because that's when a lot of breed sellouts happen. "It's cheaper [for the breeders] than building heated kennels to keep the dogs over the winters," she says.

Reames, Rosenthal, and other rescuers who attend the auctions sometimes take guff from their fellow advocates, who say they are only helping the commercial breeders by putting even more money into their pockets with every dollar that is bid. One such critic is Mary O'Connor-Shaver, an Ohio rescuer with Columbus Top Dogs who worked to get dog auctions banned in the Buckeye State.

"We have a very strong statement on buying at dog auctions," O'Connor-Shaver says. "We don't think it's a good thing. We think it's a tragic embarrassment. We always ask for an outright boycott of these auctions. We've studied the numbers, and we think that some of these dogs at the auctions are being purposely bred for sale to the rescues. We've taken a really hard stand on it because we see that these breeders are watching the rescuers to see what dogs they're buying. There's a huge Bichon rescue in the United States, and they were going to these auctions, and the breeders figured it out. And guess what: It drove up pricing. As soon as they stopped, it drove down pricing, and now they relinquish them to the rescue with no fee."

Reames disagrees. In fact, she wishes more rescuers would buy dogs out of the auctions, and she plans to buy out as many as she can.

"The way I see it," Reames says, "the dog is going to be sold at auction whether we buy it or not. If somebody bids $250 and I can bid $255 and save that dog, why wouldn't I do that?"

And just to be clear, neither Reames nor Rosenthal is against the breeding of dogs. Both are perfectly fine with people breeding dogs for sale, especially the breeds for which they have a personal affection, like Japanese Chins and West Highland White Terriers. They just don't want the breeding done on a commercial scale, the way Bob Hughes was raised to do it on his parents' farm, with dogs being impregnated and handled and auctioned by the dozens and hundreds at a time. Yes, the serious commercial breeders are all licensed, and yes, they are inspected and fined if their operations fail to meet state and federal standards, but while the breeders argue that the standards for living conditions should be similar for all animals, rescuers like Reames feel they should be far higher for dogs, because dogs are different.

"This is treating the dogs the same as livestock," Reames says. "These are domesticated animals. We have to encourage the good breeders who treat their dogs with compassion. I'm talking about people who let their breeding dogs live in the house, see a veterinarian, eat quality food, maybe there's three or four mamas, but that's all—that's how you get good, quality pets."

And for what it's worth, Rosenthal isn't opposed to the auction in Wheaton, either. She says that without it, the rescuers couldn't get to the dogs at all, because commercial-scale breeders don't trust anyone who might utter the words "puppy mill" or who has even the slightest air of being an animal welfare advocate. (Such people are more commonly called "animal rights extremists" in this part of the Midwest.) If showing up at the auction is how she can do the most good for the most dogs, then Rosenthal is more than willing to keep going to the auction. She'll hand over the money—not with a smile, but without causing a stir—if that's what it takes to inject the cause of rescue into the marketplace.

"I'm a Christian woman," Rosenthal says. "I'm nice to everyone. I go and mind my own business. One time I met a man from Arkansas. He saw my Iowa plates in the parking lot. 'Iowa,' he said. 'How's the dog business up there?' I just said, 'Oh, you know, probably about the same as it is down here.' And I just kept on walking."

While she's a regular attendee, she's obviously not a fan of the people selling dogs at the auction. She's certainly not there to make friends; she's there to disrupt their business model.

"The breeders are all about money," Rosenthal says. "If they're not making money, they'll have a kennel sellout. The dogs, the cages, all of it. They won't pay to feed them if they can't sell them. It's all supply and demand. The dog shows? They're fantasy. They're a big ego trip. These auctions, they're the reality."

Each of the three German Shepherds brought out from the back room were pregnant; they went for $510 to $550 apiece. The trio sold to a single buyer who probably went home satisfied that he'd gotten a good deal. After all, Hughes said from the podium, one of those Shepherds' fathers had been sold at auction a while back for $6,500.

The father of the teenage girl sitting in the bleachers wearing the pink sweatshirt and sparkly matching headband bought the day's only Rottweiler, a four-year-old male listed as a "nice, aggressive breeder" with AKC registration papers. The price was $600.

Hughes couldn't get any bidders for the six-year-old male Chesapeake Bay Retriever named Feldmann's Big Boy, called out as dog number 180 and so terrified being brought from the back room that he wrapped all four of his legs around the two handlers trying to calm and carry him. Nobody would even bid a single dollar, no matter how many times Hughes asked. "No sale," he finally called out as the trembling dog was returned to his cage in the back room.

When bidding seemed slow on the three Golden Retriever females, each just shy of two years old, and prices stalled in the mid-$700s, Hughes goosed the crowd, saying, "One litter will pay for all of them." They went a few minutes later for $810 apiece, right around three thirty P.M., with another hour and a half still to go before the last dog would be sold.

There were no West Highland White Terriers at the auction on that particular day, but Reames has seen plenty of them brought to the folding table over the years—after all, they've been among the more popular, in-demand breeds across America since the 1960s. A female Westie can start breeding just shy of her first birthday, and Reames often sees the younger, pregnant ones go for about $650 apiece. She doesn't always know exactly what happens to them next, but she does know, just as well as Hughes and the commercial breeders do, how the money trail develops from auction day forward. Here's how she explains it, to put into perspective how much money really is on the table inside of the auction house every time a dog's number is called:

A commercial dog breeder will get two litters of puppies out of that Westie during each of the five years after purchase. Every litter with a Westie is four to eight pups. That means a total of eight to sixteen puppies a year, or forty to eighty dogs coming out of that single Westie in five years' time. Even if the breeder sells them all as males and non-pregnant females to a broker at a discount, for $100 apiece, that's $4,000 to $8,000 going into the breeder's pocket, minimum.

The broker will then sell those dogs to the pet stores at maybe half of their retail price, or about $400 apiece. So, subtracting the original $100 per puppy, that's another $12,000 to $24,000 in income, creating a total of $16,000 to $32,000 so far from the initial dog. Yes, it does add up fast. The pet store then sells those pure-bred Westies to the public for the retail price of, easily, $800 apiece. That adds another $16,000 to $32,000 in gross income, for a conservative total of $32,000 to $64,000—every cent of it generated by that original $650 female who was sold at the auction five years earlier, and who will probably be brought back to the auction table only after her breeding production slows, when she's considered used up.

Then again, sometimes she might come back a bit early, if the owner decides Westies are no longer worth his time to breed, or if an inspector shuts down his kennel and orders it to be liquidated, dogs and all.

"It absolutely blows my mind how many of these dogs come into the auctions already pregnant," Reames says, talking about not just the Hughes auction, but also smaller ones she has attended. "At one auction, I saw a dog actually having her puppies right there at the auction. I've heard the auctioneer say, 'It's money in the bank, people!'"

The mother lode of breeds at the October auction in Wheaton was the Yorkshire Terrier. Nearly sixty of them were advertised in the preshow flier, many of them from a breeder having a kennel sellout, a breeder who provided an endorsement stating that "the quality and health of their puppies are exceptional, from the size, hair coat, and the face that everybody wants." The Yorkies would average just shy of $400 apiece by the time Hughes was done, with the most expensive one being an eighteen-month-old female who had already given birth to at least one litter of puppies, whelped when she was a year old, and who was likely already pregnant again. She went for $1,150, having earned a reputation as a good producer from a nice, young age.

More and more people were stepping down from the bleachers and shuffling toward the door as the last of the Yorkies came out. It was getting late, their funds were used up, and, depending on their reasons for being at the auction, they had either accomplished or failed at their business goals for that day. Some of them seemed happy and some seemed frustrated, but none seemed shocked or disturbed about the existence of the auction itself. Southwest Auction Service may represent different things to different people, but it is one thing for sure: the epicenter, almost square in the middle of the map, of how dogs are bought and sold in America, and of how similar dog market interests operate in nations around the world.

Virtually every player of significance is represented in the barn's bleachers, from high-volume commercial breeders to small-scale breeders alike. There are breed registries like the AKC—whose seal of approval often raises a puppy's price in the general marketplace—as well as competing registries looking to make money off the fees that come from supplying each dog's "official papers." There are local rescuers and national-scale rescue networks that turn around and market the dogs for sale to the public as "adoptable." Anybody is welcome to walk inside, raise a bidding card, and take a dog home, just as anybody is welcome to open a wallet at pet stores and in back yards and at adoption events all across the planet.

Bob Hughes, at the end of the day, is selling dogs, which are a legal and regulated product. Like him or not, he's doing it really well, in an environment that is professional, organized, and family-friendly. Lots and lots of customers are buying dogs through him, and if there were no deals to be made, then the scene would not exist. It certainly wouldn't continue to be a profit-generating enterprise a quarter of a century after Hughes became an auctioneer.

It just feels different than what most dog lovers know, of course, because when Hughes flips on the lights inside his barn, it's like shining a spotlight on every last opinion and bias about dogs, and on what society has done to the dogs themselves—all they have been allowed to become and to represent, from price point commodities to furry-footed children, generation after generation, in the name of wanting to bring them by the millions into homes every year. Many dog owners may never set foot in that barn, but they are the ultimate buyers of the product being brought to the folding table, whether they are comfortable with that fact or not.

As the last few dogs were carried out of the back room that day, one of the sellers got annoyed; the bidding on her five-month-old male Biewer Terrier had stalled at $500, probably because the dog's fur was tan and white instead of the more common tricolor with black patches. The seller stood up from her seat in the bleachers and shouted across the room for Hughes to pull the dog off the auction table: "I don't want to sell him for that! He's called gold dust. It's a rare color. I could get two thousand dollars for him over the Internet!"

After that, all that remained was the matter of offloading a pair of female Havanese. One of the buyers took some persuading; as bidding stalled and Hughes waited on her to decide whether to add to the tally, she asked for the dog to be spun around so she could evaluate her, much like a judge at a dog show. The woman ended up buying, much like a show judge might have awarded a ribbon upon careful consideration. Hughes had managed to shake $650 out of the attendees for those last two dogs, and then he pronounced the day's auction over, some seven hours after it had started and run clear through without a break.

The total day's take for the dogs turned out to be just over $110,000, and maybe thirty people were left in the barn, including the auction employees, when Hughes put down the microphone near a quarter past five. The place looked like an amusement park at the end of a frenzied day: sticky soda cans crushed and dropped wherever they fell, dirty plates of half-eaten sandwiches left on the bleachers, empty bags of chips that missed the garbage cans and landed on the floor. The staffers at the tables near the concession room had long ago packed up and gone home, and the barking from the adjacent room had gradually quieted as buyers collected their purchases and loaded them into the vehicles outside.

It had stopped raining a few hours earlier, but drivers still had to dodge the mud puddles in the dirt driveway to keep their tires from spinning as they pulled out and headed for home. One of the last vehicles to leave was a truck pulling a box trailer, one without any windows or ventilation, painted black on all sides with the logo and telephone number for a local heating and cooling company.

If anybody passed that truck driving northbound on Highway 86 out of Wheaton, they would've had no clue that there might be a dozen or more dogs inside. Yes, the dogs' offspring might find their way into homes all around the world in the years to come, but even if they'd been barking their brains out on that night, nobody was around anymore to hear them.

CHAPTER TWO

LUXURY PACKAGING

"If you can build a business up big enough, it's respectable."

—*Will Rogers*

Most of the people filtering into the cheap seats just after dinnertime on February 10, 2014, were wearing thick boots, wool coats, and warm scarves. It was the snowy season in New York City, and wind gusts whipping up Seventh Avenue toward Madison Square Garden left cheeks as red as if given a stinging slap. The singles and couples alike looked relieved as they stuffed their gloves and hats into their pockets and settled into sections numbering well into the 400s, finding their places amid the twenty thousand or so seats in the massive sports arena. It was a Monday night with schools open the next morning, which meant few of the adults had children in tow. These spectators looked no different than if they were about to see a concert or a hockey game, except that some of them carried inch-thick, purple, faux leather programs—388-page books, really—featuring a cover image of Sensation, the Pointer in hunting stance who graces the Westminster Kennel Club logo.

Sure, the programs were a splurge at $20 apiece, but they were still a fraction of the $70 or so per seat these folks had paid to be able to watch the world's most prestigious dog show without binoculars. And really, in a place where it costs $11 for a hot pretzel and a soda at one of the concession stands along the concourse, $20 starts to seem like, well, a bargain for a keepsake, especially one with gold lettering on the cover, full-page ads that look professionally Photoshopped, and a section about how to hire personal security guards for dogs through the Madison Square Garden staff.

Because they'd arrived early, these fans could watch the cameras being set up for the first of two televised nights at the 138th Annual Westminster Kennel Club Dog Show. Westminster isn't the biggest conformation dog show on the planet, but it's arguably the best known, the Rolls-Royce brand among similar shows like Crufts in the United Kingdom and the FCI World Dog Show held in rotating countries around the globe. The total field of competition for this year's show was 2,845 dogs of 187 breeds and varieties, a spectacle that is a dramatic marketing evolution from Westminster's first show, before the turn of the twentieth century, when only thirty-five breeds appeared (and a portion of proceeds were donated to the ASPCA, to help find homes for strays).

The coveted best in show title at Westminster wouldn't be awarded until the next night, after all seven group winners had been selected in two nights of televised programming, but the first of those group judging rounds was scheduled to start inside of an hour. Backstage, groomers and handlers were primping and priming the winners from the earlier rounds of cuts.

It was serious business, preparing the stage for the whittling of the remaining dogs to just seven finalists, one group at a time. Men wearing tuxedoes and worried expressions took a long, last look around the ring, whose green carpeting served as a visual substitute for grass. They hiked up their black dress pants by the knees as they squatted to smooth the edges of the royal purple carpet that marked the entrance, and they considered the angles of the flower arrangements that were barely visible to many people inside the arena, but that seemed strategically located to create the impression of a natural garden setting for the TV audience. Everything, including the imposingly large men working as security around the roped-off seats on the floor, appeared to be in place as the clock ticked toward the prime-time television hours.

Looking out over the preshow scene was sixty-four-year-old David Frei, who describes himself as having spent thirty-five years owning, breeding, and showing Afghan Hounds, and who has been the voice of Westminster on television since 1990. He smoothed his hair and chitchatted with his co-host, thirty-seven-year-old Erica Hill, as they organized their notes and prepared to exchange witty banter before a television viewership of millions. Occasionally, they'd share a chuckle, a glancing touch, and a smile, perhaps thinking about the scope of what they were about to do or the international fame this event allowed them to enjoy. The dogs registered for this year's show included 127 from beyond America's borders, with fans back home in Canada, Mexico, Japan, Australia, Brazil, Chile, Colombia, Finland, Italy, Norway, Slovenia, Thailand, and the United Kingdom. The crowd slowly filling Madison Square Garden may have seemed big, but it was nothing compared to the real audience this show is organized to reach, with Frei and Hill spreading its message about purebred dogs everywhere a television set can be tuned in via satellite throughout the civilized world.

The people with partitioned-off floor seats made their way inside closer to start time, looking resplendent as they entered the arena in their tuxedoes and full-length gowns. Women were dazzling in drop earrings, sequined fabrics, and sparkling necklaces, and even the few men dressed casually looked like models whose pressed khakis and leather loafers were fresh from the pages of *Vogue*. They were positively aglow for this, their club's biggest week of the year, and some had invested thousands upon thousands of dollars, not to mention years or decades of their lives, in the business of dogs to earn their seats front and center. A few had arrived in limousines from Manhattan's toniest neighborhoods; others had flown first class from Europe and beyond. At least one attendee was known for bringing his private Gulfstream jet from South America, perhaps enjoying the same classical music now echoing throughout the rafters of Madison Square Garden in a rare moment of calm before the Jumbotron and Purina Pro Plan dog food ads flickered to life.

The folks in the cheap seats tried to frame their cellphone selfies with the wealthy in the background, much like cruise ship passengers who find themselves in view of superyachts on the docks of Caribbean islands like St. Thomas. The lucky ones had seats that let them photograph the show ring with the AKC banner hanging over it, proving that Westminster was an officially sanctioned event. Facebook posts no doubt screamed, "I'm at Westminster!" and people handed phones back and forth, ecstatic to show off their good fortune of sitting close enough to see.

Anyone still in his chair rose to his feet as a US Army color guard marched stoically into the ring, followed by a Frankie Valli impersonator and the cast from the Tony Award–winning Broadway musical *Jersey Boys*, who had prepared a rousing rendition of "The Star-Spangled Banner." There was a hiccup in the television timing—the red lights didn't indicate that the live broadcast had started until about two minutes after the crowd had gotten up—and everyone in the arena chuckled as the announcer called out, solely for the benefit of viewers at home, "Please rise for the singing of our national anthem." Even despite the lighthearted moment, hands were placed over hearts, caps were removed from heads, and due respect was shown as the event got under way.

Then the first of the snouts and tails began to peek out from backstage, and murmurs and whispers blossomed into full-throated cheers, even up in the nosebleed sections. Michael LaFave, a breeder himself, took to the arena's microphone as he has since 2001. His face isn't nearly as well known as Frei's to viewers at home, but his voice certainly is. He eased forward and said the words the crowd had been waiting to hear since last year, in his deepest, most silky-rich tone: "May we have the Hound group in the ring, please."

He might as well have been announcing the entrance of Patrick Ewing or another New York Knicks Hall-of-Famer. Row after row of grown adults jumped and applauded. Almost every face in Madison Square Garden that night was white, and quite a few of them now turned crimson, absolutely flush with excitement. They clapped and hooted with their hands over their heads as if cheering the start of a World Cup match. They hollered for several minutes straight, all because thirty-one leashed dogs had sauntered into the building.

Viewers at home may have heard all this, but they didn't see any of the preshow buildup; the live feed instead was on a shot of the Empire State Building alight and awash in Westminster's colors of purple and gold, the same colored lights used to honor no less than Queen Elizabeth II on Golden Jubilee Day. Then the camera cut to Hill, who introduced Frei by saying, with all seriousness, "This is, in many ways, an Olympic event." The hashtag #wkcdogshow appeared in the corner of the screen, encouraging people to take to social media just as they might during the Academy Awards. Then viewers were taken backstage to meet a Portuguese Podengo, which, along with the Rat Terrier and Chinook, was making its debut as a new breed in the show. The camera lingered on the Podengo for a few minutes, much as it might while showing off a concept design from Porsche or Ferrari at an international car show. The Podengo was indeed a nice new option for buyers, soon to become available from dog dealers worldwide.

Back in the main ring, judge Douglas Johnson and his bowtie were making their presence known, ensuring that the dogs were lined up alphabetically to match their listings in the program— similar to the alphabetical arrangement used for the auction at the barn back in Missouri. At home, viewers heard Frei call dog number 1, the Afghan Hound, by her name, which was Rachel, but at Madison Square Garden, no dog would be called any- thing but a number, also the same as in the auction barn. For judging purposes, she was Afghan Hound number 7, one of nearly two dozen who had been judged earlier in the day during the first round of cuts. And while Frei told viewers at home a bit about her owners to make her seem more everyday—like a dog they, too, could someday own—the judge at Madison Square Garden cared only about her appearance. For the purposes of demonstration in the ring, the Afghan Hound might as well have been on the auction house's folding table. The identical image of her standing there being evaluated by her looks, save the glitterati all around, was uncanny.

For the benefit of viewers, Frei and Hill would continue chatting throughout the Hound Group judging, telling the home audience again and again that these dogs were akin to royalty, of historic significance, the real stuff of kings and queens. Their pace was slower than an auctioneer's, but they were selling their hearts out just the same, bragging about each dog's value in terms of heritage and legacy. They, along with LaFave, repeated marketing buzz- words, dates, and phrases that implied tradition and significance an average of once every few minutes for the television viewers. Coonhounds date from the era of America's first president, George Washington, Frei said as American English Coonhound number 6 took his turn at the podium. The fifteen-inch Beagle (distinct from the thirteen-inch variety) was introduced to the crowd as number 28, but on television she was revealed to be the grandniece of Uno, the 2008 best in show winner, prompting Hill to quip, "That's a good bloodline to be a part of."

Hill then asked Frei how common it was to see descendants of former winners in the show. "A dog show's purpose is to identify superior stock," he answered, adding, "Yes, a dog wins here, it's the sincerest form of flattery, breeding to that dog."

In other words, the show being put on display for the public may have been entertaining, but the real show going on tonight was about the business of breeding, even if few of the fans ever noticed.

Back in the stands, unable to hear any of this chitchat, were more than a few of those fans—many of whom, by now, had been given enough time to chug their first beers. When Bassett Hound number 7 trotted out, a middle-aged man in a black sweatshirt and blue jeans stood up and screamed as if LeBron James had just hit a three-point shot from deep in the backcourt. "Beautiful!" another guy hollered. "That's a good-looking dog!" a woman shouted. "Oh, look at that Beagle!" a woman breathlessly gushed. If they could have, they would have howled. The pack instinct would get only stronger as the night wore on.

Quite a few of the people cheering, along with many of the seriously invested people down in front, likely would have been disgusted by the scene at the auction house in Missouri. Yet here, under the arena lights with the $20 programs and household-name television personalities, they had no qualms at all about what was happening. The reason is simple: this dog show—which dates from 1877, the same year the railroad and steamship tycoon Cornelius Vanderbilt died—allows breeders to do business in the style of the Old Money class. They have long been savvier than the purebred owners who spend their days breeding dogs on struggling family farms and going to auction houses when they can't make ends meet. Like the first of today's so-called reality television celebrities, the people in the tuxedos and gowns figured out decades ago that, instead of banning the cameras, it was better to invite them inside and control them, to turn a breeders' event into a glimpse at the dogs of high society. They also intuitively discerned that it was better to have the money for the resulting puppies change hands away from the public eye, so the process of selling seemed far more civilized. Indeed, viewers at home wouldn't hear Frei or Hill utter a single word about the cash value of the dogs on display, but really, the only difference between the announcers and the auctioneer Bob Hughes was that they were helping to set the top, and not the bottom, of the dog market.

Judging by the B-roll footage mixed in with the live broadcast that night, the top of the market was a great place for a dog to be. Viewers at home saw a flashback segment of past Westminster winners dining at Sardi's in Manhattan like Broadway celebrities, sitting on the famous sofas of the *Today* show like movie stars, and hanging out with Donald Trump like fellow billionaires. One half-century-old highlight reel showed the Whippet who won Westminster in 1964 spliced with footage of the Beatles arriving in America that same year, equating John, Paul, George, Ringo, and Courtenay Fleetfoot of Pennyworth as cultural juggernauts, all.

"We used to breed dogs for a reason, to do a job for us," Frei told viewers on that first night of judging. "Now, they're really bred for companionship and to be part of our family."

Meaning, of course, that everybody should go out and buy one—and judging by the crowd response to the Hound group, the market was going to be quite good this year for Long-Haired Dachshunds. Number 26 drove the spectators to their feet in a chorus of cheers. "Baaaassseeeeett!" the increasingly drunken guy in the black sweatshirt and blue jeans bellowed every time there was a lull. Entire sections of fans went crazy when Bloodhound number 5 was caught stretching on the Jumbotron, just like dogs do every day in bedrooms and back yards around the world. The camera happened to be on this particular dog who yawned, and so the fans went wild.

Frei tried to put the yawning dog into context for the television audience at home, doing linguistic backflips to keep the magic alive and ensure that the Bloodhound didn't seem too, well, pedestrian.

"You always hope your dog has its moment of divine inspiration when the judge is looking at you," he said before ultimately having to admit reality. "But they're dogs."

Just how much are the Westminster dogs worth? A good person to ask is Linda Blackie, because she recently had to make the case of their enduring value to a jury.

Blackie didn't have a Standard Poodle listed in the show program at Westminster in 2014, but as the owner of Whisperwind Kennels in Altoona, Pennsylvania, she knew the scene well, having taken best in show in 1991 with a Standard Poodle officially named Whisperwind's On A Carousel and known to his owners as Peter. The Poodles she bred were fixtures on the winning stages at dog shows, especially the Poodles with Peter's DNA in their lineage. In particular, she'd had great success after breeding Peter's daughters to a British-born Standard Poodle named Gordon who was named a top dog in Finland as well as in the United States. "That combination worked beautifully for me," Blackie told *Best in Show Daily*. "It had gotten to the point where I could use the dogs that came from the Peter/Gordon breedings and know exactly what I was going to get, what kind of tail-set, carriage, coat, temperament, everything."

Peter and Gordon, of course, could not live forever, so Blackie and the dog owner Miriam Thomas contracted with Mount Nittany Veterinary Hospital in State College, Pennsylvania, to store more than a hundred semen samples from five of their champion Standard Poodles. Four of the semen samples reportedly came from dogs sired by Gordon and bred to Peter's daughters. The fifth was reportedly a son of Peter—a direct descendant of the Westminster winner.

The freezing of champion-dog semen may sound like science fiction to the uninitiated, but it is old news in the world of purebred shows. The AKC first recognized a litter of puppies conceived from frozen semen in 1981, a full decade before Peter took the top prize at Westminster. The Kennel Club in the United Kingdom has a preinsemination application it asks breeders to use. The FCI allows some national kennel clubs to permit insemination of dogs even if they've never bred naturally. It's what breeders all around the world want, because it makes the process easier. Frozen semen can be shipped for breeding dogs on opposite sides of oceans or used when male and female dogs have conflicting show schedules or just plain won't, well, get their groove on in the flesh. One storage company says an added benefit is eliminating the risk of a valuable purebred dog getting herpes. The practice of freezing dog semen is so common today that its marketing has, in some circles, become cutesy: Vale Park Animal Hospital in Valparaiso, Indiana, explains the process on its website under the headline "Freezing Future Friends (or How to Make a Pupcicle)."

Despite the everyday use of the procedure, though, things can and do go wrong, and they did for Blackie and Thomas in 2010. That's when they were told 122 of their frozen semen samples from Mount Nittany hospital had been accidentally thawed—and thus ruined.

The lawsuit Blackie and Thomas filed became a precedent-setting case when it was argued before a jury of nine women and three men in 2012. The veterinary hospital didn't argue that it hadn't destroyed the samples, but it did argue that the amount of compensation the women wanted—widely reported as more than $300,000—was far beyond the samples' actual value. It was the first time a jury had ever been asked to determine the value of a dead Westminster winner's future generations.

Arguably, the financial damages could have been in the millions. Using the same type of math that turns a $650 West Highland White Terrier from a dog auction into more than $60,000 of income in just a few years by breeding litter after litter, these Standard Poodle aficionados could have proved quite easily that 122 champion-lineage semen samples—even if half of them didn't work during insemination—would have produced more than $1,000,000 worth of puppies sold at $2,000 apiece.

Instead, Blackie and Thomas sued for the value of the samples alone, not the value of the puppies the frozen semen could have produced. The women determined the value was more than $300,000 by claiming they could have made $5,000 for every two frozen samples, according to multiple news reports. That is six times the annual median income in the United States or in England, where Peter and Gordon originated, all for the frozen semen of five dogs from their bloodlines.

The attorney Louis Glantz of Glantz, Johnson & Associates was hired to argue their case. He wasn't an expert in animal law. Instead, he had a background in real estate, elder law, estate planning, and corporations. He was about as average as people can be when it comes to understanding the inner workings of the dog show and breeding worlds, but even he knew the sway the word Westminster could hold with the general public. During the trial, he displayed a poster of Peter after his big televised win. He also used a poster of Gordon with Betty White, who, in addition to being an award-winning actress, has a long history of being involved in animal welfare causes. And to drive home the point to the jury that Peter and Gordon weren't just *any* dogs, he showed a poster of the Triple Crown–winning racehorse Secretariat, the stuff of Hollywood films and best-selling books with reverent titles like *The Horse God Built*. Destroying these semen samples, the argument went, was nothing short of denying everyone the potential to enjoy a future Secretariat of the dog show universe.

"These dogs are the equivalent of Secretariat, not like the dogs we have at home," Glantz is quoted as saying in the *Centre Daily Times*, adding separately, "Peter and Gordon were the two best Poodles the world has ever known."

While quite a few owners of Poodles might argue that the dogs lapping water from bowls on their kitchen floors are the greatest in the world, the jury agreed with Glantz and bought wholeheartedly into the business model of the global breeding community. A Westminster win, they concluded, adds value. Jurors awarded Blackie and Thomas more than $200,000—far less than what the semen samples could have produced as puppies for sale, but only about a third less than they'd originally requested.

It was a rare moment, a decision that quantified, for the first time, not the value of an existing dog, but the *potential* value of a show winner's offspring and then the offspring's offspring for years to come, even long after the Westminster winner's death. While Bob Hughes back in his auction barn might be able to tell buyers of the dogs on his folding table that one litter will recoup the whole purchase price of an individual dog on a particular day, the breeders of champion Standard Poodles and all the other breed champions whose semen was in the liquid nitrogen tanks could now tell buyers that a half-dozen semen samples would equal the cost of a new car. There doesn't have to be an auction of the Westminster winner to increase the dog's value. The dog doesn't even have to remain alive. All that's needed is an artificial vagina, a "teaser bitch," or some manual stimulation by a human hand, and the security procedures of a biohazard facility to prevent unintentional thawing.

As they say at the auctions, it's money in the bank. A frozen-semen bank, yes, but a bank nonetheless.

"Sabotage! That's not fair! Hey, judge, sabotaaaaage!"

The thirty-something woman in the mid-arena section was fast approaching apoplexy. Perhaps a vocal parent who had been thrown out of more than her fair share of Little League games back home, she was outraged by what was happening in the show ring on Westminster's closing night at Madison Square Garden. Judging had commenced for the always controversial Terrier group, whose winners have, by far, taken home more best in show honors than any other group's winners in Westminster history. The Wire

Fox Terrier alone has won more than a dozen times, while fan favorites like the Labrador Retriever and Golden Retriever have yet to win even once. The Terrier judging thus had blood pressures rising throughout the arena because those who knew the event's history knew the winner of this group had a real shot at winning the whole shebang.

This Little League mom's favorite, the Miniature Bull Terrier, had endured the misfortune of being called out in alphabetical order after the Airedale Terrier and the Bedlington Terrier and the Cesky Terrier and all the other pre-M Terriers—all of whose handlers had used tasty treats to guide them around the ring. More than a few of the treats had landed on the green carpeting, and they were enough to distract the poor thirty-pound Miniature Bull Terrier, who sniffed at them with total disregard for the enormity of everything else going on. The handler was utterly, visibly frustrated by what was likely a thumbnail-size piece of hot dog or chicken. It might as well have been a steaming pile of excrement, stinking up the dog's sixty seconds of fame. Whatever it was, it smelled delightful to the Miniature Bull Terrier, who broke proper gait while the judge was watching.

That was what set the fan off. The crooked madness of it all— the stark raving lunacy—was just too much for the Little League mom to bear.

"Oh come *on!*" she shouted, throwing up her hands in disgust and turning to strangers all around her, airing her grievances to anyone who would listen. "How is that even right? Are you people kidding me? This whole thing is rigged!"

"I'm okay with it," her friend said, sitting beside her with a smirk and thinking about the Komondor, from the Working group. "I'm still rooting for the one that looks like a mop. This only helps his cause."

A row ahead of them was a bubbly brunette of a certain age who had made the trip to New York City from Boston, Massachusetts, just to see the Westminster show. For her, it was like going to a movie premiere, getting to sit in the audience and critique the handlers' outfits as if she were an *E! Fashion Police* host on a red carpet. The bubbly brunette comes every year and always starts out by scanning the floor seats for faces she recognizes. One year, she says, she caught a glimpse of Martha Stewart. But her all-time favorite year was the one when the arena crowd started doing the wave.

"You should've seen the people down front in the tuxedos and gowns," she recalled. "They looked around and their faces—oh, their faces—you could just see them thinking, 'What *are* the peasants doing? Are they revolting?'"

Of course, none of this shouting and commentary had gotten onto the television broadcast from night two of the show; instead, the viewers at home had once again been duly informed about the epic nature of what they were witnessing. Erica Hill talked about how Westminster was "one of the world's greatest events on one of the world's greatest stages," working with her co-host to mix the words *venerable, esteemed, admired,* and *loved* into sentence after sentence. David Frei, meanwhile, encouraged the audience to believe that they, too, could have a purebred just like the ones in the ring. "They're doing the same things at home that your dog is doing: stealing food off the counter and shedding on your black clothes," he said. Occasionally, viewers got to see NBC television personality Alicia Quarles interviewing the handlers of dogs who won their groups, with Quarles's African American skin supersized on the screen, offsetting all the lily-white faces in the crowd and giving viewers at home the sense that Westminster was a multicultural event.

The on-air banter continued straight through the night's judging, stopping only for commercial breaks. One of those was at 9:38 P.M., when the people inside Madison Square Garden got to hear something that was not aired for the public at home. Michael LaFave, over the arena's loudspeakers, addressed the Garden crowd directly, telling them that if they had come to see the best of the best, they were in the right place—and that if they were looking to add a dog to their lives, they should note that none of the dogs here at Westminster came from a pet store or a puppy mill. These dogs came from breeders who *care.*

The announcement was unexpected, and it shot many people in the arena to their feet, making clear what they saw as an absolute distinction between what they were doing and what went on in places like Bob Hughes's barn. The applause hit a crescendo so loud, so fast that it nearly drowned out LaFave's last few words. Nobody appeared to feel a sense of irony about the fact that Madison Square Garden's address was Seventh Avenue, also known as Fashion Avenue in Manhattan, or about the fact that the purebred dogs Westminster held up for the world as the most stylish—the "must haves" on television—would soon be churned out in big quantities by those puppy mills they disdained and sold as knockoffs just like the handbags on city corners at the end of Fashion Week. If they felt a sense of complicity in the big picture of the world's dog industry, they didn't show it, although the self-congratulatory applause was kept off-camera, just to be on the safe side of hubris. The breeders and fans at Westminster seemed proud to be recognized for doing an entirely different thing, as opposed to doing the same thing differently, from the people back in Missouri.

Another commercial break hit after the final judging of the groups, and with no announcement from LaFave to rile them up, the crowd took matters into their own hands by starting this year's attempt at the wave. Unlike during the year the bubbly brunette had first seen the wave receive shunning glances from the elites down in front, this year, some of the women and men in gowns and tuxedos joined the fun.

"Oh look!" the brunette cried from high above them, pointing and gasping. "Look at that! They're doing it!" She clasped her hands with delight, as if watching a baby take her first steps. "I wonder what they're saying to each other," she mused to nobody in particular. "Like, is there a wife down there going, 'Reginald, darling, just do it. Lift up your arms, dear.'"

As the cameras prepared to return from the commercial break, security guards multiplied by the dozen. Large men in dark jackets with hands folded in front of them stood not only near the roped-off seats, but also near the bottom of virtually every aisle. It was like the last few minutes of the Super Bowl or the final countdown of a March Madness tournament: They were ready to use bodily force, if necessary, to stop any overenthusiastic fan from rushing down into the ring.

"I wonder where the PETA people are," the brunette said, looking off to the sides for members of the group People for the Ethical Treatment of Animals. "They try to buy the seats where they know the cameras will be pointing. One year they got on TV for a few seconds. That's why all the extra security is here now. Nobody wants that happening again."

It was ten thirty P.M., and though the house lights had been on throughout both nights of Westminster judging so far, they now dimmed, making the arena as dark as the streets outside. The dogs selected as finalists for best in show were about to come out for the grand finale. LaFave—before the television returned—told the crowd, "We highly encourage you to cheer on your favorite." Madness ensued as spotlights began to swirl around the ring. Flashbulbs from cellphone cameras twinkled like stars throughout the arena. Anyone looking carefully, down in front, could just make out the small red lights turning back on atop the television cameras, with the place in a frenzy as seven dogs reentered the ring.

Yawning Bloodhound number 5 was back and still clearly the fan favorite based on the rise in decibels his presence created. Applause was strong, too, for the Wire Fox Terrier. Also running into the ring one after another were an Irish Water Spaniel, a Portuguese Water Dog, a Miniature Pinscher, a Standard Poodle, and a Cardigan Welsh Corgi. Again, they all were called by number, not by name, though this time their names did flash on the Jumbotron for everyone in the arena to see.

On television, viewers were told about the awe-inspiring achievements these seven dogs had made. Together, they had more than 520 best in show wins from other events. Four of the finalists had more than one hundred wins apiece on their résumés. The handler of the Wire Fox Terrier had won a Westminster best in show before, and the dog at the other end of his leash, nicknamed Sky, had already taken the top honor at both the National Dog Show Presented by Purina and at the AKC/Eukanuba National Championship. "A win here," Frei told TV viewers, "would be sort of our triple crown of dog shows."

Nobody mentioned on television that Sky was about as big money as dogs could get, a dog in whom wealthy people owned shares, like a corporation, with financial backing that had originated among the upper classes in South America, Europe, and beyond. They included Victor Malzoni Jr., a construction magnate and owner of Hampton Court Kennels in Brazil who sponsors the campaigns for a half dozen show dogs a year in the United States plus more at shows in Europe. (If the name Malzoni sounds familiar, it's because it graces the towering symbol of big business in Brazil, a 786,000-square-foot, black-mirrored office building on São Paulo's Faria Lima Avenue, which is that nation's version of Manhattan's Fifth Avenue.) Another of Sky's owners was Torie Steele of Malibu, California, who made her fortune helping Italian fashion designers such as Valentino and Versace enter the US market with her flagship Torie Steele Boutique on Rodeo Drive in Beverly Hills, California, and who was the second wife of the billionaire Sam Wyly, who has owned everything from the craft store chain Michaels to the Maverick Capital hedge fund.

Tonight, though, for the viewers at home, the dog was simply Sky. Inside Madison Square Garden, he was Wire Fox Terrier number 11. And having achieved his star-studded entrance along with all the other dogs, he now stood with his handler and awaited the arrival of Betty Regina Leininger. The Canadian native and former breeder of German Shepherds was some 1,500 miles away from her adopted hometown of Frisco, Texas, serving as best in show judge in New York City that night. As the house lights came back up, Leininger was escorted into the ring as if coming down the aisle at a wedding, "looking quite regal," as Hill told the audience at home, in her Westminster purple gown with rhinestone-bejeweled straps and matching high-heeled shoes. Her posture was absolutely perfect, as if she'd been taught to balance a book atop her blond coiffure by lifting her nose and chin into the air, just so.

And then the dogs were judged, one by one, just as they'd been in the previous rounds. Bless the heart of that Bloodhound: This time, instead of stretching, he shook his head and flapped his ears for the camera, sending the crowd into spasms. When Sky "stacked"—stood proudly on all fours as if he owned his tiny piece of the green carpet—fans cheered as if he'd done a backflip on command. "Coooorgieeeee!" a man shouted from somewhere in the arena, quickly drowned out by dozens of people screaming, "Blooooodhoooooouund!"

Leininger was unswayed by the heckling, walking calmly to the judging table to write her selections for the record. When she revealed the Standard Poodle as the runner-up, the crowd went against the tide and booed. "Nobody likes the Poodles," the bubbly brunette quipped in the stands. "It's those haircuts. Really, what are they thinking?"

And then, Leininger pointed to Sky, the big winner of the night. LaFave announced him over the loudspeakers as "the Wire Fox Terrier," and again, the crowd exploded in cheers.

Sky's handler lifted him into the air, as exuberant as a man who'd just won the lottery. People with security passes rushed in to congratulate him while Frei and Hill bade goodnight to the television audience, and the little red lights atop the cameras went dark for the last time. Large men in suits then strung a gold-colored rope around Sky and his handler, a demarcation line not to be crossed by anyone, including the journalists pacing impatiently with cameras in hand. Just before Sky's official photograph was taken for posterity, his handler gave him a quick brushing to be sure every hair was in place.

Frei stepped down from the media booth and onto the green carpet, flashing his credentials as he ducked under the rope and took his place among the dignitaries. The scene looked like a banquet hall after the buffet shuts down, with lots of older men slapping one another's backs and talking about how to settle up the bar tab. Classical music returned over the loudspeakers, and the losing dogs vanished back into the bowels of Madison Square Garden. As the cameramen began to break down their equipment, a proper receiving line took shape waiting for Sky to finish his photo shoot and prance into history. His owners would win no cash prize on this evening, but their rewards would surely come for years, if not decades, in the future.

In the stands, people rushed for the exits, jamming the escalators that led down from the arena and into the wide concourse hallways. Most were putting back on their thick boots, wool coats, and warm scarves, about to head into the cold February night air, happy they'd gotten their money's worth at a good show. A few stopped at the official Westminster booths to buy commemorative shirts on the way out.

One woman, though, wearing a fine evening gown of neutral color, stood off to the side, clearly growing upset as the crowds passed her by, often without even noticing her. She appeared to be in her sixties, with makeup perfectly applied and lipstick recently freshened. She had an entourage around her of four, maybe five other people, some younger and others her age. She was miffed to the point of tapping her toe as a security guard blocked her from the small side door she was trying to access.

The guard looked tired, as if it had been a long night and he just wanted to get home to his kids. He held a walkie-talkie up to his mouth with the cool indifference of a man who had been asked "Do you know who I am?" more times than he cared to remember.

"Yeah," he told an unseen gatekeeper listening on the other end of the radio, all the while keeping his imposing, six-foot-plus frame between the woman and the door. "I have a lady here with some people. She says she's the owner of the dog that won the whole thing."

Behind that door, for the cognoscenti allowed inside the golden ropes, the party was just beginning. The woman was keen to join them, and she likely planned to wait there, aggrieved with her lips pursed and her toe tapping in the public hallway, until her rightful place was acknowledged and she was allowed to enter.

CHAPTER THREE

BRANDING, BY BREEDING

"Business opportunities are like buses: There's
always another one coming."
—*Sir Richard Branson*

How modern society got to a point that includes huge dog auctions and globally attended dog shows is a story that can be told beginning about a week before Christmas in 1798, when a group of like-minded men got together for an invitation-only meeting in England. They were led by Francis Russell, the fifth person to hold the title of Duke of Bedford. He was an aristocrat through and through, albeit one with a penchant for carving his own side paths in life, a quality perhaps best displayed when he abandoned the tied-back hairstyle of the day in protest of a government tax on hair powder. Russell also owned and bred racehorses, and he had a general interest in agriculture. On the day he sat down to chat with his fellow bluebloods near the turn of the nineteenth century, dogs weren't even an afterthought, but the ideas discussed in that room would lead to what we know today as dog breeds in the auction houses and show rings and breeders' kennels alike— all because these men of the highest standing, back in their day, wanted to tap into the public's insatiable curiosity about fat cows.

That's right: much of it started with fat cows. Dogs weren't the stuff of the moneyed class at the time. Instead, agricultural animals like oxen, pigs, and cows dominated the public discourse. The heftiest heifers, when put on display, drew record attendance among curiosity seekers of all economic means in England. Commoners handed over shilling after shilling to stand five deep and crane their necks for a glimpse at the most swollen, fattened cattle the patricians could produce. The fact that the wealthiest men of the time got together in a backroom and decided to charge attendance was pretty much inevitable. Their first livestock shows were so successful that the exhibitions became annual events, adding pigs and hens and other barnyard brethren into the judging mix, with the cattle bulging farther and farther beyond their natural bone structures every year, so that the crowds grew larger and larger all around them.

By 1843, no less than Albert Francis Charles Augustus Emmanuel of Saxe-Coburg and Gotha—the husband of Queen Victoria—was a participating exhibitor in the open fields where people gathered under the sun to view the newest specimens. It fast became fashionable for people of means to commission portraits of their cattle in bucolic settings, always with the animals' bodies turned broadside, to show off their most valued physical quality: girth. Stud books were created to record bloodlines, and lineage was seen as more important than the animal's usefulness or practicality on the farm. Breeding options were no doubt negotiated and settled over dinner parties at long tables and while gentlemen sipped properly aged Scotch in private studies.

The backlash started with butchers, who protested that the meat from the behemoths was too fatty to eat, although, as Harriet

Ritvo writes in *The Animal Estate,* choice cuts from show-winning carcasses "were purchased by great ladies who liked to serve roasts that could be identified by name." The weekly magazine *Punch* started publishing articles about how breeding for looks made the animals sickly, sometimes barely able to walk or even move under the mass of their own midsections. Critics complained that judges were rewarding animals whose existence was at best ridiculous and at worst detrimental to livestock as a whole.

At this time of the copious cows in England, social hierarchy reigned. There was virtually no chance that working-class people could rise and join the ranks of the elite. They could attend all the exhibitions they wanted, and they could have all the talent in the world for breeding livestock, but at the end of the day, raising prizewinning oxen and cows was expensive. Big animals needed big land, big food, and big transport systems that cost far more than everyday people could ever hope to invest. One had to be wealthy even to consider partaking in the game, a roadblock that bothered, quite terribly, those who saw a future of fairer standards among all people in society.

The *concept* of prizewinning animals, though, was free for all to consider—and it was far more easily and economically applied to the dogs of Victorian England.

Before this time, hardly any average people kept dogs in their homes. Some of the elites did, though, and in that sense they could be copied. Dogs may have been a part of people's lives dating from the earliest days of hunter-gatherers, but it wasn't until this point in history that dogs started to become what we know today as pets. By the mid-1800s from London to the suburbs, everybody who dreamed of being anybody was getting a dog, naming her, and taking her home.

Shows comparing dogs with one another became popular in the same vein as the livestock exhibitions, and the value of purebred dogs shot skyward in England around 1880, with kings and queens and dukes and duchesses and other royalty positioning themselves to decide which dogs deserved to win and pass on their bloodlines. The upper class anointed itself as the controlling membership in the earliest breed clubs, which were groups created to define what made, say, a Great Dane a Great Dane, and to help set the standards by which all dogs of their particular breed would be judged. (Today, these groups are often called *breed parent clubs*.) "It was almost as though members of the decadent upper classes, whose real influence was declining rapidly, were struggling to keep an upper hand in the only way they still knew how: as arbiters of taste," writes Michael Brandow in *A Matter of Breeding*. The trend made its way across the Atlantic Ocean, too, with fanciers copying the same blueprint for financial success. The dog shows began in New York and grew throughout the late 1800s. Up-and-coming socialites formed parent clubs for various breeds. P. T. Barnum's Great National Dog Show, held during the 1860s, became a precursor to today's Westminster version. By 1908, when a Model T Ford automobile cost $825, top purebreds were being sold to the wealthiest Americans for $1,000 to $5,000 apiece.

The initial dog breeders in England fast became outraged that working-class people were breeding dogs to enter into what had always been "their" animal shows, but the average people loved the idea of being able to hobnob with the elites and saw their dogs as no different. (Sound familiar?) It all became a bit unwieldy, with the earliest dog show rules being rather willy-nilly, and for order of some sort to prevail, a classification system had to be devised. That is how more than two-thirds of the breeds recognized today were created, just a century and a half ago. Prior to this time, dogs had been characterized not by their looks but by their purpose, be it hunting, herding, or something else. That changed in 1874, a full decade before the AKC was formed, when the first edition of the *Kennel Club Stud Book* was printed in Britain. Whereas in 1800, when dog shows were unheard of and a fancier could almost count on two hands the number of dog breeds recognized in the Western world, by 1890 about sixty breeds were being displayed at hundreds of dog shows annually, sometimes with nearly 1,500 dogs competing. This was the same era when Barnum—against cries of animal cruelty by Henry Bergh, founder of the ASPCA—created a circus that displayed exotic animals like elephants all around the globe, and a time when the first world's fairs were being produced throughout Europe and the United Kingdom to show off the newest products for consumers on a global scale. As the dog shows became more standardized, they, too, introduced new products in the form of new breeds, and it seemed natural to put the dogs, like so many other animals, on display for the public's entertainment.

How were the breeds defined? The same way the four hundred or so recognized breeds in the world today are created: through negotiation and petition among breeders. Were those standards ideal for the dogs? Sometimes no more than they were for the morbidly obese cows. At this time in England, for instance, breeds like the modern Bulldog were born—complete with traits that, still today, cause the dog to suffer, including making it hard for the dogs to walk, breathe, or give birth to puppies. The critics saw this many, many generations ago, right at the start, with one describing the Bulldog craze in the 1800s by writing, "The disgusting abortions exhibited at the shows [were] deformities from foot to muzzle." Today's critics are only slightly less biting, calling the Bulldog "a curious blend of Victorian sensibility and gothic horror" before adding that Bulldogs are among the most expensive breeds for veterinary care today.

But the shows went on, and the common people figured out how to breed and own dogs that looked the same as the ones the rich people possessed. Consumer demand only grew as society continued its shift toward economic mobility among the classes.

"They wanted people to know at a glance that they had a first-rate dog which had cost a lot of money and had impeccable lineage," says Vanessa Woods, a research scientist today at the Duke Canine Cognition Center and co-author of *The Genius of Dogs*. "The easiest way to broadcast this was by the dog's appearance."

The majority of breeds, in other words, were developed just like today's Louis Vuitton scarves or Jimmy Choo shoes or Fendi clutches that visually announce a person's economic standing—or at least what the person wants other people to believe about her economic standing. When average, aspiring people in mid-1900s America started watching the Westminster dog show on television and buying purebreds in such great quantities that they led to puppy farms and dog auctions, they were only furthering the mentality begun a century earlier in England, that the breed of one's dog was an extension of oneself within the growing middle class.

Today's high ratings for televised dog shows like Westminster and the continued existence of groups like England's Kennel Club, the AKC, and FCI confirms that, as the calendar now turns closer to the mid-2000s, society has hardly changed its thinking at all.

"To me, breeds are like a designer handbag," Woods writes. "People like the way they look and the hype behind them. They buy into stereotypes (Border Collies are the smartest, Labs are the most faithful, etc.) and then they match up how they see themselves with the marketing behind the dog."

Why should anyone believe Woods's opinion about breeds? Because she's among the first people in history to study the scientific evidence behind the marketing that today's dog owners, their parents, their parents before them, and their parents before them have been presented for more than a century and a half.

Woods's co-author and husband, Brian Hare, founded the Duke Canine Cognition Center and teaches in Duke University's Department of Evolutionary Anthropology and Center for Cognitive Neuroscience. Hare had the chance to study monkeys, which humans have long considered closer to their own genetic makeup than dogs. He happened to notice something surprising while working with the supposedly superior animal species: his dog, Oreo, could understand human gestures the monkeys didn't even notice. This random observation made Hare curious about studying how dogs think and act, a practice that had long been considered unworthy of serious researchers' time and effort.

Hare and Woods, who is known for her research of bonobos, or great apes, joined a growing number of cognitive scientists and ethologists who, only since about the mid-1990s, have been shaping the modern study of dogs and trying to prove, or disprove, what most everyday dog lovers take for granted when talking about dogs and breeds. These experts are applying the scientific method to stereotypes, and they say they've learned more in the past decade about how dogs think than mankind learned in the entire previous century.

Given the history of how most breeds came to be, perhaps there's not much need for a spoiler alert here: The early science shows that, contrary to popular belief, modern dog breeds are almost exclusively about looks and hardly at all about temperament or what makes a dog a good addition to a family.

"Science is still really at the frontiers of answering what traits are inherited and when this occurs," Woods says. "We know through [Russian experiments with silver foxes] that aggression is hereditary, but not enough to be able to predict the temperament of a dog. For example, some of the sweetest dogs are rescued fighting dogs. Scientifically, there is really no way to know for sure, and it certainly isn't by breed. A Rottweiler puppy has an equal chance of being a loving member of the family as a Golden Retriever puppy."

Janis Bradley, another early adopter into the first generation of canine science, agrees. She has been trying to separate fact from stereotype since 2001. That's the year a thirty-three-year-old San Francisco woman named Diane Whipple became news across America, when a neighbor's pair of Presa Canarios mauled her to death while she was entering her apartment after grocery shopping. According to an expert's testimony, one of the dogs, weighing 125 pounds, stood on its hind legs and used its forelegs to pin the five-foot-three, 110-pound woman against a wall. The second dog, of similar size, heard the commotion in the building's hallway and joined the frenzy. After about six minutes, Whipple was on the ground, stripped of her clothes and unable to move, having been bitten seventy-seven times. She died several hours later from massive blood loss and asphyxiation from a crushed larynx.

The horrifying death, Bradley recalls, spread paranoia about dogs across Northern California the way an earthquake spreads fear of aftershocks. It was almost as if the entire human population was showing signs of posttraumatic stress, triggered by the mere sight of some dogs—and Bradley wanted to know if the reaction was warranted based on a single, highly publicized event.

"I was working at the San Francisco SPCA, teaching dog trainers and working with dogs who were being referred to me with aggression issues," she says. "People were getting afraid of dogs. My friends with German Shepherds would walk down the street, and other people would cross to the other side. People were really sensitized. I was scratching my head. I work with the supposedly high-risk dogs, and most of the people I know professionally do this, and I don't know anybody who has been seriously shredded by a dog. I started looking into the research to see if I was aberrant, if my experience was unusual."

Today, Bradley is director of communications and publications for the National Canine Research Council in the United States. The group's mission is to synthesize the most current, most scientifically defensible information about the human–canine bond, from researchers at places like the Duke center as well as the Family Dog Project in Hungary, and then to share it with decision makers and everyday dog lovers.

Like Woods, after looking at the current scientific studies, Bradley could not be any clearer in her opinion of modern-day breeds. The notion is pure folly, she says, that a dog's breed indicates much of anything beyond the way it looks. As much as breeders and kennel clubs worldwide may advertise outright or imply quietly that certain breeds are likely to have predictable temperaments when brought into homes or to serve our families better as pets, the science thus far simply does not support that assertion.

"Nobody was ever breeding for the kinds of things that pet owners care about anyway, for lack of a better term, for personality traits, they've never been bred for it," Bradley says. "Nobody has bred for general friendliness or unfriendliness or playfulness or any of those things. Nobody has ever tried to breed for those things."

She adds, "The inclination among geneticists now is that it wouldn't be practical to do anyway, because most likely, a low threshold for getting angry, those kinds of things, those are what geneticists call polygenic traits. There are a whole bunch of genes involved, so you're not going to find that it's anything you can breed for. It's going to remain more complicated than that."

As an example of how misguided dog lovers have become about the meaning of breeds, Bradley points to Greyhounds. What are Greyhounds known for? Racing. So much so, in fact, that breeders won't use Greyhounds as stock unless they're eager to chase. It's what scientists call an evolutionary bottleneck, meaning no Greyhound gets to pass on his or her genes unless that attribute is present.

Even with such rigorous selection, according to Bradley, the science shows Greyhounds today are eager to chase only slightly more than the average among all dog breeds. She's seen this reality in her own living room, too, where she keeps two Greyhounds as pets and many others coming through as foster dogs. In terms of personalities, they're no different than all the other dogs she's ever known as a trainer.

"I've worked with thousands of dogs of every possible mixed and purebred description, and now I'm involved with the Greyhound rescue people," she says. "I have some sense of the scope across the species. I just listen and don't say anything when the Greyhound people tell me they're the best."

She adds, "I've never met any people [involved with any particular breed] who didn't think their breed was special. The refrain is pretty much always, 'They're not like other dogs.' I had dozens and dozens of foster Greyhounds, and I have to say, they seemed like *dogs* to me."

Why, then, despite increasing bodies of scientific evidence, do so many dog lovers maintain with such fervor that theirs—whatever they choose—is the best kind of dog, or that purebreds in general are the best dogs money can buy?

"I think it's because humans like pattern and prediction," says Dr. Jane Brackman, a California-based expert on canine genetics and domestication. "In nature, things are random, but humans have a tendency to take random design and create meaning out of it. You're talking about a very visceral level of humanness. You want to take the chaos of nature and create a design, something you're controlling. I can only think that's why people want purebred dogs."

Interestingly, attempts to standardize how dogs look may actually be changing them more than anyone understands. Brackman's studies include a look at the number of words that define each breed—the official standards of size, shape, and features that breeders use to distinguish, say, a Redbone Coonhound from a Treeing Walker Coonhound. In some cases, the definitions about how certain breeds should look have gotten much longer, and therefore more specific, which is how one breed can be split off into others. For instance, in the 1500s, a cynologist named Jonathan Caius defined a Spaniel using forty-seven words. By comparison, each of the thirteen Spaniels recognized as purebreds today by the AKC has a breed standard containing more than two thousand words, Brackman says. It's like the difference between defining a chair in five words (something on which one sits) and a wing chair in nineteen words (something on which one sits that has wings mounted on its back and stretching down to the armrest). Adding words narrows the definition and can create a new style, or breed, of anything. The moniker Ascob Cocker Spaniel, for example, may sound somehow ancient and related to royalty, but it was created to stand for "any solid color other than black."

As some of the definitions have changed, so have the interpretations of what the words mean, to the point that even the same exact breed standard could have meant one thing a century ago but a different thing today. "Some breed standards describe a dog as powerful," Brackman explains. "The word hasn't changed, but what the word means in relation to what is powerful today has. Consequently, dogs get bigger. So even in breeds that have standards that remain unchanged, change can occur nonetheless."

Vague words in breed standards, too, can lead a breed to evolve from one thing into another. If a breed standard states, "the shorter muzzle is preferred," then inevitably, breeders trying to win in the show ring will create dogs with shorter and shorter muzzles. The result is dogs whose heads are flattened to the point that they have trouble taking in air through their deformed snouts.

All the while, Brackman says, breeding to these standards to achieve any single physical thing often unintentionally leads to other things. "What geneticists have discovered in only the last decade is that in dogs (and probably other animals as well), many traits are prepackaged, not à la carte. For example, if you select for a broader head, you'll get thicker legs as well." In some cases, breeding for physical characteristics may mean affecting things like health and behavior, too. "When people see dogs, they see shape and temperament," she adds. "In actuality, most genetic variants control traits we can't see at all."

Consider herding dogs, which comprise about ninety breeds today. Seventeen of them have a mutation that was, until recent times, unknown to even the most successful breeders. The mutation allows some newly invented medications to travel into the dog's brain, causing illness or death. Breeders didn't realize they were selecting for this mutation until veterinarians started giving dogs the modern drugs. The mutation was invisible and likely genetically coupled to something else that fit the "ideal" physical breed standard.

"It just hitchhiked in with other traits, or whatever prevented the problem was inadvertently thrown out with other traits people didn't like," Brackman says. "Even though the breed looks the same in 1900 as it does today, that doesn't mean there haven't been changes. Maybe we just can't see them."

Some mutations, she says, are tolerated because dog lovers feel they are a reasonable trade-off to get the desired look—but in other cases, continuing to buy some purebred dogs because of their style only makes the dogs themselves miserable.

"I'm a sucker for English Setters," she says. "They have health issues like thyroid deficiency, allergies, and some dysplasias of both hip and elbow. My Setters and I can live with that. If other diseases affect your favorite breed causing severe difficulties, pain, and suffering, then the buyer/pet owners should do the right thing. Who decides when enough is enough? It's the pet owner who bears the emotional loss and financial costs of veterinary care for unhealthy dogs. If a breed is suffering from genetic disease, don't buy that breed."

It's going to take more than a hundred years for scientists to enjoy the same amount of time kennel clubs have had to convince dog lovers of their beliefs about breeds, and the notion of breeds will no doubt persist well into the next generation of dog buyers, at least. Many stereotypes are so deeply ingrained that dog lovers shake off contradicting evidence as an affront to common sense. Golden Retrievers have always been beloved, they think, without knowing that during the 1900s the breed's name was changed from the plain-sounding "yellow" to make them more marketable. Labradors have always been sought after in all their forms, dog lovers believe today, without realizing that during the 1800s the yellow ones were killed at birth because black was the more popular color of the day. The Boston Terrier, dog lovers might argue, must have a historic New England lineage, when in reality, the dogs started out being promoted by a group calling itself the American Bull Terrier Club. The name of the breed was changed near the turn of the twentieth century to make American buyers believe the Boston Terrier was as fabled a breed as those whose names included well-known English places like West Highland, Yorkshire, and Staffordshire.

Given how long some stereotypes have had to bake into the brains of dog buyers everywhere, it's going to be a long while before many will be able to acknowledge that they're choosing breeds primarily because of physical attributes—and not in any measurable way because of temperament or health.

"It's perfectly fine to have a personal preference, primarily visually," Bradley says. "It's a little like picking a boyfriend. First, you start by how they look and what appeals to you. The difficulty is when you start reading a whole lot more into it than that. I like chocolate and you like strawberry: that's fine. Everybody has a right to have the kind of dog they want. That's a perfectly reasonable expectation. The place where people get into trouble is when they attach behavioral expectations to that."

Americans who love Border Collies brought lawyers to the fight about what constitutes a dog breed—about who gets to define and own the meaning of each brand. Donald McCaig dubbed the effort not just a skirmish but instead the "Dog Wars" in his memoir about the battle.

It happened twenty years ago, in 1995, when the AKC began to recognize Border Collies as a breed eligible for conformation dog shows like Westminster. Until that time, Border Collies had competed only in obedience and tracking trials as a "miscellaneous breed," because for several centuries the dogs had been bred for skills, primarily the herding of sheep. They often didn't even look like one another, which meant they didn't fit neatly into the breed standards. Many Border Collie breeders and owners wanted them kept out of the show ring, horrified at the idea of their favorite dogs being bred to look alike and sold as Border Collies without possessing any of the traditional skills, and afraid that copycat breeders would soon fill large-scale puppy farms with lookalikes of whatever the breed standard required.

"Working Border Collies come in many sizes, colors, and appearances," McCaig explains. "Historically, breeding for conformation destroys working abilities in a few generations. We didn't want that to happen to the world's most useful working stock dog."

The AKC operates by designating a parent club to be the official standard-bearer for each breed. In 1994, when the AKC decided it wanted to include Border Collies in its conformation shows, it wrote letters to three different Border Collie clubs, asking if one would like to be designated the AKC parent club. The clubs were split in their responses, and in 1996, the AKC designated the Border Collie Society of America as the official parent club. The opposition, including McCaig, drew funds from a donation-filled Border Collie Defense Fund in a legal attempt to overturn the AKC recognition outright, or to require the AKC to register the show dogs as something other than Border Collies—to protect the breed name that had, for so long, been associated with behavior instead of looks. They used lawyers and the media, and they tried to get help from politicians. Ultimately, though, they failed. All three existing Border Collie clubs would not come together in the legal action, and the AKC registrations commenced while the infighting among the breeders continued, to the point that the legal case was fatally weakened.

The experience was like a newly carved stake being struck into the landscape that show breeders had been mining since the mid-1800s. It proved that even today, if a registry like the AKC can get just one group of breeders to buy into the existing paradigm and become a parent club, anointed much like the royalty of generations past, then the registry can continue to add new breeds to the books and the dog shows indefinitely.

"Unfortunately there are now two distinct breeds: the Border Collie and AKC Border Collie (aka Barbie Collie)," McCaig writes two decades after the loss. "A few Border Collies look like Barbie Collies, not many Barbie Collies can work livestock. The downside is that naïve puppy buyers might be taken in by the AKC breeder who knows nothing about stock work but claims his/her dogs 'could work, if only . . .'"

The United States Border Collie Club continues to encourage owners to register their dogs not with the AKC, but instead with such groups as the American Border Collie Club—which is just one example of single-breed clubs that do not always agree with the actions of all-breed clubs like the AKC. One Border Collie breeder went so far as to have all puppy buyers sign a contract stating that if even one puppy were registered with the AKC, then legal damages of $10,000 would be due. The puppy buyer may have been stunned to learn that options exist for purebred registry beyond the AKC in America, but there are, in fact, many, including individual breed clubs as well as the all-breed ACA and APRI. Some breeders say the ACA and APRI were formed in direct opposition after the AKC raised its per-dog registration prices and, in one breeder's words, "got snotty to deal with."

The American registries don't always agree with one another about breed standards, just as the AKC, the Kennel Club in England, and FCI don't always agree at the international level. These differences have led to more threats of legal action as the years have gone on and the breeds have multiplied worldwide, with all kinds of breeders threatening to sue various clubs for various reasons, including to protect their share of any particular breed's business.

In 1999, Labrador breeders went to US federal court and filed a class action lawsuit against the AKC over its changing of breed standards to favor one size of Labrador versus others. In 2005, FCI, meeting that year in Argentina, kept breeders in the emerging dog market of Japan happy by officially creating two Akita breeds: the American Akita and the Japanese Akita. In 2012, an American Coton de Tuléar breeder sued the AKC, trying to prevent registration for many of the same reasons the Border Collie people had cited years earlier. (She lost, and the Coton de Tuléar made its Westminster dog show debut in 2015.) In 2014, a Dutch citizen named Jack Vanderwyk with residences in France and the United Kingdom wrote an open letter to the Kennel Club protesting the way it registers Labrador Retrievers, threatening to take the matter to court if the British club continued to recognize standards being accepted by the AKC across the pond. Around that same time in 2014 in Canada, breeders of French Bulldogs were going mad about proposed changes to the breed standard by its national club, saying future French Bulldogs would look nothing like their forebears.

As more and more of these incidents get publicized, along with critiques about the health and welfare of show dogs bred solely for looks, the legitimacy of breeds and breeders in the most developed dog markets erodes. In the United States, for instance, McCaig says the power of the AKC has diminished in the years since the Border Collie dustup.

"The AKC is increasingly irrelevant," he writes. "At the time, they were all powerful. The AKC, as breeders put it, could 'put you out of dogs.' They are less powerful and poorer today. Their registration figures have plummeted since the Dog Wars. Their number one problem today is conformation breeding practices often produce unsound dogs, which is becoming common knowledge. Instead of 'AKC REG' being a guarantee of quality, increasingly it's seen as the opposite. The AKC can 'recognize' any breed they want, but some breeds (Jack Russell Terrier, English Shepherd, Border Collie) have formed successful single-breed registries."

Even the AKC admits to challenges of perception in recent years and has begun a campaign to make the word *breeder* as beloved as it used to be—although instead of blaming the shifts in public attitudes on disgruntled breeders or new scientific studies, the kennel club instead cites animal welfare organizations as its primary problem. In the fall 2013 edition of *Ruff Drafts*, the newsletter of the Dog Writers Association of America, AKC Board of Directors Chairman Alan Kalter wrote: "There is no doubt that prejudice against breeders has impacted our breeders, our sport and the public's ability to enjoy the unique experience of a purebred dog in their lives. Just twenty years ago, a purebred dog was the dog to have in your life. Twenty years ago, a responsible breeder was viewed as a respected resource. Twenty years ago there were virtually no important legislative efforts aimed at eradicating all dog breeding. What changed in those twenty years? The noble quest to give every dog a 'forever' home was co-opted by the animal-rights organizations as a method to raise funds for their mission to completely eliminate pet ownership."

Kalter is right about the fact that animal welfare groups have made a dent in breeders' business model, and he's right that some animal rights activists have called for an outright end to owning dogs (more on those issues later), but the reality is that when it comes to eliminating pet ownership, there isn't any real danger. About thirteen million people in the United States and Western Europe alone buy dogs every year, and demand is rising throughout many other parts of the world. Plenty of breeders are still hard at work selling existing breeds as usual—and trying to create even more new breeds to entice us all.

Could the German Blabrador be the next great breed, someday standing right alongside the Pointers and Labradors and Bloodhounds at dog shows, and in such high demand that it goes for top dollar at the auction houses?

Ken Anderson sure hopes so. He and his wife, Abby, have spent fourteen years producing all kinds of puppies at their Sugarfork

Kennels in Goodman, Missouri, and they have a breeding stock of about ninety dogs today. They take great pride in the dogs they sell to pet stores and direct to the public via the Internet, primarily to buyers from New York, New Jersey, Florida, and California. Over the years, they've been asked by telephone about a half dozen times whether they are a puppy mill, likely because of the volume of dogs they produce. Abby asks the callers what a puppy mill is, and she says most callers define it as a filthy place where the dogs are mistreated. She and Ken work hard not to fit that description, and she quite visibly frets about every puppy having a good and loving home. The Andersons are pro–spay and neuter, too, often having the surgery done themselves before sending the puppies to their new owners. "If they don't want to breed the dog, then do the thing that's responsible," as Abby puts it. "I'm big on Planned Parenthood when it comes to the animals."

The Andersons invite anyone who buys a puppy from them to visit their farm, and they regret that a lot of shoppers turn them down, opting instead to "click and ship" the puppies. Anyone who had taken up their offer to visit Sugarfork on a sunny afternoon in November 2013 would have seen the Andersons' bigger breeds, like the Boxers and Dogues de Bordeaux and Bulldogs, romping inside enclosures nearly the size of ball fields while most of their smaller breeds, like the Brussels Griffons, Pugs, and Shih Tzus, were in stacked cages. Occasionally, a few of the dogs in the stacked section would growl and bark at one another through the enclosures, but Ken tended to them, making sure they couldn't get near one another to cause any physical harm. All of the dogs looked clean and physically healthy, and most of the dogs seemed content, with a few of the larger dogs chasing one another around the pens as if at an off-leash dog park in center city Philadelphia or Los Angeles.

One dog, though, stood apart on the farm that day. He was pitch black and had the run of the place, bopping and loping around with his tail wagging and his ears flopping and his tongue dangling out of his wide mouth with a goofy smile. He was special at Sugarfork, and he seemed to know it. As Ken sat down to take a break from the day's chores in all the kennels, this particular dog sauntered up to him and sniffed around his camouflage pants, eager for some of his master's attention.

If an everyday dog lover had seen this pooch on the street, the reaction would probably have been that he was a mutt with some Labrador in him.

"This is him," Ken said with a grin, sitting up in his chair and petting the dog with the satisfaction of a proud papa. "The German Blabrador."

Ken invented the German Blabrador after breeding a Labrador to a Bloodhound, and then breeding the resulting puppies to a German Shorthaired Pointer. So far, he has produced two litters, and he says the ACA has offered to register the third generation officially. It would show up on the ACA website right between the Gelockter Bichon and the German Broken-Coated Pointing Dog, a few lines above the German Shepherd in the alphabetical list of breeds.

Is that the same as worldwide recognition by the AKC, the Kennel Club in Britain, and FCI? No—but give it time. The Rat Terrier, Chinook, and Portuguese Podengo introduced at Westminster in 2014 also had to start somewhere and work their way through the registries. The Portuguese Podengo, for instance, while just accepted by the AKC in 2013, has been approved by the Kennel Club in England since 2004. FCI published its version of the breed standard in 2008. With time and effort, there's no reason the German Blabrador can't also become recognized worldwide as a new style of dog available to the general public with credentialed paperwork.

So far, Ken says, the German Blabradors he has created are all great at hunting deer antlers, and since things are going so well, he and Abby are just as excited about continuing the project as they are about breeding their other dogs. After all, that's what breeders do, and they are proud to do it in a way that keeps buyers coming back, even if their puppies never set one paw in a show ring like Westminster's. Their pride is in producing healthy, happy pets that people want to take home.

"You can breed two champions and get junk," Abby says, waving her hand as if to dismiss much of the hullabaloo that surrounds certain breed standards today. What matters to her is creating puppies who become valued members of people's families. And she has plenty of customers, so she must be doing something right.

That same logic applies to her competitors, too. While the Andersons don't advertise the prices they charge for their puppies, some of their competitors are striving to drive prices as high as possible by turning dogs into show ring champions—and receiving inquiries from customers all around the globe.

CHAPTER FOUR

FREELANCE PRODUCERS

"Quality means doing it right when no one is looking."

—*Henry Ford*

Colleen Nicholson didn't sense that anything was wrong when a woman and her five-year-old daughter came to visit. Not at first, anyway. They seemed like perfectly lovely people who wanted to buy one of the Doberman Pinscher puppies Nicholson had listed for sale. The pups were still too young to travel on that day, so the mother and daughter also spent plenty of time with Nicholson's adult male Doberman, Magnum, and he loved them both. They seemed like the kind of people who would give a dog a great life—the only kind of people Nicholson ever allows to buy puppies from her Kelview Dobermans business in central Pennsylvania, where prices ranging from $2,400 to more than $3,500 usually weed out anybody who doesn't intend to treat a dog as a valued member of the family.

"The puppies were six weeks old, and we hadn't met her husband," says Nicholson, whose sister works with her to ensure everything is in place before the puppies grow old enough to leave. "We want to meet everybody. She'd say, 'Oh, he's a surgeon, he's busy,' but we insisted. They came on a Friday night in separate cars because he was coming from the hospital. He got out of his Mercedes, and he was this little squatty guy, and his posture was just pure arrogance. We brought Magnum out—Magnum, who loves the world—and he stopped short and growled at him. We asked him to wash his hands, thinking maybe it was the antiseptic smell from the hospital, but it didn't help. So now, our red flag is up. We trust Magnum's instincts.

"I said, 'I'm sorry, clearly something is wrong, so I'm going to give you back your deposit,'" Nicholson remembers saying.

The surgeon did not take her decision well.

"He started pacing back and forth and then he started shouting, 'You can't do this to me! I can buy whatever dog I want!'" she recalls. "Then I turned my back to get his check, which I hadn't cashed, and he grabbed a lamp. The mother put the daughter behind her. She'd obviously seen that before. Magnum was by my side. If that guy had gotten any closer . . ."

Nicholson's sister called for help, including the police, but in short order the man stormed out and drove away. The family never contacted Nicholson again, but the surgeon did come up in conversation during the following months at regional dog shows.

"We heard he got a German Shepherd," she says, shaking her head with disgust. "Somebody gave that guy a dog."

As hard as it is to believe, the only thing standing between some of the highest-priced puppies in the world and whatever people want to do to them is often a single human being's integrity. When it comes to the small-scale end of the breeding business, the breeders and the buyers can get away with pretty much anything unless another person stands in their way. It's just as true of breeders who sell dogs to a surgeon with anger issues as it is of breeders who follow the surprisingly common practice of killing Boxer puppies at birth simply because they're born with white fur. At this end of the industry, regulators are virtually nowhere to be found. Everything the dogs endure, as with so many dogs around the world, boils down to human character and decency.

Nicholson is what's known in the dog industry as a hobby breeder, which means a small-scale seller of dogs who usually turns out one or two litters of puppies a year. Hobby breeders often describe themselves as people trying to better their breed, and they produce pet dogs as well as show dogs. That's why the prices for Nicholson's puppies have a range: She charges more for the ones who have the most potential to win judges' attention in the future. Hobby breeders usually are involved with breed clubs and registries, they sometimes invest more money in testing for potential health problems than other breeders, and they generally are people who let their adult dogs live in their homes as members of their families, just as Nicholson did with Magnum. They often breed dogs as an income-generating hobby, just as the label implies. Nicholson, for one, earns her day-to-day living as a real estate agent.

Legally speaking, though, a hobby breeder is no different than a back yard breeder, which is anybody who has a litter of puppies and offers them for sale. A back yard breeder might be somebody whose dog gets accidentally pregnant, or who sells a few litters of puppies each year with no desire to do anything but make a quick buck. In the eyes of most governments worldwide, hobby breeders and back yard breeders fall into the same category: noncommercial and unregulated. In America, breeders aren't inspected by federal agents if they have fewer than four breeding females. The level at which legal regulation begins differs from nation to nation—in the United Kingdom, a breeder must own at least five females, for example, while in Ireland, it's six or more intact female dogs—but generally speaking, laws that regulate breeders are based on the notion that smaller is usually trustworthy. The US government says hobby breeders need no regulating because they "already provide sufficient care to their animals." The British Parliament took up a debate about puppy farms during 2014 while altogether ignoring the small-scale breeders. Frankly, nobody even knows who all the hobby and back yard breeders are, let alone where they are, so any inspectors trying to find them and regulate them would be utterly, hopelessly lost.

The lack of regulation means that standards vary wildly among small-scale breeders, which is how a lamp-wielding surgeon can get turned away by Nicholson while receiving a warm reception from a breeder of German Shepherds. Hobby breeders are, for the most part, free to conduct business however they see fit. If they aren't trying to win at dog shows, which would require them to register their dogs with a group like the AKC or the Kennel Club in Britain, then there's no reason for them to do anything at all beyond breeding a puppy somebody will pay money to buy.

Nicholson got into hobby breeding after buying her first Doberman in 1978 from a back yard breeder, a man she later realized was the epitome of everything that is wrong with the small-breeder end of the dog industry. Somebody had taken her to a dog show, and she'd fallen in love with the look of Dobermans. She did what most dog buyers did in those days: looked in the newspaper classified ads to find a Doberman puppy for sale.

"I paid three hundred seventy-five dollars," she says. "It was a guy with a few Dobermans. He had both the parents there, the place wasn't dirty, and he was friendly, but the dog had diarrhea and was vomiting from the time I got home. The dog never got right. He always had chronic issues. And he had a nasty temperament. We went to a conformation class, and at four months old, he was trying to bite the judge."

Nicholson remembers calling the breeder and asking for help. After all, $375 was a lot of money back then, the equivalent of about $1,400 today. The price, she'd thought, should have been some indication of quality. "They said, 'You got your puppy, we got paid, we're done,'" she recalls. "It was an ugly education."

The dog died of cancer at age four, and Nicholson decided she could set a far better example personally for the breed that had left her so smitten. "Our whole intention was to better the breed and make great puppies," she says today, after twenty-five years in the breeding business with her sister. "We would never treat people the way those people treated us with our first dog."

Dog shows fascinated Nicholson, so she also took up handling as a hobby, showing other people's dogs in the ring for a fee and learning, a little more each time, about which qualities mattered to her. She cared about temperament and health because of her previous experience. She could see that some dogs were more trainable than others. She began to learn what physical qualities met the AKC breed standard. Nicholson wasn't exactly shopping while she was handling, but she was always on the lookout for a great puppy, and one day, she saw a four-month-old Dobie who made her swoon.

"The woman tells me it's a thousand dollars," Nicholson says with a laugh. "I'm twenty years old at the time. I've got about a hundred dollars, but she'd seen me showing dogs."

They made a deal for Nicholson to work off the rest of the price by forgoing handling fees, and that's how she ended up bringing Magnum home. He was everything she'd imagined even before that awful night with the surgeon. The Doberman was sweet, beautiful, smart, protective, and great with kids—the kind of dog lots of people might want. Part of the deal was that she'd allow the woman to breed Magnum, and that's when she started paying visits to the experienced breeder's home to learn about newborn puppies, when she wasn't asking around elsewhere. "This whole time I was still showing dogs, and I was picking the brains of the old-school breeders," Nicholson says. "I was learning how the sire brought this quality and the female brought this other quality."

Magnum was bred five times in his life. The first time Nicholson tried with her own female, she got twelve healthy puppies—but the mother wouldn't produce any milk. She had the dog spayed and found her a calm life among people in a nursing home. "This is my hobby," she says. "It's not the dog's hobby. Some dogs love to be moms. Some don't. It's not for everyone, and that's okay."

She has spent as long as a year trying to choose a stud for her females, whom she doesn't breed before age three because she doesn't think they're yet mature enough to handle motherhood. "I think at three, they're mentally ready to be a mom," she says, adding that by age three, the dogs have had all their major health tests and been in conformation dog shows enough times to earn champion status. "The dog is settled enough that it can be a responsible mother. You can breed them younger, but it's not okay. A twelve- or thirteen-year-old girl can have a baby, but should she? It's pretty basic common sense."

Nicholson typically breeds her dogs less than a half dozen times throughout their lives before allowing them to retire as pets in her home. She says they live out their days playing with other Dobermans and have plenty of access to the two grass-covered acres that surround her house when they're not separated in their crates. She expects everyone who buys a puppy from her to give the dog that same quality of life, and she is available to owners of her pups right up until the inevitable end.

"When your puppy is twelve and a half and dying, I am supportive," she says. "I am helpful. You're not just buying that puppy. You're buying into my knowledge."

Last year, Nicholson says, she had about fifty people, many of them repeat customers, on a waiting list for the twelve puppies she produced—and she doesn't even let them choose their own dogs. She learns each puppy's temperament and then matches them to each buyer's lifestyle, offering only the puppy she thinks will do best with each family. Retired senior citizens, for instance, will never get the most energetic dog in the litter, no matter how much they love the pup's color or are willing to pay. If a person doesn't want the puppy she offers, then Nicholson moves on to a buyer she believes will give the dog a top-notch life. Plenty of people on the list are willing to take whatever dog she gives them.

Another thing she refuses to do is ship puppies to people who want them sent by plane after finding her on the Internet. Buyers have to come to her home so she can evaluate them before handing them a dog in person—and each bill of sale requires the new owner to complete at least one level of obedience class with a professional trainer. She also takes handling fees of about $85 per showing from owners whose dogs she brings into AKC-sanctioned rings, and she reserves the right to use at least some of the dogs she sells for breeding purposes, although that doesn't always happen.

"We could breed more, but we are making a choice not to make a living off the animals," she says. "Two acres next door came up for sale a while back, and we could've bought it and expanded, but we didn't."

She'll even tell buyers, with brutal honesty, that not all of the puppies she produces have been perfect. Life is not perfect, she says, and even the best breeders can't guarantee that nature won't take a wrong turn. When she talks about bettering the Doberman breed, she means aiming for puppies who are physically sound, have good temperaments, and show no signs of common Doberman health problems such as hip dysplasia, the bleeding disorder Von Willebrand disease, hypothyroidism, or cardiomyopathy. But twice in the past thirteen years or so, she had puppies born with problems she could not predict. One had juvenile renal disease and had to be euthanized at just over a year old. The other puppy was born about a decade later with only one kidney.

"With that dog, I gave them the option of a new dog or their money back, and they took the money and used it for vet bills," she says. "The dog lived to be two. It was heartbreaking."

Neither of those dogs, of course, was bred to create more puppies—which is the real rub for Nicholson when it comes to small-scale breeders who say they're just like her but in fact care about nothing but sales, like the man who bred the first Doberman she owned. Buyers sometimes disappoint her, too. She has known well-respected people in the show dog world, including one veterinarian who stunned her by allowing puppies Nicholson had bred to live in disturbing conditions, to the point that Nicholson bought at least one of the dogs back. She avoids some of her fellow hobby breeders as potential partners because she repeatedly sees their dogs being born with health issues or bad temperaments, and she knows as well as anyone that some hobby breeders with respectable credentials would have given that abusive surgeon a dog, cashed his check, and continued with business as usual.

She sincerely wishes all puppy buyers would investigate breeders like her as thoroughly as she investigates them. Doing so would solve a lot of the problems dogs are forced to endure.

"A full-time breeder is not necessarily a professional," Nicholson says. "When I say professional, I am talking about integrity, loyalty, honesty, trust. I'm talking about character you should be proud to have."

It's important for buyers to ask questions, she says. Then ask more questions. And more still. If any breeder, even one who seems to have impeccable references and is charging thousands of dollars, won't answer every question or make eye contact, move on. The governments of the world may think small breeders are generally more trustworthy, but Nicholson, based on her years of experience, does not always agree.

"Never," she says, pausing for emphasis, "never *ever* make assumptions."

A utilities meter reader, sent to do an everyday house check on usage for May 2014, was the first person to notice the smell. It was wafting like invisible, toxic clouds from inside the house in Paoli, Indiana, a small suburb of Louisville, Kentucky, where neighbors mostly keep to themselves.

The meter reader called the Orange County Sheriff's Department, and Chief Deputy Josh Babcock arrived soon after. He and his fellow officers pulled air-purifying respirators over their faces to protect their noses and throats from burning in the putrid ammonia stench. They walked around the house, often not believing what they were seeing: two to three inches of feces in some places where dogs were walking. Kibble had been tossed atop the muck, though there was no water in bowls or anywhere else the pups inside the home could reach. Nine Poodles were packed into three cages, and another twelve Poodles were free to roam through the sludge. Some had maggots living in their skin, including under their eyelids. A veterinarian later shaved nine pounds of matted hair and feces from a single dog, with some of the clumps nearly the size of baseballs.

"In twenty years of law enforcement," Babcock told reporters, "it's one of the worst homes I've ever been into."

Then came the truly shocking news from WLKY News, WBIB News, and WDRB News: The breeder charged with animal cruelty was named Laura King. Her references, if anyone buying a Poodle puppy from her had asked, could have included Metropolitan Veterinary Specialists in Louisville, where she worked as a veterinary technician during evening hours. Plenty of dog owners knew her and trusted her, based on the care she had given their pets, and she apparently thought she could maintain that façade, having called her boss to describe her sudden absence from work not as involving a possible jail sentence but instead as a family emergency. Her colleagues found out about the charges only by seeing the story on the local news. They'd been aware she was a Poodle breeder, but nobody had ever visited the Paoli home. The people who knew King and worked with her—every last one of them an animal care professional—said they were as stunned as everyone else to learn what appeared to be the horrific truth.

A lot of dog lovers trust people like vet techs and might look to them and veterinarians first when it comes to locating a responsible breeder. Buyers think they're up to speed because they've seen the commercials on television and the advertisements imploring everyone to be on the lookout for irresponsible breeders trying to make a fast buck by keeping hundreds of dogs at a time living in squalor. Nobody wants to support the so-called puppy mills, so dog lovers look for people selling dogs who seem small scale and honest, and who come with a good reference from a trusted friend or veterinarian.

That may have been a reasonable practice in the past, but nowadays, the world's worst small-scale breeders know it's what the buyers are doing. Sellers are adapting their business practices and marketing stories accordingly. The least responsible are making themselves look an awful lot like the Colleen Nicholsons, to the point that buyers often can't tell the difference when handing over cash to bring a puppy home.

Despite the huge scope of the breeding business worldwide, many of the people dealing in purebred puppies are still tiny, independent producers. Consolidation has not yet come to this industry the way it has in others, and because so many of the breeders are freelance operations, they often end up doing business however they please. The AKC and the Kennel Club in Britain each have inspection programs that purport to give buyers some kind of a legitimacy guarantee for breeders who turn out just a couple litters of puppies a year, but criticism reigns on both sides of the Atlantic about how few breeders the associations ever actually inspect. In 2013, the AKC acknowledged that it had no idea how many breeders in America owned AKC-registered dogs and that it had just nine inspectors covering the entire nation. Also in 2013, the Kennel Club released data in Britain showing it had inspected less than 4 percent of breeders admitted into its Assured Breeder Scheme that year, and that 90 percent of new breeders—nine out of ten—who had previously registered at least five litters of puppies, and who had been given the right to use the "Assured Breeder" label when talking with customers, had never been inspected at all.

Even breeders sanctioned by these groups as experts can turn out to be charlatans who keep adult dogs in miserable conditions while selling their puppies as top grade. It can go on for years. In January 2013, the AKC reported that it had stripped the dog show judge and Chihuahua breeder Margaret Ann Hamilton of all privileges for a decade. The action came after authorities in Washington State searched two homes and, according to the *Seattle Post-Intelligencer* and the *Issaquah Press*, found about a hundred dogs living in feces-covered stacked crates, walking in neurotic circles from constant confinement, and desperately in need of medical care, some so badly malnourished their jawbones were decomposed or gone. Yet like the accused vet tech in Indiana, Hamilton had outstanding references as a small-scale breeder if anyone buying a Chihuahua puppy from her had cared to ask.

What's even scarier for conscious consumers trying to buy dogs from responsible sources is that operators like King and Hamilton were reportedly working alone, or at most with the help of a spouse. In some parts of the world, animal welfare advocates say this game of tricking buyers of purebred puppies has expanded not only across city and state lines but also national borders, and it is now best described as multinational organized crime, or a "puppy mafia." Buyers are on the lookout for massive mills or farms when the new problem is sometimes a network of irresponsible small-scale breeders working together—in a way that can be invisible to regulators who, like buyers, are watching for larger-scale abuses.

"Not all of these are about mass breeding farms," says Julie Sanders, the United Kingdom manager for Four Paws, an international animal charity with offices throughout Europe as well as in South Africa and the United States. "Some of them are about dealers in Eastern Europe having as many as three thousand breeders, and they are collecting from different breeders because they need puppies on the go at different times."

Sanders has had a front row seat since UK officials relaxed the nation's dog import laws in 2012, bringing them in line with European Union standards. Before that change, a dog could get a rabies shot and then had to wait six months (the disease's incubation period) before entering the United Kingdom. The regulation was relaxed to make it easier for everyday people to travel across borders with their pets, and it created a loophole now being exploited to sell far younger puppies from Eastern Europe, where animal welfare laws are looser. The targeted buyers are unsuspecting, high-paying people in major Western European cities such as Amsterdam, Berlin, and Madrid, and ultimately throughout Britain.

The numbers during just the past few years show the zeal with which Eastern European breeders are pouncing on the new business opportunity. Between 2011 and 2013 alone, the number of dogs entering the United Kingdom from Poland, Romania, Hungary, and Lithuania rose from two thousand to twelve thousand. Romania, in a single year, had an increase in dog exports to Britain of more than 1,000 percent. Often, Sanders says, the puppies arrive shockingly young and sometimes sick, with forged vaccination papers and whatever else the sellers need to offload them to buyers who think they're getting a good bargain on a purebred dog.

Sanders, working with an undercover team posing as wholesale buyers, traced some of the puppies to one typical source: an animal market held every Sunday in Poland next to the regular market selling food, clothes, and other goods. She saw Chihuahuas, Miniature Pinschers, Staffordshire Terriers, Siberian Huskies, German Shepherds, Beagles, Maltese, Yorkshire Terriers, Spaniels, and more, all lined up alongside the goats, horses, ducks, geese, and other animals for sale. The dog dealers had signs claiming to be adoption organizations—which Sanders says makes it legal to sell individual puppies there—but in fact were offering pups for sale en masse, creating the starting point and setting the sales quotas for the networks that transport the dogs to the deepest-pocketed puppy buyers in Germany, the Netherlands, Spain, and Britain. The numbers of pups coming out of such places can be shocking; one dealer in Slovakia estimated that he alone distributed more than ten thousand dogs a year across Europe.

"It's extremely sophisticated," she says. "We were told when we were doing undercover filming at the puppy market that we had to buy more than ten puppies a month, and we were told to buy more because some would die en route—but not to worry because we'll still make the money. They allow for a percentage over what you want, which is your wastage. It's a stressful journey for puppies, from Poland to Europe to the UK. They may not be given food, water, or anything."

The puppies are moved by land across Europe on the cheap, in trucks that may have no ventilation nor meet any other commercial standards. They're then often taken by boat into the United Kingdom, Sanders says, because inspections at seaports are less stringent than at airports. Trucks collect the puppies at the seaport dock, or UK-based dealers meet the shippers on the side of a nearby road, and then the puppies are distributed to private homes throughout Britain, with just a few being offloaded at every stop. That way, they can be made to look like newborns from small-scale, individual breeders and everyday people, who advertise them on the Internet to duped buyers who think they're giving money to fellow Brits who treat dogs responsibly.

"We've been told that some people try to purchase the breeds that match the dogs they have in the house, so people don't ask questions," she says. "Some people give a lame excuse, such as they're selling it on behalf of a friend. Recently we were told they're bringing the mothers over with the puppies because the puppies are so young, and so the mothers can be there to sell the puppies, then they bring them back to the puppy farms, which are horrendous."

The reality for savvy, small-scale breeders or even networks of them today is that the law, or lack thereof, makes it easy to cut corners pretty much anywhere in the world—and the fact that more and more people shop for dogs on the Internet provides a steady stream of customers to the worst offenders. Websites can be made to look nice when real-life conditions are deplorable. Even trusted online brands, sites many people regularly support with business in other areas, can be part of the problem when it comes to dogs.

"Next year, we're targeting classified ad websites, including eBay, in 10 countries where we operate," Sanders said about a 2016 campaign, explaining that eBay doesn't sell animals, but it owns a number of classified ad sites worldwide where animals are advertised, including Gumtree in the UK, which is similar to Craigslist in the United States. "Classified ad sites are helping to fuel the trade in puppies with a lack of regulation. They are being exploited by illegal and irresponsible breeders and sellers, with disastrous consequences for the animals."

Dog lovers can shake their heads at the magnitude of it all and at the way abuses are infecting parts of their lives they thought were pristine, but the reality is that no matter how many laws are enacted or investigations are done, buyers are often the only stopgap that can prevent the abuses in the first place. They are far too often the only ones in a position to decide whether a small-scale dog seller is a Colleen Nicholson or an international smuggler. No matter where dog lovers look around the world, unless a small-scale breeder is accused of animal cruelty, often buyers are the only ones ever aware that he is selling puppies at all.

"As long as there is demand, there will always be suppliers," Sanders says. "If there is money to be made, people will do it."

Stefano Paolantoni is the owner of Dell'Alberico Kennel in Italy's bountiful Chianti region, a place whose residents know more than a little about how to grow and sell products the rest of the world admires. Today, Paolantoni is recognized as a world-class breeder of Lhasa Apsos, Maltese, and Toy Poodles, but he got his start much as Colleen Nicholson did halfway around the world, with a single dog. He then chose a different path, producing more and more puppies year after year, showing how a single breeder can become an international player whose dogs now have ties throughout Europe, in the United States, in Japan, and in Russia.

As a child during the 1970s, Paolantoni had a German Shepherd he took to field trials, where dogs are judged on skills instead of looks. He heard about the conformation dog shows and became curious, and he met a woman named Annigje "Annie" Schneider-Louter, whose Van de Warwinckel Kennel in Holland had been the first to bring Lhasa Apsos into the Netherlands, from Belgium and England, in 1965. Schneider-Louter was also a Lhasa Apso judge, which means she not only was producing the first litters of the breed ever to be born in Holland, but also was helping to shape the breed standard all across Europe.

When she befriended the young newcomer Paolantoni, he was ecstatic and saw his way into the business under the wing of a seasoned pro.

"She was my mentor and later became a very important friend," he says. "She trusted me so much, and she sold me a beautiful male who was already a multi-champion, named Mi-Don Van de Warwinckel. In my opinion, everyone needs to have a good mentor for breeding. This is absolutely the most important thing for having success."

It didn't take him long, with her help, to make his own mark. By 1978, Paolantoni's Dell'Alberico Kennel was recognized by the Italian Kennel Club and by the FCI, and he imported some additional Lhasa Apsos from the United States to breed Marlo's Rocky Road, who became one of the most winning Lhasa Apso show dogs in the world. One of Rocky Road's sons, Ulderigo Dell'Alberico, was named the top all-breed dog in Italy in 1999. Soon, the Lhasa Apso puppies Paolantoni produced had buyers waiting not only throughout Europe, but also in the United Kingdom and the United States.

That's not to say he was raking in the big bucks. The total market for the breed remained small, he says, and financial gain never became his focus. Even if he'd wanted to get rich by churning out an endless stream of puppies, there just weren't enough buyers out there.

"If you have decided to breed Lhasas, it's only for passion and for nothing else," he says. "I think money is the last thing you should be focused on when you decide to breed dogs, even if you breed more popular dogs that can be sold quite easily."

Paolantoni next decided to branch out into breeding not only Lhasa Apsos, but also Maltese, which he thought he could improve with help from a partner, Franco Prosperi of Cinecittà Kennel. "At that time, the breed was not so popular like it is nowadays, and the main reason we started is that the breed was not well represented in Italy, which is the country of origin," he says. "I never thought to become rich with Maltese, and I never thought to breed just to breed. Our goal was to get the same quality I got with Lhasas."

They bought some Maltese from the United Kingdom and America, and one of the dogs they acquired had already won championships in the United States and in Europe. His name was Shanlyn Lolly O'Malley, which didn't exactly roll off people's tongues in Tuscany with the kind of flair it might have in Dublin, but the dog nevertheless became the foundation male for all the Maltese that Paolantoni has since produced and marketed as the most stylish of Italian dogs.

His Maltese puppies are now sold throughout Europe, the United States, and Japan, and quite a few of them have become top winners at dog shows worldwide. One dog, Cinecittà Breve Incontro, which he sold to a Swedish couple, was at one time the most-winning Maltese in Europe, named a world champion three times as well as a top all-breed dog in Denmark.

As the saying goes, success breeds success, and now Paolantoni is further expanding his business, this time looking to the East instead of the West for his foundation stock.

"I wanted a new goal, and I decided to find a breed I liked, and this was the Toy Poodle," he says. "Japan and Russia were the two countries where the dogs were the best quality at the moment I started with them, and this was the reason I imported my first dogs from there."

He is now working in collaboration with the Japanese breeder Toshinori Omura from a kennel called Smash, whose dogs have earned honors at Westminster, the FCI World Dog Show, and national shows everywhere from Croatia to Denmark to France. Again, Paolantoni says, his goal is not to cash in on market trends, but instead to better the breed standard and ensure the health of the dogs.

"If you are going after customers who are requiring 'teacup Poodles' or 'mini-Toy Poodles,' then of course you become a commercial breeder," he says. "A responsible breeder is not breeding according to the requests of the market. He is breeding to improve the breed and to keep it at a high level."

Another thing Paolantoni keeps at a high level is his number of dogs. He has about eighty of them now among the three breeds, although not all of them are still of breeding age. He turns out about twenty litters of puppies a year from a kennel near his home. The kennel spans three levels and encompasses nearly 6,500 square feet. He uses the first floor for grooming with an assistant and for housing puppies with their mothers until they are at least twelve weeks old. The breeding dogs and the older dogs have access to an outdoor garden, while the dogs headed for show rings are kept on the third floor, away from dirt and distractions, and instead get their exercise and training on a large terrace.

Paolantoni is fine with the number of dogs in his care, and the way he talks about them implies that he does all he can in terms of their health. In fact, he wouldn't have his business any other way. He's not the kind of breeder who keeps the dogs until they're used up and then discards them. He treats them as much like pets as a lot of people who have just one or two dogs at home.

"At my home, I always have a couple of dogs who are sleeping in my bed," he says. "I can't easily keep down the number of dogs because I always keep my old dogs. My oldest dog died when he was over twenty-three years old."

And while eighty dogs may seem, to some people, like an awfully high number, it is actually a common sight on puppy farms throughout the world. In those places, far more than twenty litters of puppies a year are being produced—and those dogs don't always get to live until they're old. Most of them have never even imagined, let alone been given a chance, to sleep in a human being's bed, and the only thing they have to do with dog shows is filling the demand created by them.

CHAPTER FIVE

BIG PRODUCTION COMPANIES

"The mainstream is always under attack."
—*Bill Gates*

Dave Miller would like to support a local dog rescue group someone mentioned to him. The seventy-five-year-old's attitude may surprise some people, because he's one of the proudest commercial dog breeders in the world. In fact, at the time of this writing, he was president of the Missouri Pet Breeders Association, which claims to be America's largest and oldest group of its kind and is based in a state that produces, by some estimates, more than 30 percent of the dogs sold in pet stores nationwide. At the website for his business, Monark Puppies, Miller doesn't talk about dog rescue at all. Instead, he explains that on his farm, he raises beef cattle, quarter horses, dogs, and grandchildren. Anyone who visits can stand with him among the outdoor pens containing fifty or so adult Newfoundlands, Beagles, Shiba Inus, Corgis, and

Puggles. He pets the dogs and accepts their kisses with a smile, and he will tell you unequivocally that he's every bit as much a dog lover as the smaller-scale hobby and show breeders—which is one reason why the local rescue group's appeal for donations caught his attention.

"They go and get the dogs out of the shelter, and they put the dogs into foster homes, and from there they find the dogs a home," Miller says. "Now that's something that I could get behind. And I'd like to send those people some money, you know, make a donation.

"But first," he says, raising his more than six-foot frame fully upright, staring out from beneath the brim of his cowboy hat, and wagging his index finger, "they're going to have to stop calling me a puppy mill."

Miller and his wife, Judy, began raising dogs in 2003 because, as they started aging into the senior citizen class, they found the pups easier to handle than larger livestock on their farm. On the day that put them to the decision, Judy was watching from the window while Dave got tangled with a quarter horse out in the front yard. He was nearly hurt. "That's it!" she insisted, as Dave recalls. "She told me riding horses was for youngsters."

Dave had been a bird hunter and raised some hunting dogs, so he and Judy tried raising other kinds of dogs, too. They never planned on having the dozens of adult dogs they now keep, but they happened to get in on the Puggle craze of the early 2000s in America, and in their first year with just three females, they sold $10,000 worth of Puggle puppies alone. They eventually invested about $180,000 to build kennels that meet state and federal requirements, and their farm grew to become one among about 2,600 commercial puppy operations in the central United States large enough to require licensing by the federal government. As of 2012, Dave says, they were putting about $690 worth of supplies, salaries, veterinary care, and other needs into every puppy they eventually sold. They grossed $140,000 that year and kept $60,000 as net income, give or take—still a heck of a lot more than most dairy farmers bring home in the area, just the same as it was in this part of Missouri back in the 1950s.

The Millers sell puppies to brokers and pet stores as well as directly to consumers online, and while they may get $1,600 apiece for their Newfoundland pups, overall they average about $1,000 per dog. It's enough, he says, to provide for the family members and employees who help with the feeding and watering of all the dogs each day. "Judy could make more money being a greeter at Walmart," Dave says. "But you see the people here, our niece, our grandkids, and it sustains our family."

It also keeps the lights and heat on inside of the sixteen-by-eighty-foot mobile home where he lives on the farm with Judy and their grandchildren. The dimensions are noteworthy because anyone who walks around the Monark property will immediately notice that some of the dogs enjoy living spaces larger than the humans do. The Millers have open-top fenced enclosures with grass and gravel bottoms that are about thirty feet wide and eighty to a hundred feet long, big enough for even the largest Newfoundlands to work up a jaunt and play. Two to five dogs live in each pen, depending on the dogs' size, and the spaces are as clean as any back yard where pooches hang out at private homes. For shelter, the Millers provide dog houses with cedar-chip beds along with insulated water stations to prevent freezing—an important investment given that on this particular day, while afternoon temperatures were balmy, the wind chill at night would go down to twenty-two degrees Fahrenheit. Newborn puppies are not expected to stay outside in that weather; they are kept with their mothers in mostly enclosed buildings with roofs and heated beds that provide a fifty- or sixty-degree environment even if the temperature drops to zero degrees outdoors.

"I would defy anyone to raise a puppy in their home that's as well cared for as our puppies," Dave says, reaching out and rubbing behind a few ears as any dog lover might. The dogs in all the pens get excited when he, or anyone else, comes around. They jump and are sweet, wanting attention and offering kisses—big, wet, drool-laced slobbery ones, in the case of the Newfies who rest their front paws atop the gates and wag their tails like friendly neighbors. Dave says the dogs' enthusiasm for human contact is a sign of proper socialization, something he works hard to achieve with every dog on his farm.

Dave and Judy also make a point of telling buyers they do not breed their dogs until they're at least a year or two old. After that, they breed them about every six months, and most of their females give birth to five or six litters while living on the Monark land. After that, Judy takes the lead in finding each dog a home, being sure to explain the dog's life to date so there are no problems with adjustments into a more family-oriented, and often more rambunctious, lifestyle where the dog is allowed to live indoors with people. Judy says her efforts to place the dogs in homes while they're still relatively young is yet another thing that sets Monark apart from the region's less responsible commercial breeders, who breed the dogs into old age and then kill them, claiming it's the only humane thing to do because, at that point, the dogs can't adjust to another lifestyle. It happens more often than she'd like to see in this part of Missouri, a state that, according to one recent report, is home to 20 percent of the worst puppy mills in America, places where breeders have been caught with everything from dogs in cages so small they can't stand up to a frozen four-week-old Shih Tzu left outside in minus-nine-degree-Fahrenheit weather.

Nothing like that is being alleged at the Millers' farm, where government inspectors are a regular presence and every puppy is born of dogs registered with the AKC or APRI. Dave says the AKC's representatives, too, have been to his farm to do DNA testing and verify each pup's parents. He values that level of quality control, as well as the level of buyers the AKC sends his way. "We get a lot of our leads from the AKC classifieds," he says, adding that those particular buyers don't try to chip away at his asking prices the way others sometimes do. "They are high-quality buyers."

To the people who accuse him of raising dogs like livestock, always outside in enclosures like pigs, Miller does concede that there is a similarity, but probably not the one animal welfare advocates want to hear: "It's no different than cattle," he says. "If you don't take care of them, they won't produce." Locals say the Monark setup rates an eight or nine on a scale of one to ten, as commercial breeding operations go, and the Facebook endorsements the Millers receive from buyers are endlessly glowing. Calling their farm a puppy mill does more than hurt the Millers' feelings; it makes them angry, given how differently they operate from people who, at least back in the old days around here, raised puppies inside chicken coops and old dishwashers.

In fact, they say, it's insanity to equate every pet store dog with a puppy mill dog, as so many advertising campaigns do. Their dogs are sold in pet stores, they say, and their puppies as well as their adult dogs are cared for and treated with respect. As breeders, they are licensed and inspected at the federal, state, and local levels. The transport companies that take their puppies to the pet stores are licensed and inspected, too. Then the pet stores at the end of the line are licensed and inspected. There is oversight at every step along the way to ensure the dogs' health and safety—a far different scenario than when any buyer enters into a one-on-one contract to buy a puppy from a small-scale hobby or back yard breeder, or, for that matter, many nonprofit dog rescue groups.

And despite the accusations levied against him because of the number of pups he produces, Dave says, even if the whole pure-bred dog market came crashing down, his dogs would still enjoy comfortable lives as long as he had the ability to take a breath or walk a step.

"If we had a complete sellout tomorrow and if I were so broke that I couldn't buy dog food, we'd find a way to keep the ones who needed taking care of," he said, raising his eyebrows and looking over his shoulder to see if his wife happened to be watching him through the house windows. "Judy wouldn't stand for her dogs being mistreated."

Are Dave and Judy Miller running a puppy mill? Is Dave right to wave his finger with disdain when people put that label on him? Is it right to call a commercial kennel like the Millers' a puppy mill if the dogs never live inside a home, snuggle with a human on a sofa, or walk on a leash in a park, but otherwise are kept in conditions that meet all local, state, and federal regulations, receive veterinary care, and by all assessments seem happy and friendly and clean, and then produce puppies for many satisfied customers?

Is the way the Millers breed dogs on a commercial scale different enough to put them into a category other than the one that describes, say, someone like breeder Joy Wise? In July 2014, animal control officers near Cumming, Georgia, did a compliance check at Heavenly Kennels, where Wise claimed thirty-five years of experience and offered Chihuahuas, Miniature Schnauzers, Yorkshire Terriers, and other puppies for sale at online prices from $350 to $750. According to *USA Today* and the *Marietta Daily Journal*, Wise had been cited two months earlier—for 264 animal cruelty offenses, 264 animal neglect offenses, and failure to obtain a business license—and had been given a chance to clean up her property and correct the dogs' living conditions. Instead, officers said, things had worsened by the time they returned and even more dogs had been brought in. They found pooches living in their own feces and in overcrowded cages. Some were trying to sleep atop their food bowls, which were more comfortable than the open wire floors. "More than 350 Dogs Seized from Suspected Puppy Mill," read the *USA Today* headline. One dog gave birth to five puppies just a few hours after being seized. Many more were pregnant, and four dogs had puppies recently born.

What about the breeder Margaret Elaine Komorny? Is she the same as, or different than, Dave and Judy Miller? The same month when authorities took Wise's dogs, the seventy-seven-year-old Komorny was sentenced in Livingston County, Michigan, on animal cruelty charges, with local media calling her a puppy mill operator, too. According to the *Battle Creek Enquirer* and the *Livingston County Daily Press and Argus*, Komorny had been keeping ninety-one dogs at her Raisin Tree Farms kennel, where she claimed twenty-five years of experience and specialized in the sale of Whoodles (a combination of Wheaten Terriers and Poodles). Two of her dogs had to be euthanized for medical reasons after they were found living among dozens in overcrowded, feces-covered, urine-soaked cages with no food or water. Dogs had ear infections, burst eardrums, tumors, various worms in their stool, rotted teeth, and feces so matted in their fur that they scalded the males' testicles.

Or how about fifty-six-year-old Rebecca Van Meter? How does she compare with Dave and Judy Miller? The same month Wise and Komorny were brought before the law, according to WRCB News and the *Chattanooga Times Free Press*, police visited Van Meter's property in McDonald, Tennessee, an unincorporated area outside of Chattanooga. Officials had received an emergency call about the conditions dogs were enduring there—an accusation that was a far cry from what puppy buyers saw at Van Meter's website, Queen Elizabeth Pocket Beagles and Bears, where the business name was above photos of smiling kids with puppies and the message "placing therapy puppies with special needs children and adults." Sheriff's officials and workers from the local SPCA found 247 dogs in stacked kennels and pens covered in feces, urine, and standing water. Some of the dogs had mange and staph infections. A number would need several months' worth of veterinary care. "This situation helps bring focus to the need for stronger legislation," Charles Brown, the director of a local agency, told the *Times Free Press*, "because anybody can just set up a puppy mill."

All dog lovers have come to know the terms "puppy mill" and "puppy farm" in recent years. They appear on the news and in fundraising letters from animal welfare groups showing horrific photographs and asking for donations to shut down the big-scale breeders who treat dogs badly. The substandard kennels mentioned here are far more than an American phenomenon; US border patrols regularly turn up puppies being smuggled into California from puppy mills in Mexico. Ireland's reputation as the puppy farm capital of Europe became so widespread that laws were enacted in 2012 to crack down. Recent reports show that Hungary and Slovakia are now among the Eastern European nations entering the trade. In Japan— where the culture stresses conformity and fads grow fast—puppy mills spring up to cash in on hot breeds such as the Siberian Husky, whose sales skyrocketed from a few hundred to sixty thousand in a single year after the breed was featured in a television show.

But what, exactly, *is* a puppy mill? There is no legal definition, even according to leading animal welfare groups. If a puppy mill is defined as a large breeding operation, then legally operating people like the Millers are looped in with all the rest. If a puppy mill is defined as a place where dogs are kept in squalor, then it must include some one-dog back yard breeders along with the multinational smugglers, which means kennel size is irrelevant. Perhaps the best anyone can do is to say a puppy mill is a commercial breeding operation that puts profits above the well-being of dogs, but given that definition, some show dog breeders qualify, too. After all, those who continue to produce breeds like Pugs with ultra-flat noses and the resulting constant breathing problems, and to sell those puppies for thousands of dollars apiece, are arguably putting profits above the pooches' well-being. What about Colleen Nicholson, the show-quality Doberman hobby breeder? She crops the ears of her puppies, a practice that is legal and sought after by puppy buyers in America but that is banned as animal cruelty in many other parts of the world. Is she putting profits above the well-being of dogs with every $3,500 pup who goes out the door?

Even the so-called dog experts are vague in their definition. Remember the announcement made over the loudspeakers, but not for television viewers, at the 2014 Westminster Kennel Club Dog Show? The one saying with great pride that none of the dogs in the ring that week were from a puppy mill? The distinguishing factor was nothing quantifiable, and in fact nothing more than what people felt in their hearts: that they were breeders who *cared*. That's what the announcer said. It's the same argument used by Dave and Judy Miller, and by Colleen Nicholson, and probably by many people arrested on animal cruelty charges, too. Puppy mills, at the end of the day, are kind of like pornography in modern society: everybody thinks they know it when they see it, and buyers are instinctively opposed to it, but beyond that, the lines are blurred, and dog lovers keep buying the product the worst offenders are producing. If that weren't true, then puppy mills and pornographers would have all gone out of business many, many years ago.

Even breeders themselves can't agree on how to come at the issue of the largest-scale breeders, and they can be more vicious than any trained fighting dog if someone from their own team drifts too far toward the animal welfare side in the debate. A thirty-year veteran of Collie breeding named Ted Paul learned this the hard way in 2009, when lawmakers in his home state of Oregon introduced a bill that would limit the number of dogs a breeder could own. The number they settled on was fifty. They decided to choose a number, and for better or worse, they landed at fifty-one or more dogs constituting a puppy mill.

If some everyday dog lovers feel like that's a generous place to draw the line, Paul agrees. "It seems like an awful lot of dogs to me, too," he says today. "It was looked at as, people who have already gotten themselves into conditional problems where they have too many dogs, they can cut back and still have a career in dogs."

At the time the legislation was introduced, Paul testified in favor of it at the state Capitol building in Salem. He first listed his credentials: AKC dog show judge, breeder of champion Collies, past president of the Collie Club of America, past president of the Pure-bred Dog Breeders and Fanciers Association, and past president of the Cleveland Collie Club. His reputation could not have been more impeccable as a member of the breeding community, which is why he was listened to so carefully as he told the lawmakers he thought the law was an excellent idea. "My concern with the people who operate puppy mills is that they are callous, ruthless animal abusers who will breed any two animals they think will sell," he later told the HSUS, expounding on his testimony for the general public. "They are in it only for the money, and in their greed they treat animals as a cash crop deserving of no favors, just torture."

His language was harsh, and the backlash was both swift and personal. *Traitor* was one of the, well, kinder words some breeders seethed in Paul's direction. They accused him of being two-faced, of calling himself a proper member of the fancier community while aligning himself with what they deem the aggressive animal rights agenda at the HSUS. The *Dog Press*, which covers dog fanciers, ran the all-caps, we're-declaring-war-style headline "DOG SHOW JUDGE OWES APOLOGY." Bloggers called on the AKC to suspend Paul's privileges for conduct detrimental to the sport. Breeders shouted for more enforcement of animal cruelty laws instead of new laws that paint all large-scale puppy sellers with the same dark, tainted brush. Paul stopped receiving invitations to judge at dog shows. Some breeders urged past show winners to return the ribbons he had awarded them, shipping them back in disgust. One can only imagine the packaging they had in mind to leave on his doorstep.

"I think it was general politics that made it so harsh," Paul says now, with the benefit of hindsight. He still stands by his testimony five years later, and he still believes that limiting the legal number of dogs a breeder can own is the only solution, but he laments the fact that various types of dog breeders and animal welfare advocates have become so polarized that they can barely have a conversation about the puppy mill issue, let alone resolve the problem. It's almost like working with far-right conservative and far-left liberal politicians: never, no matter what, even if the entire dog industry implodes as a result, shall they ever give an inch or find common ground between them.

"You've got to find the people that are honest, willing to do whatever is necessary to make things work," Paul says today, "and boy, those are few and far between."

Elizabeth Brinkley is an example of a breeder Paul might describe— and who would describe herself, too—as having zero interest in compromise. The sixty-one-year-old owner of Dante Kennels near Richmond, Virginia, has been breeding Shetland Sheepdogs since 1974 and has spent the past fifteen years also working as a legislative liaison, going into the behind-the-scenes meetings where dog-breeding laws are written in multiple US states—and trying to put a stop to agendas like the one Paul endorsed.

Brinkley is not a large-scale commercial breeder herself; she is an AKC Breeder of Merit (self-described as "never inspected") who owns nine dogs and turns out one, maybe two litters each year, selling the puppies for $600 apiece. Her dogs have been champions in America and in Britain, and she is proud to have "best in show" from multiple events on her résumé. Her dogs rotate turns living inside her home and in a converted eight-by-ten-foot tool shed with access to two outdoor runs, each twenty-five feet wide and the longer one about a hundred feet long. She'd let all the dogs live inside at once if she could, but, she says, her landlord won't allow it.

Many people would say that, as breeding operations go, Brinkley's setup in Virginia is at the opposite end of the spectrum from Dave and Judy Miller's farm in Missouri, with Brinkley's being far more like a small-scale enterprise than a large-scale one—but she stands firmly on the side of commercial breeders like the Millers, for what she sees as the good of the entire puppy-producing industry.

"First of all, the animal rights movement invented the words 'puppy mill.' It didn't exist thirty years ago," she says. "I've been in kennels with a hundred dogs and they're fantastic, and I've been in hobby breeder kennels that I wouldn't let my dogs near. It's not about the numbers. It's about the care."

The problem, as Brinkley sees things, is that lawmakers are so busy trying to come up with new laws that they're failing to provide funding and staffing to enforce the animal cruelty laws already on the books. Officials may have good intentions when they enact everything from limits on the number of breeding dogs to outright bans of dogs in pet stores because of alleged ties to puppy mills (now the case in some three dozen North American cities, including Los Angeles, San Diego, and Chicago), but those tactics won't solve the problems that exist. What lawmakers should be focusing on, she says, is not the number of dogs, but instead the number of staff members—both in their own policing agencies and at kennels of all sizes. Her argument is that having three hundred dogs on a property is no problem if, say, you have a big tract of land and twenty employees to handle the dogs' daily needs. That's fifteen dogs per person, close to the same workload many small-scale breeders have at their homes, where nobody questions the dogs' care at all.

Brinkley bristles at what she calls "hobby breeders and snobby breeders" who raise their noses in disdain when discussing their large-scale commercial brethren or applaud anti–puppy mill announcements at shows like Westminster. The simple fact, she says, is that without the commercial breeders, there wouldn't be enough of the popular purebred and cross-bred puppies, like the Maltipoo, to satisfy consumer demand. Large-scale breeders are a necessary part of the industry's continued existence, she says, because of the sheer quantity of puppies the world's dog lovers seek to buy. And in having that opinion, Brinkley is in total agreement with the rescuer who went to the Southwest Auction Service dog sale and said Westminster is the dream, but the reality is filling consumer demand through setups like Dave and Judy Miller's farm. Big demand, quite simply, requires big supply.

She also believes that any incursion into the rights of the largest commercial breeders is, by definition, an attack on the business of all breeders. People who treat dogs badly, Brinkley argues, are going to treat dogs badly no matter what laws are passed. They may have one dog, or they may have a thousand. Either way, nobody can legislate morality. Laws affect only those breeders who follow them, and that rarely means people who keep dogs in squalor—but it always means people like Dave and Judy Miller, her own Dante Kennels, and the world's most responsible show dog producers.

"I don't want these puppy mills or substandard kennels or whatever you want to call them staying in business, but I also don't want laws passed that are going to put me out of business," she says. "A lot of the big muckety-muck AKC breeders want to pretend it's going to go away, that it doesn't affect them. It may take a really well-known breeder getting busted for the light bulb to go off over some of these people's heads."

She adds, "Those attacks are not just against the big breeders. They're attacks on all of us. If our enemies succeed in taking out the big breeders, do you think they're going to stop? We're next, all because we won't stand up for one another. We need to stop pointing our fingers at people and start dealing with the dogs."

And actually, some officials outside the United States are approaching the so-called puppy-farm problem with thinking along the lines of Brinkley's: it's not about the number of dogs, but instead about the health of the puppies. While US lawmakers are debating how many dogs are too many for a breeder to own and shutting down pet store sales from coast to coast, other nations are focusing instead on the quality of puppies to reveal bad breeding practices. Since 2012 in Ireland, for instance, all puppies have been required to be microchipped so that unhealthy litters can be traced back to the source. Some parts of Australia require the same, as does Denmark and the island nation of Cyprus. England will require all dog owners to implant microchips by 2016. Dogs entering Japan from other nations are already required to be microchipped, and dogs entering European Union nations from foreign countries need either a microchip or a tattoo of identification.

Can microchip registry information be faked? Sure—all it takes is a breeder providing a false telephone number to the microchip company from the start, and the breeder will never be found. It's another example of how unscrupulous people will find a way to do bad things, which is one reason the approach hasn't taken hold in America. Legislative attempts to pass mandatory microchip laws have failed in large US states including California and New York, at least in part because of organized opposition from the AKC. As with breeders like Brinkley and the Millers, the AKC takes the position that responsible breeders and dog owners shouldn't have to face undue government requirements, and the AKC includes mandatory microchipping in that category.

That's not to say that breeders like Miller and Brinkley are against government intervention altogether. They want the lousy kennels that cast a negative light on their own operations to be inspected and shut down just as much as all dog lovers do. And to be brutally honest, as far as animal cruelty goes, Brinkley thinks some top show dog breeders are just as guilty as some so-called puppy mill owners. They'll alter dogs—including cutting them so their ears and tails will stand just so—for no reason other than to earn a nod of approval from a judge, and sometimes in ways that are deemed animal cruelty in other parts of the world. "They think they're better than the puppy mills, but some of them get just as greedy as the puppy mills do," she says. "It's not about the breed. It's about winning. That twenty-five-cent ribbon means more to them than the dog. It's pure, plain, and simple about ego. To me, that's just as much animal abuse as a substandard kennel."

At the end of the day, the whole of the puppy mill language overtaking the breeding community has made Brinkley not only defensive, but also what she describes as defiant about telling people she's a breeder. When she utters the B-word, they gasp at her as if she's a criminal. Their eyes go dead cold because, she says, animal rights activists are convincing the general public "that every dog should be raised as a puffy pink poodle on a pink pillow." That's just not the reality—and it hasn't been for quite some time now, even though each generation likes to think of itself as smarter than its parents or grandparents when it comes to buying dogs. There have always been small-scale, top-dollar breeders, but the vast majority of people buying purebreds have long shopped from the commercial-scale producers, whether they bought from them directly or through newspaper classified ads or in places like pet stores or, most recently, by way of the Internet.

"It's a case of, do you want to shop at Macy's or do you want to shop at Walmart?" Brinkley asks. "Because the stuff at Walmart is not as well made, do we take away your option to shop there? The American public should have the right to choose."

As things stand today, that right to choose is intact around the world, and it's currently being defended, perhaps most vociferously, by a single company processing tens of thousands of puppies a year—as fate would have it, about a half-hour's drive up the road from Walmart corporate headquarters.

CHAPTER SIX

THE MEGA-DISTRIBUTOR

"We are currently not planning on conquering the world."

—*Sergey Brin*

Michael Stolkey takes a measured breath before holding open the heavy, thick door that precious few outsiders ever get to walk through. "This is why people hate us," he says, taking a few strides into the hallway on the other side. "The kennels."

Stolkey is director of corporate sales for the Hunte Corporation, a privately owned business in Goodman, Missouri, that is at best wary, and at worst paranoid, about letting newcomers inside. The company, which opened in 1991, is likely the biggest legal distributor of puppies to pet stores across America, and it has long operated with great secrecy, hunkering down against the cries of animal welfare activists and allowing only carefully prescreened visitors to pass beyond this threshold. The business of readying puppies for transport to stores is conducted here in a well-honed, legally regulated, and systematic way, and the company's sheer size, along with its supply chain of commercial and other breeders, are the stuff of great speculation and contempt. No conveyor belts or robot arms are at work, but even Henry Ford would be impressed with the assembly line nature of operations. It's one of the things that make Hunte a big, easy-to-loathe target. Animal welfare activists have, among other things, followed the company's trucks into the field and locked their drivers inside with the puppies, likely screaming from the asphalt about how the humans deserve to be trapped inside a cage alongside the dogs they're selling in mass production style.

Nobody was locking anybody inside the door to the kennels on this day in late August 2014, when routine operations were busy, but not hectic, thanks to the seasonal lull in puppy sales. The doorway opened into a brightly lit, white hallway so long that it seemed almost to disappear into the distance of the $10 million, at least 200,000-square-foot facility, in much the same way hallways in large, sterile hospitals vanish into a labyrinth of the unknown. Workers wearing different-colored scrubs to indicate their job titles—veterinarian, technician, assistant—walked calmly to and fro, some with empty hands and others carrying one puppy at a time, petting them and cradling them as any dog lover might. A Siberian Husky pup, a baby Boxer, and a Shar-Pei with hair still growing into his face folds were among those being ferried back and forth to the photography room, the grooming room, and the surgery suite, giving the place an atmosphere similar to a large nursery filled with cuteness and coos.

One or two people have managed to sneak undercover cameras into the kennel section over the years, and YouTube videos show a bit of what goes on outside the public eye, where thirteen numbered doors line the long corridor's right side. Inside each one are rows of kennel-style cages like the ones used in veterinarians' offices and animal shelters. Some are large and some are small, to meet

USDA regulations depending on each puppy's height and weight. Two levels of the enclosures are on either side of every room, with the levels separated by a stainless-steel catch basin that is easy to clean after urine and feces falls through the metal-grate floors. Each room is climate controlled and separately ventilated to prevent the spread of airborne diseases, and each appears to contain about a hundred of the enclosures, which are the holding spaces for the tens of thousands of puppies the company distributes each year.

At the height of operations before the 2007 global recession, the industry giant was buying about ninety thousand puppies a year from breeders and distributing them to Petland and other retail stores not only in America but also in other parts of the world, marketing them in Europe with expectations of global sales and hoping to further increase Hunte's annual revenues at that time, which were $26 million. Since the economic crash—which shocked the usually recession-proof puppy business by shrinking the supply of puppies coming from US breeders and slashing sales figures at the pet stores—Hunte's business has been halved and shrunken back to domestic distribution only. Today it moves about forty-five thousand puppies a year, which likely means it is still the biggest distributor in the world's biggest market for dogs.

The purchasing of the pups happens on Tuesdays, which are known as "buy day" here inside the kennels. Hunte officials say they acquire puppies from USDA-regulated commercial breeders along with hobby breeders all around the middle United States, including not only Missouri and nearby Arkansas, but also Kansas, Iowa, North Dakota, South Dakota, Indiana, Illinois, and Nebraska. Hunte agents fan out in climate-controlled vehicles outfitted with a scaled-down version of the kennel ventilation and enclosure systems, and they drive hundreds upon hundreds of miles each week, going door to door and offering breeders wholesale prices for their puppies along with the kenneling systems and supplies that are part of Hunte's vertical business model. The agents are not the final buyers, but are instead the facilitators who keep the product pipe-line moving. They are in the field every Friday through Sunday, and they're back in Goodman with truckloads full of puppies by Monday night, in time for "buy day" procedures that start Tuesday morning, when local dog breeders are invited to join the agents in offering puppies Hunte may want to buy.

Some of the dogs are purebreds with registration papers from the AKC, APRI, or ACA—founder Andrew Hunte once told AKC officials his company is the kennel club's biggest customer in moving dogs that buyers later register with AKC for a fee—while other puppies who come in on "buy day" are designer cross-breeds, like Goldendoodles, that regularly prove popular with retail con-sumers as well. The owners of pet stores nationwide send Hunte their wish lists based on local demand, and Hunte tries to fill them through its network of breeders, though it also works with whatever dogs are available during any given week. If, for instance, Wei-maraner sales happen to be slow in the pet stores but a respected breeder of Weimaraner puppies shows up with a litter, Hunte will still buy the dogs, to help keep the breeder in business until demand from consumers picks up again.

"We will always take the puppies," Stolkey says, explaining that good breeders need a consistent buyer for their dogs to make their own business models work. Hunte wants to support the best breeders, he says, because doing so maintains a solid supply of healthy, desirable puppies overall.

The minimum age of puppy Hunte will accept is eight weeks, and no dogs are accepted who weigh less than a pound and a half—because the company has learned that the ultra-small puppies usually lack an immune system developed enough to survive the move through the system into pet stores. The company also turns away puppies from USDA-inspected commercial breeders who have received a direct violation, which typically means a problem that affects a dog's health as opposed to, say, a substandard kennel enclosure. When a direct violation occurs, Hunte doesn't strike the breeder from its books entirely; the company instead sends its agents into the field, offering supplies and educational materials to help get those breeders back up to snuff, so business can resume in the future. The company is smart about making money at both ends, for sure, which is either an admirable business strategy or a bottom-feeding one, depending on the point of view.

A Hunte veterinarian leads the goings-on every Tuesday inside the buy room, where he stands behind a scale (the average weight of accepted puppies is six and a half pounds) and examines the incoming puppies one by one. The kennels are built to house in the neighborhood of 1,300 dogs during the busy season, which suggests that on some buy days, the pups are receiving a pretty fast pass, maybe just a few minutes each, because of the sheer quantity of evaluations that need to be done. The veterinarian determines whether each incoming puppy is grade A, B, or C based on how closely the puppy reflects breed standards, Stolkey says. ("You don't want somebody thinking it's a Westminster winner when it's not.") Hunte then offers each breeder a sliding scale of payouts that also are affected by seasonal supply and demand, including Christmastime booms. The dollar figures are kept private, but they are definitely wholesale, far below the retail prices set for the dogs when they get to pet stores.

When the company opened, it turned away about 30 percent of the incoming dogs because they had things like heart murmurs, bad hips, and eye problems, but today, with Hunte's sheer buying power having set the wholesale market's standards, less than 10 percent of the puppies coming into the building fail to make the grade. It's a similar business model to the one used by Tyson Foods, the world's largest processor of beef, pork, and chicken, with headquarters less than an hour away. Tyson, like Hunte, owns none of the farms where the animals are raised but nevertheless often has a strong say in how they are bred and how much the farmers earn. Animal farmers basically have two options: sell directly to consumers at full retail price, or sell to distributors at wholesale price. Many puppy farmers choose the latter and work with Hunte because they lack the time or skills to do the retail marketing and sales themselves, especially with a newly imposed federal rule designed to prevent US breeders from putting up a website and shipping puppies to buyers sight unseen.

The puppies Hunte accepts are microchipped and preenrolled in the AKC's Reunite program, which is designed to help owners find dogs who go missing—and which is another moneymaker for the kennel club, in addition to the purebred registration fee, if the puppy's final owner continues the Reunite membership into consecutive years. Then all of the pups spend six days inside the thirteen kennel rooms getting baths, nails clipped, ears cleaned, surgery for things like hernias or undescended testicles, and watched for signs of behavioral issues. Occasionally, if another operation is already being performed, the puppy will also be spayed or neutered.

As standard procedure, every puppy receives a battery of preventive medications intended to wipe out anything harmful already in his system, and to ward off anything new from taking root. These include a vaccine against distemper, adenovirus, parainfluenza, and canine parvovirus. Hunte dogs also receive pyrantel pamoate for intestinal helminthes (worm-like organisms), fenbendazole for prevention of giardia (intestinal parasites), sulfadimethoxine for prevention of coccidia (also intestinal parasites), and treatment for prevention of external parasites, such as fleas. Every puppy's drinking water is infused with Pet Aid, a supplement used to reduce gastrointestinal stress and help maintain appetite, and puppies weighing less than two and a half pounds, or who are generally thin, also receive a Nutra-Gel supplement to prevent hypoglycemia. If a puppy needs more than the regular protocol, veterinarians prescribe medication on a dog-by-dog basis.

Inside each of the kennel rooms, the dogs certainly look clean and healthy, and their barking echoes loudly enough to drown out most conversation. The slamming of the metal enclosure doors to lock them is sometimes jarring, at least to the human ear, but more than a few puppies have no problem sleeping through the noise. The air smells much like wet dogs after playtime in a river but otherwise has no stench, a testament to the climate control and ventilation systems that make working inside the kennels surprisingly easy on people's noses. It's true that the puppies in Hunte's care have nowhere soft to lay their heads inside the enclosures with metal-grate floors, nor any toys to play with or chew because they could spread bacteria—a lack of stimulation that probably frustrates the ones who are teething. It's also true, Stolkey says, that the pups spend virtually the entire six days inside the enclosures, twenty-four hours a day.

On the other hand, the system doesn't seem to affect most of the pups in any immediately evident way, as was clear on this Thursday, two days after intake, when most of the puppies seemed generally unstressed, with only a handful out of hundreds shaking or cowering. At least half of them kept right on snoozing even when people walked through, and others jumped and pawed at the enclosure doors, barking and whining for attention. The kennels at Hunte are not representative of how most dog lovers treat young puppies, but they are highly reminiscent of the kennels in many veterinarians' offices and publicly funded shelters—and Hunte's are brighter, cleaner, and less crowded than some shelter kennels, for sure.

When a Hunte worker notices something that affects a puppy's health, as was the case with a Yorkshire Terrier puppy walking in endless circles on this particular day, the dog gets extra care to try to correct the problem, including sometimes being placed in larger, mobile enclosures on the floor with more space to move around. Hunte also has what Stolkey calls a "sick puppy room" with about forty enclosures where puppies who show problems after intake are sent for upgraded care with equipment, including nebulizers. A separate, similarly sized room with its own ventilation system is used for puppies who get sick during transport to pet stores and are returned. Five veterinarians and eight veterinary technicians are among the staff of one hundred and seventy-five, along with additional support staff members who do everything from cleaning the enclosures to taking each puppy's photograph for upload so pet stores can place orders online.

Virtually all of the workers have smiles on their faces and seem both happy and proud of their workplace, and they are under constant watch, with even the surgical suite's three V-shaped steel tables being wide open for viewing at all times through glass windows across from the kennels in the long white hallway. While Hunte may seem secretive to the public, inside the building, it would be hard for any worker to do anything harmful to a dog without a witness, at least in the kennel area.

In the far back of the building that most people never visit, where some companies might cut corners on construction or cleanliness, the Hunte operation looks virtually identical to the clean, well-lighted area the public sees right inside the front entrance. It's in the back where the USDA-regulated trucks are loaded, each with a version of Hunte's ventilation, climate control, and kenneling systems to keep the puppies as healthy and clean as possible while en route to pet store displays. The trucks are loaded inside a cavernous, multistory, weather-protected garage that opens onto a big private parking lot, spaces that, even when mostly empty, hint at the high volume of business Hunte's infrastructure can accommodate. Parts of the facility reportedly were expanded with two USDA loans totaling close to $4 million, both issued in the early 2000s before the global recession, and both of which Hunte officials say the company was paying back ahead of schedule before the economy crashed.

Most of the trucks are bound for pet stores, Stolkey says, adding that the company also will ship puppies by air if there is consumer demand. The trucks, including the cabs, cost as much as $350,000 apiece to outfit, he says, and Hunte has about ten of the biggest trucks, which, with the exception of the Thermo King climate systems, look just like rigs hauling produce, furniture, and other goods all along America's interstates. Most everyday drivers of sedans on the same roadways would have no idea puppies were even inside, given the bland white exterior panels that are noticeably free of the company's logo, to avoid attracting attention.

Each truck is handled by two drivers who take turns sleeping in bunks up in the cab. They're trained as what the company calls "care technicians," able to administer some medications and look for signs of common stress-induced problems or illnesses that can arise during the two- to three-day transfer process to pet stores. Each truck is equipped with a GPS system that, Stolkey says, ensures the trucks stop every four hours so the drivers can check the dogs' condition, food, and water, and clean the kennels. The air refreshes throughout the truck completely every three minutes, he adds. LED lighting remains on inside the trucks at all times so the puppies can see, making it less likely they will become disoriented and further stressed.

Stress, after all, often leads to sickness, and Hunte claims that pretty much everything it does is based on maintaining the puppies' health. The motive is of course not entirely altruistic; a solid cash flow would prod even the worst company to treat the dogs decently. Sick puppies at the end of the line don't sell, and puppies who don't sell are just plain bad for business.

Headlines about puppies being burned alive are also bad for business, which is why each truck in the Hunte fleet has a fire suppression system, a safeguard installed after sixty puppies headed for pet stores died in a 2006 truck fire in Lowell, Massachusetts. There hasn't been a similar accident since, but that fire remains one of the four main things for which Hunte is regularly criticized. The second is its supply chain, which includes a lot of large-scale breeding farms that animal welfare activists call puppy mills, portraying Hunte as the savvy, virtually invisible middleman that floods pet stores across America with puppy mill dogs, hiding the nature of their origin from puppy-loving consumers.

The third criticism is one of the major headline makers, often written as "trenches full of dead dogs." It stems from a violation notice from the Missouri Department of Natural Resources, which received an anonymous complaint on November 5, 2003, from what Hunte calls a disgruntled employee, about the company's disposal methods. The actual complaint describes "mass puppy graves," but the letter that state inspectors sent the company uses the more-often-repeated language, saying the trenches where Hunte was burying dead dogs were correctly built but improperly spaced, and that a broken sewer line was discharging wastewater into a tributary of a local creek in violation of the state's Clean Water Law. The notice also stated that Hunte was burying more than one thousand pounds of dead animals each year, surpassing the local limit, a claim Hunte says was inaccurate. The company has since taken the state's suggestion to move to an incineration method of disposal, which, as the state wrote in its 2003 letter, is more environmentally friendly, less labor intensive, and more apt to create a better public image.

"Anybody in agriculture knows where there's life, there's death," Stolkey says by way of explanation. "Where there's health, there's sickness." The company does not reveal the percentage of puppies who die in its care, but common sense indicates that if the percentage were large, then Hunte would have been out of business long ago. Working backward from numbers that are available, Hunte is moving about forty-five thousand puppies a year at an average weight of six and a half pounds per puppy. That's a total of 292,500 pounds' worth of dogs. One thousand pounds, the state limit for burial, would equal less than 0.5 percent of the dogs. Even if the percentage is ten times as high, the company would still most likely qualify as a no-kill facility, which means saving at least 90 percent of the dogs from severe illness and other problems, according to guidelines followed by more than five hundred communities with animal shelters designated as no-kill across the United States.

Sick puppies are a reality of life, and they sometimes become part of the sales process despite the company's systems and procedures. As the existence of Hunte's own return room evidences, not all of the puppies make it into pet stores in good health. Hunte's team says respiratory problems are its biggest challenge, what with most of the puppies being away from their mothers for the first time and becoming stressed with snotty noses or coughs, not unlike children going to school at the youngest standard ages. Hunte deals with a lot of the same issues large-scale shelters encounter, and because its dogs are ultimately sold in pet stores at high prices, consumers tend to get even angrier at the sellers than, say, buyers at shelters when sick puppies make their way into homes.

Hunte at one point had an F rating with the Better Business Bureau, which received four complaints about the company during a three-year period and another 657 complaints against Petland stores, which are one of the primary destinations for Hunte-distributed puppies. While Hunte officials say they no longer distribute dogs internationally, Ohio-based Petland has stores in Canada, China, Japan, Mexico, and South Africa. The two firms are entwined in multiple ways, with Hunte's founder also owning at least one Petland store. Thus, when oversight agencies and animal welfare activists talk about Hunte, they also talk about Petland, because that's the brand in the supply chain that puppy buyers will recognize. Most people who buy a pet store puppy who gets sick wouldn't think to file a complaint against anybody but the pet store owner, even if the dog was actually in Hunte's care far longer than in Petland's.

As evidence of sick puppies in the Hunte-Petland system, a 2010 Better Business Bureau report cited lawsuits by former owners of three Petland stores in Tennessee, Indiana, and Ohio who said they received sick puppies from Hunte. One said more than half of the sixty to sixty-five puppies he received were sick, another said several puppies he received from Hunte died of parvovirus within weeks, and a third said he had to spend some $40,000 in veterinary bills caring for Hunte puppies. In 2009, those claims were included as part of a class-action lawsuit filed against both Petland and Hunte by the HSUS, which argued racketeering and cited additional complaints about sick puppies from thirty-one people who bought dogs at the end of the retail line. A judge dismissed Hunte from the proceedings in 2010 without any findings of guilt, and ultimately all the racketeering charges against both Hunte and Petland were dismissed.

Ryan Boyle, Hunte's vice president of sales and operations, doesn't deny that sometimes puppies get sick. He says the company faces "buy day" problems similar to those encountered by shelters and rescue groups, which cannot always verify a puppy's health care prior to entering any facility. "We have the same struggle here, to make sure the puppies got their vaccines," he says. "We ask for the labels but we don't have a video of the breeder administering it."

Dr. Bill Oxford, a veterinarian at Hunte, says the company's "buy day" check, six-day holding period, exit-day check, and additional check by the pet store's veterinarian upon arrival two or three days after leaving Hunte's kennels constitute a process that exposes most immediate health problems. Boyle admits that the only thing any company—or rescue group, for that matter—can truly guarantee when it comes to puppies is a sound system of checks and balances, which Hunte believes it does well. "The six days is incredibly important from the breeder to the pet store," Boyle says. "The best-regulated path to market is through this facility. I don't think anybody can doubt it."

Nor, to Stolkey's thinking, can the other half dozen or so puppy distributors in the United States make the same claims. "Go up the road to our competitor," he says, almost as if making a dare. "See if they'll let you go in."

Temporary respiratory illnesses, parvovirus, and the like are different from lifelong genetic health problems, which are another often-criticized aspect of purebred breeding in particular. Hunte does offer a multiyear refund guarantee against genetic health problems on every puppy it sells, a guarantee it is able to make in large part because of a proprietary software system that flags problems throughout the Midwest breeding community.

"We probably have the largest genetic database in the world," Stolkey says, based on the number of dogs Hunte has processed in its nearly quarter century of doing business. It's not an unlikely boast; even with today's business being half the size of what Hunte once enjoyed, it's a reasonable guess that well more than a million puppies have come through the Hunte buy room and kennels. The AKC claims to have the world's largest database of canine DNA, but Hunte may indeed have the largest database of troublesome breeders. "We have eyes on the ground," Stolkey adds. "My agents will come back with photos of USDA-licensed kennels, and we'll say, 'Okay, we have to get to work here.'"

In fact, the desire to eliminate sick puppies is the entire basis on which the Hunte Corporation was founded. As hard as it may be for some animal welfare advocates to believe, Andrew Hunte started his business for the same reason many of them got into the cause of rescue: to get more healthy puppies out of the system and into people's homes.

Andrew Hunte, a native of Barbados, got started in the pet store business in Florida. He knew little about the farms where so many puppies are born, but he quickly grew upset about regularly receiving shipments of sick puppies from breeders in the Midwest. He became more and more frustrated as it happened time and time again, until one day, in the 1980s, he decided to drive out from the Sunshine State to look around the places where the puppies were originating. It was the age of Ronald Reagan, the time of a boom economy in which farmers could make a lot of cash breeding puppies as cheaply as possible. Hunte poked around the Midwest and realized that what was happening with the dogs was, to his eye, disturbing.

"He thought, 'No wonder I'm getting sick puppies,'" says Greg Brown, Hunte's marketing director. "People raised their dogs like livestock. There was no manual."

Hunte set out to put himself between the breeders and the pet stores, to institute quality control that he felt needed to exist not only for the breeding and pet store businesses to thrive, but also for the health and proper care of the dogs. The list of industry firsts Hunte now claims is long—and shows how few standards of care existed among breeders and pet stores just thirty years ago. Hunte says it was the first company to move animals in specially built vehicles, to develop an air purification system for kennels, to forgo housing more than two puppies in each enclosure, to segregate puppies from different breeders to prevent cross-contagion, to hold hobby breeders to USDA-compliant standards, to develop products like the nutritional supplement Puppy-Aid and the nonalcohol (and used everywhere throughout the facility) Hunte Hand Sanitizer, and to encourage the USDA to amend its regulations and ensure puppies younger than eight weeks are never bought or sold.

That last advancement is especially significant, because in challenging USDA standards as not good enough, Andrew Hunte placed himself right alongside many of today's animal welfare advocates, who say that even modern-day regulations fail to ensure a reasonable quality of life for breeding dogs and their puppies on the farms.

Hunte also instituted an annual Breeder Educational Conference, which has been held every year since 1999. It's a two-day event featuring speakers and exhibits along with tours of the Hunte Corporation, to show everyday breeders how Hunte believes things should be done (and what products are for sale to help do it, at conference-special prices). The conference is akin to secondary education for breeders aiming to be professional when dealing in dogs, much like conferences organized by Best Friends Animal

Society for rescuers trying to set higher standards in that segment of the dog business. In 2013, the Hunte event speakers included a researcher discussing the positive effects of early neurological stimulation, an Oklahoma State University representative talking about biosecurity, and USDA representatives hosting a town hall discussion about regulations. In 2014, the lineup featured a University of Missouri College of Veterinary Medicine expert on whelping, an AKC representative talking about health tests, and a USDA regional director explaining laws about Internet puppy sales and foreign imports.

"We're writing the playbook here," as Stolkey puts it, which, by analogy, makes Brown an interesting new assistant coach working to rehabilitate Hunte's image. Brown previously handled marketing for a YMCA branch and knew nothing of the dog business, and he joined the Hunte team to help the company open its doors and tell its story—to try to stop the spread of rumors about things like "trenches full of dead dogs" and the physical threats of violence he says Andrew Hunte, now about seventy years old and in failing health, regularly receives.

Brown is especially keen to discuss Hunte's policy of finding a home for every dog who enters its doors, including those who get returned, by using in-house networks that operate similarly to small-scale nonprofit rescue groups, putting the word out through social media, and matching special-needs dogs with the right owners. Even the returned puppies are great, Brown says—and that includes his own Boxer and Mastiff, one of which got sent back because of asthma, a condition Brown says his family easily controls.

The company also is trying to do its part to help other homeless dogs when possible, Brown says, but it faces resistance because of the political divide between breeders and rescue groups, particularly its adversaries at the HSUS.

As an example, Brown says, after Hurricane Katrina struck New Orleans, Louisiana, in 2005, Hunte packed its climate-controlled trucks full of dog food, water, and veterinary supplies and had them ready to roll from Missouri down to the bayou to help the overflowing animal shelters. "The trucks were loaded," Brown says, shaking his head at the all-stop order he says the company received from the HSUS coordinator in Louisiana. "He called and said, 'We don't want *your* help.'" (The HSUS did not respond to a request for fair comment about this accusation.)

That dismissive attitude was similar to the one Brown says the company received when it offered to help outfit a shelter in western Missouri, where Hunte thought it could improve kenneling, ventilation, and other systems to prevent the spread of disease. Its overtures there were rebuffed, too, Brown says, and Hunte ended up making a $50,000 donation instead—all the while continuing to be lambasted by animal welfare groups seeking the public's support.

"It's a very good motivation for donations to have a bogeyman, somebody to blame," Brown says. "We're big, so a lot of times it's us."

He says he's had phones slammed down on him by rescue groups of all kinds after he called with overtures of partnerships. Yes, of course, there's money to be made in selling Hunte products and kenneling systems to rescue advocates, but to Brown's way of thinking, Hunte's years and scope of experience include things that could benefit shelter operations, and thus all dogs, even ones in which Hunte has no financial stake. In Missouri, for instance, why shouldn't the local shelter have systems just as effectively designed as the ones inside the Petland store Andrew Hunte operates? If the goal is to get dogs into homes, then maybe Hunte has some things it could teach the rescuers about distribution and sales.

Brown also spends a great deal of time sifting through hate mail with subject lines like "Christian devils," a label that comes from the way Andrew Hunte has intertwined his company with religion. Operations are indeed based in the Bible Belt, and a two-hundred-seat chapel is on site, fully modernized in megachurch style with four projectors, a quartet of discotheque-worthy ceiling-mounted speakers, and at least sixteen spotlights, all pointed at the altar, or stage, where a young pastor with a guitar stands before a backlit cross. Wearing a gray polo shirt, blue jeans, and a hint of stylish beard scruff, he sings religious songs alongside a small band, gives people a place to discuss what's troubling them, and leads prayers every Thursday from two until three o'clock. Hunte workers may attend what's known simply as chapel on company time and with full pay.

On this particular Thursday, about forty of them chose to sit for the talk about the Second Commandment: You shall not make for yourself an idol. According to the pastor, it means putting one's faith in God above all else, and not being distracted by any other religions or primary focuses, be they television or lucky rabbit's feet or even puppies.

A reading was offered from the New American Standard Bible, Romans 1:22–25, which states:

> Professing to be wise, they became fools, and exchanged the glory of the incorruptible God for an image in the form of corruptible man and of birds and four-footed animals and crawling creatures. Therefore God gave them over in the lusts of their hearts to impurity, so that their bodies would be dishonored among them. For they exchanged the truth of God for a lie, and worshiped and served the creature rather than the Creator, who is blessed forever.

The lesson: man is made in God's image and should strive to honor Him. Animals are not the same. For those who know the true path to salvation or, arguably, to success, it's paramount to remember that dogs, like everything else, have their rightful place. It's the natural order of things.

With that in mind, the workers filed out of the chapel, some returning to the kennels, all in a calm and neighborly fashion, ready to meet the demands of puppy buyers for many years to come. It is, after all, consumer purchases that fund every last nickel of Hunte's success, and every bit of success that everyone else in the supply chain enjoys.

That's how things have always been when it comes to dogs, since long before Hunte even existed. As America's mega-distributor of pet store puppies, Hunte may be the current bogeyman, but the core product it's selling is almost as old as the nation itself—and so is the marketing message that keeps getting so many people to buy in.

CHAPTER SEVEN

MARKETING THE MESSAGE

"Salesmanship is limitless."

—James Cash Penney

J ust before eight o'clock Eastern time on the morning of February 14, 2013, many people across America turned on their televisions to watch the news. It was a Thursday, so most were half-listening as they hopped into the shower and got dressed for work, but if theirs were among the hundred million or so homes that received CNN on that day, they likely paused their routine and stood close to the screen for at least a minute to take a better look. Reports about Israeli-Palestinian politics or soldiers at war in Afghanistan may not have piqued their interest, but this particular segment, near the top of the hour, sure did. A table full of media personalities led by anchorwoman Soledad O'Brien was gushing over a little black dog nicknamed Banana Joe.

It was the moment dog-loving Americans tune in for every February, the moment when they stand half-dressed in front of the TV and let their toothbrushes dangle from their mouths while they coo, the moment when, even if they've never attended a dog show in their lives, they are invited to fall in love with the newly crowned Westminster-winning royalty dubbed "America's Dog."

The first thing many viewers tried to do was pronounce Banana Joe's breed, *Affenpinscher*, which doesn't roll off the tongue like *Labrador* or *Poodle*, and which hardly anybody had ever heard of before that week. But now, all over television in a constant barrage of interviews on channel after channel, the rare Affenpinscher suddenly became one of the best-known breeds in the world's biggest market for dogs. Banana Joe, who was born and bred in the Netherlands at the Tani Kazari kennel, had just won the 137th Westminster Kennel Club best in show title, and he was making the media rounds with his entourage—like any other celebrity with a business message to manufacture.

Westminster had been Joe's eighty-sixth competition win during the nearly six years he'd been alive, which means he averaged about fourteen dog show wins a year. He'd taken top honors in Belgium, the Netherlands, Luxembourg, and Germany. He was a hard-working show dog, to say the least. His owners weren't on camera with him at CNN; in fact, the dog wasn't allowed to spend a single day living with anyone but his handler, Ernesto Lara, during periods when he showed, because any undue influence on Joe could interfere with his training, and thus his chances of winning in the ring. The schedule no doubt infringed on possible in-the-flesh breeding times, too, but that was all about to become history. When asked what was next on Joe's agenda, Lara told the television audience, "Now, I guess, he's going to have a quiet life, and maybe a lot of girlfriends will come his way."

Laughter filled the studio, and then O'Brien chimed in—trying to ask a serious question that simply was not part of the message Joe was there to promote.

"I have to imagine that he's valuable," she said. "You joke about that, but he's valuable for breeding, right?"

David Frei, sitting next to Banana Joe with the wide smile of a practiced salesman after nearly a quarter century of representing Westminster, deftly maneuvered around the issue of money and instead answered in a way that made Joe sound like an everyday pooch: "Well, that's what dog shows are all about, is finding the next generation of healthy, happy dogs and the greatest dogs to put into your breeding program. We want more Joes out there in family homes, sitting on the couch, being loved by everybody."

With O'Brien's attempt to interject even a hint of reality having been duly quashed, CNN went to commercial like every other competing network would that week during similar segments, and like so many programs do when covering dog show winners after similar events like Crufts and the FCI World Dog Show in other parts of the globe. To her credit, O'Brien had tried to get at the root of what was actually going on, instead of merely following the "isn't he adorable" script. Many other popular television hosts couldn't even see that they were being used as widgets in the purebred-marketing machine.

On *ABC World News Now,* the report by anchor Diana Perez equated the little black dog with Super Bowl sports heroes as well as beauty pageant queens, even going so far as to interlace a Miss America pageant clip of a red-bikini-clad blonde with shots of purebred show dogs getting manicures and doing Pilates. *Wall Street Journal Live* called its video coverage, unambiguously, "Faces of the Canine Stars." When Banana Joe, Lara, and Frei brought their promotional tour to the popular morning talk show *The View,* co-host Whoopi Goldberg introduced the dog with a huge grin, calling him "the amazing Banana Joe," co-host Elizabeth Hasselbeck let Joe drink water from her mug, and co-host Joy Behar quipped, to huge laughs, "The bitches will be coming out of the woodwork." Co-host Sherri Shepherd asked about personality, giving Lara his cue to tell viewers at home the dog was like "good people," a wonderful pet. Frei also got his on-camera moment so he could introduce that year's newly accepted breeds, the Treeing Walker Coonhound and Russell Terrier, in case any viewers had other dog-shopping desires.

Each of these television programs—those under the auspices of news as well as those labeled entertainment—was designed to leave the message firmly planted in viewers' minds that Banana Joe and all the purebred Affenpinschers like him were great family pets, and that everyone should adore them and go out and buy one. Dog lovers had no idea what they'd been missing all these years with their Cocker Spaniels and Bassett Hounds and—dare anyone say it—mutts.

Affenpinscher madness immediately descended on the tiny Affenpinscher breeding community. *Bloomberg Businessweek* reported at the time that precisely seven Affenpinscher puppies were for sale in the entire United States, and that only twelve AKC-recommended Affenpinscher breeders existed in all of North America. Getting a puppy from one of them would run a buyer about $2,500, though they could be found with commercial breeders for as little as $400. That pricing wouldn't last, though, as breeders popped up all over the place trying to cash in on the Westminster win; less than a year later, Affenpinscher puppies would be on websites like PuppyFind.com without registration papers at an asking price of $1,500. Their price had nearly quadrupled in the market, and their presence at puppy farms and small breeding operations alike had blossomed thanks to all of the media attention.

Banana Joe, meanwhile, continued being marketed as a dog who was now going home to his human mom and dad, the happy returning champion of the family, darn near an American hero, just like all purebred dogs could someday be if owners bought the right puppy. But in reality, the only thing that might stay in the United States was Joe's frozen semen, to be stored for breeding. Joe was co-owned by Zoila "Tina" Truesdale of Attleboro, Massachusetts, whose husband runs the International Canine Semen Bank. Banana

Joe had spent only part of his time with the Truesdales since being born from a pairing of Kyleakin Space Cowboy and Bling Bling V Tani Kazari in Holland. Much of Joe's years in America had been a dedicated schedule of traveling to dog show after dog show with Lara, who lived in Bowmansville, Pennsylvania, a good 350 miles away from the Truesdales. But Joe wasn't going to Pennsylvania to retire, either; instead, "America's Dog" was going to the Netherlands, where he had spent the first three years of his life and where he'd now be returned to his co-owner, breeder Mieke Cooijmans, who sees him as a walking piece of art.

"He's moving to Holland," William Truesdale told Boston.com amid the media frenzy. "He's pretty much done all that he can do. The little guy has been around. He's got a lot of frequent-flyer miles!"

And truth be told, if anyone cared to ask, Banana Joe probably wouldn't be happy if there were already any other dogs in his new home.

"He isn't really what we call a player with other dogs, but he's absolutely fascinated with human beings," Truesdale told reporters. "He is very, very perky, playful. He's like a little wind-up toy. He just goes and goes. And, of course, that's what charms the judges."

"A little wind-up toy that goes and goes" is not exactly a viable sales pitch when trying to get someone to buy a family pet. Neither is "high mortality rate at birth," which has long been the case with the Affenpinscher breed. But nobody asked about general problems with purebred standards on the major US television networks that week; the assumption was that Joe was yet another top-of-the-line purebred dog from a top-of-the-line breeder, an assumption that quickly translated into consumer demand. The phone was ringing like Sunday morning church bells inside the home of Jude Daley, president of the Affenpinscher Club of America. She and her colleagues were flooded with requests from would-be Affenpinscher owners, and the calls came more frequently as the dog's media tour continued. No matter what station dog lovers watched, they were spoon-fed the same message: Affies like cute little Banana Joe were the newest must-have commodity.

The well-honed process of marketing purebreds was so conditioned into Americans' thinking that it took two, maybe three minutes of airtime to convince viewers of Joe's greatness, even at eight o'clock in the morning, when they were paying only partial attention and still sipping their first cups of coffee. Heck, a lot of people actually believed that his story was drop-what-you're-doing, stop-brushing-your-teeth, must-watch news.

It was Thanksgiving weekend in 1996, and Pati Dane was standing outside a South Florida movie theater, holding the leash of a sixty-pound Dalmatian named Shiloh. She'd chosen Shiloh specifically for the day's outing because the dog was calm and well behaved with children. It was a good thing, too, because as the movie theater doors opened, the families flooded out in a rush after the premiere showings of Disney's *101 Dalmatians*. The kids were on sugar rushes from all the candy and soda, and poor Shiloh was bombarded by the sometimes dangerous exuberance of little hands and faces coming at her without warning—and with excruciatingly loud squealing.

"The kids would come out of the movie theater and run to our booth screaming, 'Mommy! Mommy! Dalmatian! Dalmatian!'" Dane recalls. "The parents were totally oblivious."

By the time the parents got to her and Shiloh, Dane had her literature and her talking points from Dalmatian Rescue ready. She knew what had happened about a decade earlier, in 1985, when Disney had rereleased the original 1961 cartoon version of *101 Dalmatians*—and AKC registrations for the breed had increased spectacularly, from about eight thousand puppies a year to nearly forty-three thousand. This time around the puppies on the screen weren't even animated. They were real, and every kid in sight was begging to get one.

Dane stood calmly with Shiloh by her side and told the parents that Dalmatians can live sixteen or seventeen years. That's a long commitment to make, she said; these kids will be off to college and the dog will still be in the house. She explained how energetic a dog the size of a Dalmatian can be. How much exercise they need. How destructive they can become, as any dog might, if they're ignored like a toy—like the stuffed Dalmatian doll she had there at the table as a prop to help make her case. She then encouraged them to think about the coming Christmas holiday, and she asked them to buy the toy dog instead of making an impulse decision with a living animal. Look at how big Shiloh is, she said as the little kids stood next to the adult dog, sometimes dwarfed by her mass. Dalmatians grow up and need a lot more than a puppy you can hold in one hand like the cutie-pies in the film.

Her effort did some good, but she and her colleagues in the Dalmatian rescue community were simply drowned out by the tsunami of marketing that comes with a blockbuster Disney film. By January and February, when Americans were tossing out their used-up Christmas trees and returning unwanted toasters at the shopping malls, Dalmatian rescuers were already seeing the spotted puppies flooding into shelters. People had bought them impulsively, and the reality of dog ownership had set in fast. It had taken only a few weeks for Dane's worst fears to come true as the movie continued to be shown in city after city. The Humane Society of Boulder, Colorado, saw a 310 percent spike in Dalmatian drop-offs. The Humane Society of Tampa Bay in Florida said its increase was 762 percent. Dane herself received 130 dogs needing new homes—a number that usually took her more than two years to accumulate. The same trend occurred in other parts of the world, too, as the movie was released in additional markets. British Dalmatian Welfare, for one, reported a sharp increase after the film played in the United Kingdom.

When Disney released *102 Dalmatians* in 2000, the nightmare started all over again. Dane's usual intake of thirty or forty dogs shot up to over one hundred. The spikes weren't quite as severe when the DVDs came out after that, but even to this day, when the movies play on television, her phone occasionally rings. Some of the puppies are dropped off by families in the daylight after they realize they've made a mistake, while others are dumped by the litter and left in darkness, most likely from opportunistic back yard breeders whose cash crop didn't look enough like the movie Dalmatians to turn a profit.

"They'd drop them off in boxes. Based on the appearance, absolutely, it was because they didn't look like the dog in the movie," Dane recalls. "This one family came, I think the puppy's name was Pepper, a very large, purebred, magnificent-looking male. They brought him and were jumping for joy and said, 'Okay, we're going out to lunch now, thank you, you just made our weekend.' There was no education, no thought into the future of their lives and how they were going to care for the puppy."

Dane has been involved in Dalmatian rescue for a quarter century, and she has seen nothing that floods animal shelters with her favorite breed like movies on the big screen. Producers in all visual media tend to use purebreds when including dogs as characters because if something happens to one, they can usually find or breed another one who looks similar enough to slide into the role. A Dalmatian has never won best in show at Westminster, so it's impossible to say whether the crush of interest would be similar based on news coverage, but Disney reportedly grossed more than $320 million from *101 Dalmatians* and more than $180 million from the sequel—hundreds of millions more than any dog show brings in, with far more people being influenced who may never watch a dog show at all.

"When a movie comes out like that and we get a lot of people who start breeding, they don't necessarily have good intentions in mind," Dane says. "People in South Florida were breeding in their back yards under horrible conditions. They'd breed anything that had spots. We were seeing inbred Dalmatians, fathers bred to daughters, that type of thing, but also a tremendous amount of Throwbacks, which are Pointer-type mixes. Anything that had a spot, they were breeding. It was all about making money and the supply meeting the demand."

A video game, a direct-to-DVD animated sequel, and a live theater musical have since followed, and when the musical was touring, a dog trainer telephoned Dane to get some dogs to put on stage in Florida. The trainer had no idea that the mere existence of the theater production might have the collateral consequence of endangering a lot more dogs in the future.

"We were approached by the trainer from Orlando who was looking for this and that and wanted us to sign all of these releases," she recalls. "I know a handful of the Dalmatian rescues in the country did that, but I just felt a disloyalty to my breed. I felt like I was aiding and abetting, encouraging the thing that I've been trying to curb for a number of years. I just couldn't do it with a clear conscience."

The real rub, Dane says of the movies, is that Disney included a storyline about a blue-eyed Dalmatian—which encouraged more than a few unscrupulous breeders to aim for that look and discard the rest. The same phenomenon struck a different breed during the late 1990s, when Taco Bell used a Chihuahua named Gidget in its runaway-craze commercials with the catchphrase "*Yo quiero* Taco Bell." Just like the blue-eyed Dalmatian, Gidget wasn't representative of the Chihuahua breed standard. She was too tall and too fat with a low-hanging rear end, not to mention an oddly shaped head and a stretched muzzle that made show dog judges cringe. Longtime and arguably responsible breeders wanted nothing to do with Chihuahuas who looked like her.

But buyers sure did. Gidget's look, plastered all over televisions in ads for two-for-ninety-nine-cents tacos, became the thing to have. That included her tan fur, even though Chihuahuas come in lots of colors, including black, white, gold, and mixes with different splashes of hues. Breeders aiming for the long-published standard didn't change what they were doing—and many of them argue, to this day, that there was no increase in Chihuahua popularity because AKC registrations did not climb—but spur-of-the-moment back yard breeders and some commercial breeders were more than happy to accommodate demand with puppies who were sold as purebreds even though they likely didn't qualify for purebred papers. These more opportunistic breeders cashed in on litter after litter of dogs who had the look that was wanted, and some of them in the Midwestern United States talk fondly, even now, about what a great time it was for Chihuahua sales.

People involved in Chihuahua rescue do not have the same kindly recollections, because soon after the boom, they started seeing the Chihuahua abandonment numbers spike, just like Dalmatian numbers skyrocketed after the Disney movies. One Chihuahua rescuer in New Jersey said calls more than doubled over the previous year, all because of thirty-second television commercials. "Sure, it's fun to see Chihuahuas on TV," Annette Mellinger of the Chihuahua Club of Mid-Jersey told Philly.com, "but the only ones benefiting from the sudden popularity are the puppy mills and wholesalers who are distributing to stores."

For the Jack Russell Terrier, the television sitcom *Frasier* was the flashpoint. It premiered in 1993 in the United States as a spinoff of the wildly popular *Cheers* and ran for eleven seasons, winning tens of millions of fans along with thirty-seven Emmy Awards and an audience far beyond US shores. British viewers in 2003 named Frasier Crane one of their favorite characters from the United States, second only to the cartoon dad Homer Simpson. *Frasier* is still in heavy rotation through syndication today. People can't get enough of actors Kelsey Grammer and David Hyde Pierce, or their comic foil, a Jack Russell Terrier known on the show as Eddie.

In real life, his name was Moose—and he should have been held up as the poster child for successful rehoming of a challenging, willful, would-be abandoned purebred puppy. His original family in Florida struggled to housetrain him, stop him from chewing, quiet his barking, end his digging, prevent him from escaping, and end his climbing of trees (he'd go straight up them, as high as six feet). Then he chased a bunch of horses and killed a neighbor's cat, and the family decided they couldn't stand the behavior anymore. That's how he ended up in the possession of a company that trains dogs for use on television and movie sets. They, too, found him incorrigible, often shredding things and standing on tables. Nevertheless, they turned him into such a household name that his photograph made the cover of *Entertainment Weekly*. The headline played into his image not as a dog with a tough temperament requiring the attention of professional trainers, but instead as a handsome stud: "He's Hot. He's Sexy. He's Purebred." The writers in the magazine's creative department probably thought the cover blurb was hysterical.

Jack Russell Terrier breeders didn't appreciate the joke. "As the show grew in popularity, so did the breed," recalls Catherine Brown, who has bred Jack Russells since the mid-1980s. "The only good thing was that Kelsey Grammer's character had a love-hate relationship with the dog. His disdain, that's what kept things from being even worse."

At the time *Frasier* went on the air, she says, there wasn't a major Jack Russell rescue organization in America. There had never been a need for one. The small-scale breeders might get a call once in a while for help with finding a dog a new home, and they did so quietly because they could, with relative ease. Then the show went gangbusters, and the number of breeders joining the Jack Russell Terrier Club of America, she says, shot up from a few thousand to more than nine thousand. A Jack Russell Terrier could suddenly be had not for the usual price of $850 to $1,500, she says, but instead for $150 or $250 from the most opportunistic new breeders who would sell the pups to anyone for quick cash. Soon after, the number of people trying to get rid of Jack Russells they'd purchased on the cheap and on a lark exploded to the point that Brown had to install a dedicated answering machine on her telephone line.

"I was getting calls at midnight," she remembers. "One guy wanted me to come in the middle of the night because he was in New York City and his dog was shedding. Truly. It went from eight dogs on the list to twenty-five, then fifty. When that happened, I said, 'Hey, I can't do this anymore.' That's when we became a 501(c)3" dog rescue charity.

Frasier was on the air for more than a decade, and Moose started to get old. Brown was among the breeders who received a photograph of him when trainers started seeking a stunt double. He was fairly representative of the breed, she says, but had ears too much like a hound, which is how he ended up being bred to create his own replacement. That dog's name was Enzo, and most viewers didn't notice his sliding into the program, but Moose sure did. They had to be kept apart. They rode in different sections of the car. They were walked separately. Otherwise, they'd fight—another fact that failed to make it into the public's consciousness.

Some naysayers argue there's no evidence of media-generated spikes in breed popularity, whether from news segments about dog show winners or popular movies and television shows, but today's booms are reruns of the same storyline that has played out since long before most modern-day dog lovers were born. Today, people know the Disney Dalmatians and the Taco Bell Chihuahua and *Frasier's* Jack Russell Terrier, but a dog named Rin Tin Tin was the first global example, about a century ago. He was a French-born German Shepherd who was saved from World War I and taught some cool tricks in his adopted home of America. In 1923, Rin Tin Tin scored his first starting role in a Warner Brothers film called *Where the North Begins*. It was the age of silent films, nearly twenty years before Humphrey Bogart and Ingrid Bergman starred in *Casablanca*. Rin Tin Tin's name was featured right under the title in the movie's promotional poster, where George Clooney's might be today. Warner Brothers promoters urged theater owners to put crates full of puppies in their lobbies, to bring in even bigger crowds of dog lovers at the premieres, and *Where the North Begins* earned the equivalent of about $5.5 million today. The dog made not one or two sequels, but twenty-four more screen appearances that played in theaters far beyond America's borders. He translated easily; all Warner Brothers had to do was change the pre-talkie film's dialog frames from English to, say, German. To keep the gravy train going, Warner Brothers at one point paid Rin Tin Tin almost eight times as much as his human co-stars, a cool $6,000 per week, the equivalent of about $80,000 per week today.

And in 1925, the German Shepherd for the first time topped the Boston Terrier as America's favorite purebred dog, according to US registrations. Britain saw a spike, too: In 1919, just fifty-four German Shepherds had been registered with the Kennel Club there. By 1926, it was more than eight thousand. No official statistics exist, of course, about the number of German Shepherd puppies bought from back yard breeders and never registered with kennel clubs, but if human nature indicates anything, it's that there were plenty to be had. Rin Tin Tin's celebrity, backed by the Warner Brothers marketing team, proved even stronger than national boundaries, and litter after litter of Shepherds rode on his coattails and into homes as Americans' favored breed until 1936, more than a decade after his first major film and continuing several years after his death.

There is simply no arguing the power of the media in the dog industry worldwide today. It's what people like Dane, Brown, and their fellow rescuers see. They've gotten to the point where they gear up for it and arrive at movie theaters on premiere nights, bracing themselves off to the side with a dog on a leash, trying against all hope to stem the inevitable tornado of demand followed by destruction that mass exposure to specific breeds creates.

"The AKC is not in the trenches like we are," Dane says. "They weren't walking through the shelters like we were and having to pick or choose. They weren't getting dogs like Pepper thrown over their gates on a regular basis."

In Britain, one trophy-winning dog who made headlines similarly to Banana Joe was a Pekingese officially named Yakee A Dangerous Liaison. His nickname was Danny, and he beat a staggering twenty thousand other dogs to win best in show at Crufts in 2003. But soon after Danny's big victory, when his image was being flashed around the world as the dog of the moment, he became the subject of scuttlebutt everywhere from Savile Row in London to the Guggenheim Museum in Manhattan. Hobnobbers were atwitter with gossip about the rumor that Danny, in order to take the grand prize, had undergone a facelift.

Cosmetic surgery is a huge no-no according to dog show rules set by the Kennel Club, which sanctions Crufts in Britain the same way the AKC sanctions Westminster in America. Ultimately, Danny was cleared of the accusation and allowed to keep his ribbon, and the Yakee kennel continued to win prizes with dogs just like him, taking best of breed honors in 2004 and 2005, and turning out one of Danny's sons, Yakee If Only, who became the top-ranked dog in all of America in 2005. As the scandal faded into history, Pekingese lovers everywhere breathed a deep, satisfying sigh of relief.

The only one who couldn't breathe easier was Danny. It turned out he had, indeed, undergone surgery, not to change his looks but instead to relieve an upper airway obstruction. Such health problems are common in dogs who, over the years, have been bred and inbred to produce faces that are more and more squashed and, in some cases, virtually flat—not at all like their ancestors, but highly appealing to modern show judges and buyers. Their skulls are what veterinarians call brachycephalic and are common not only in modern versions of the Pekingese, but also in many other sought-after breeds like Pugs and French Bulldogs.* Some of the

---

* Brachycephalic dog breeds include the American Bulldog, Boston Terrier, Boxer, Brussels Griffon, Bull Mastiff, Cavalier King Charles Spaniel, Chinese Shar-Pei, English Bulldog, English Mastiff, French Bulldog, Japanese Chin, Lhasa Apso, Neapolitan Mastiff, Pekingese, Pug, and Shih Tzu.

dogs have been mutated to meet dog-show standards until there's pretty much no snout left at all. Many people hear them chugging for oxygen and think, "It's just how that type of dog breathes," but that wasn't the case until breeders altered and squished their skulls over time. The dogs who are celebrated today fall asleep sitting up. They snort and gasp all the livelong day. They can't cool themselves the way other dogs can. Danny had a telltale sign of that last problem, even after surgery: anyone who looks closely at some of his winning photos from Crufts will see that he had to be placed on an ice pack while posing next to the trophy, so he wouldn't overheat before the photographers were done making him a star, one who would now be in demand worldwide as a stud to breed more dogs just like him.

Danny's story was one of several told in the one-hour documentary *Pedigree Dogs Exposed*, which had its debut on the BBC in the United Kingdom on August 19, 2008. The show was about how breeding dogs to win at conformation shows—purely for looks—has created "the greatest animal welfare scandal of our time." It included heartbreaking footage of Cavalier King Charles Spaniels suffering from a genetic condition called syringomyelia, in which the desire to give them exaggerated brachycephalic facial features has left their skulls too small for their brains, causing them to writhe, scream, and roll in constant pain. The documentary also showed video of German Shepherds winning in show rings with backs so sloped and hind legs so shortened that critics called them half dog, half frog. Clips showed Boxers having genetically induced epileptic seizures, and a breeder defending the practice of culling—killing as a matter of practice—healthy, happy Rhodesian Ridgeback puppies who happened to be born without the cosmetic ridge of fur along their spine.

The point of *Pedigree Dogs Exposed* was that breed standards are artificial rules that sometimes defy nature and reward the wrong qualities, promoting inbreeding for looks and causing a lot of genetically induced agony for more than a few of the countless puppies bred from dogs held up as the best in the world. The show featured interviews with weeping owners who had bought into the purebred marketing, purchased expensive dogs with pedigree credentials, and then watched in horror as their beloved pooches suffered and died, no matter how much money was spent on veterinary fees. Several graphic scenes of medical footage punctuated the message in ways that likely gave some viewers nightmares.

When the hour-long program faded to black, for many dog-loving Britons, it felt as if time had momentarily stopped. While less than half the pet dogs in the United States are believed to be purebreds, they make up as many as three-quarters of dogs living in homes in the United Kingdom. The realization that some breeding practices were in fact causing immense suffering to the dogs was staggering. On that night, from Piccadilly Circus to the shores of Southampton, the more than three million dog lovers who had watched the show sat back in their living room chairs, looked down at their beloved pets, and gulped. Hard.

"Media monsoon with a dash of typhoon-grade hysteria" is a reasonable description of what followed. Internationally famous dogs like Banana Joe and Danny soon had nothing on the documentary's writer and editor, Jemima Harrison, who had tuned in that night from her thatched cottage in Wiltshire with a few friends and the handful of people who had helped to produce the program. "Just watching the response on social media was amazing," she recalls today. "The phone started ringing before it was finished airing. Then it all went mad."

The BBC, she says, had feared a legal injunction prior to the broadcast, so the press had gotten a look at *Pedigree Dogs Exposed* only the day before it aired. The next-day explosion of coverage, in addition to the public's strong response, kept the issue of health problems in purebred dogs on the front pages in Britain for months. Someone left dog poop on the executive producer's doorstep. Registries of Cavalier King Charles Spaniels—the screaming dogs with too-small skulls—plummeted. Harrison's face was plastered everywhere as both a heroine to all canines and a villain casting unfair aspersions, depending on viewers' loyalties. "Burn the witch!" was one of the kinder comments made about her. Some people were crudely colorful in finding ever more creative ways to call her a doggone bitch.

Ironically, the program had come to be because Harrison was a purebred dog lover. She had a Flat-Coated Retriever named Freddie who died at the ripe old age of fifteen, in 2003. Somebody told her she was lucky to have had him so long, because on average, that breed dies by age eight or nine of cancer. The comment made her curious. She'd been a print journalist writing about other topics since the 1980s, and her love of dogs and her aching heart from Freddie's loss got her to clicking around the Internet. "Anybody with a couple of brain cells and Google, well, it's just so obvious," she says. "When I started to research other breeds, I just got more and more shocked. I couldn't believe what I was uncovering, and I couldn't believe nobody else had done it."

The fallout from her documentary was swift and severe. To this day, the airing of *Pedigree Dogs Exposed* remains the only time since dog shows became popular in the mid-1800s that the public stopped, considered the current reality of the dog industry, and at least temporarily halted the purebred marketing machine. It started with big-name sponsors pulling their money from Crufts. Then floods of letters and criticism battered the Kennel Club, some of whose members received personal, frightening threats. Breeders, long used to being cheered by fans during events like Crufts, instead reported everyday people spitting at them in the street. The BBC, which had broadcast Crufts for forty-two years, shocked the nation by taking it off the air beginning in 2009. It was akin to America's networks relegating the Westminster show to Internet-only status. In the midst of the outrage, Britain's most influential television producers simply pulled the plug and said, "We're not willing to be a part of this anymore."

It was not the dog show's death knell, but it was definitely a hoisting of the bell in the public square. And as any good marketing guru knows, once the message is corrupted to an extent that national media consider it toxic, there has to be a public perception of change for the business to proceed. It's the same with politicians exposed as having torrid affairs or priests caught fondling children. The institutions behind the people need to at least present an appearance of meaningful contrition and change before the public will return as devoted followers of their message.

The rehabilitation of Britain's dog-breeding world thus began in earnest. Various sizes and shapes of bandages were applied in an effort to stop the bleeding of the industry as a whole. The Kennel Club amended its policies to ban the culling of dogs for cosmetic reasons, and it reviewed all its breed standards, ultimately creating quite a few new ones so breeders would no longer be encouraged to aim for features like flat faces, giant skin folds, and bulging eyes that inhibit a dog from breathing, walking, or seeing. (Yes, those things had to be written down as an official standard for some breeders to agree to them.) The Kennel Club also banned the breeding of parent dogs to their puppies, and the breeding of sibling dogs, which, until then, had apparently been common practice to get the look that won judges' hearts. A national dog advisory council was started, and the Kennel Club created a £1.2 million (about $1.9 million) facility to create genetic tests that breeders might someday use to screen out diseases like the one that creates skulls too small for dogs' brains.

Not long after, Harrison was back at the BBC putting the finishing touches on *Pedigree Dogs Exposed: Three Years On*, a sequel that showed how, despite the changes, the overarching problems with health and welfare remained. The program talked about a champion Boxer from a kennel owned by a Crufts judge being used to sire nearly nine hundred puppies—several dozen of whom were believed to have genetically inherited juvenile kidney disease. It showed one whistleblower from the original documentary being booted from her breed club for speaking out about health concerns. It featured a veterinarian saying he believes many dog owners simply don't realize how much their dogs are suffering to achieve modern looks. It included a member of the RSPCA taking yet another shot at Crufts, saying that tinkering with beauty pageants will never be enough—that the dog shows have to be about health and welfare for the problem to be brought under control.

"There was a big campaign run to try and stop the sequel, and the BBC did get a little worried," Harrison says. "The amount of meetings that I had to go to with lawyers and editorial policy for the sequel—every letter of every word in that film was watertight."

In the end, the sequel wasn't nearly as shocking to the public as the original. It confirmed that problems remained, but by that time, the supporters of breeding had figured out how to manage their response more effectively, especially with all their new standards in place. Crufts, having aired only on the Internet in 2009, was picked up by the television channel More4. Millions of viewers returned to watch, even after an Imperial College London study showed the extent of inbreeding in ten breeds—Akita Inu, Boxer, Chow Chow, English Bulldog, English Springer Spaniel, Golden Retriever, Greyhound, German Shepherd, Labrador Retriever, and Rough Collie—had left the dogs at risk of birth defects and genetically inherited health problems, so much so that, in some parts of the world, including Germany, the lack of remaining genetic diversity would qualify them as endangered species.

By 2012, with the media rehabilitation effort continuing, a new Kennel Club rule was in place requiring dogs in fifteen breeds to undergo health checks after winning best of breed before they would be allowed to compete for best in show—and at that year's Crufts, only nine of the fifteen winners anointed by the judges passed the veterinary screenings. The so-called best Basset Hound, Bulldog, Clumber Spaniel, Mastiff, Neapolitan Mastiff, and, yes, the Pekingese, less than a decade after Danny's big win, were shown the door before the main event. While they may have been pretty, veterinarians deemed them unhealthy. And then, to cap off that bad-news year for the breeding community, former Crufts host Ben Fogle (England's version of Westminster front man David Frei) announced that he believed his beloved Labrador, Inca, suffered from fatal epilepsy because of standard breeding practices, and said he was glad the BBC had taken Crufts off television.

Pedigree Dogs Exposed aired in the United States only on BBC America on cable, and on a few PBS stations, Harrison says. It never got the wide exposure it enjoyed in Britain. No other program has ever been aired in America that explains the topic so powerfully. Nowadays, Harrison continues to push her message through a *Pedigree Dogs Exposed* blog and social media. She's not against purebred dogs in general—"I love my Flat-Coated Retrievers; I just want them without the cancer," she says—and she hopes that someday, breeders will accept her point that dogs shouldn't have to suffer and die young so people can achieve artificial standards of excellence. Breeding for looks *and* for health should be the standard, she says, even if it means cross-breeding for a short time to let nature correct the genetic flaws humans have perpetuated to the point that they seem commonplace.

"The Americans have shaped their dogs differently from the Brits, and of course they're all breeding to the all-being standard," Harrison says. "There's nothing standard here. It's like trying to tackle someone's religion. You can't argue it with logic intact. Once you realize it's not cute, and you see a Pug or a Bulldog gasping for air in the street, it just breaks your heart."

She adds, "Some studies have shown that the average death of today's Dobermans is around six. It's absolutely horrific. And you get breeders saying, 'Well, you have to love them a lot because you don't have them for long.' It's as if it's a given, and they're unaware of how powerful they could be in changing things if they just saw it differently."

Wherever there is a middle-class audience of dog buyers still to be reached, though, the purebred message and media coverage continue to spread. A record 4.6 million people reportedly tuned in to watch Crufts in 2014. In that year alone, the Westminster Kennel Club issued more than seven hundred press credentials to media outlets from more than twenty countries, and its website had about twelve million page views from more than 170 countries. About twenty thousand dogs were registered to compete in the 2014 FCI World Dog Show, held that year in Helsinki, Finland, with some of the pups coming from as far away as the Philippines, Australia, Peru, Brazil, Japan, and Russia.

Of course, reporters from news outlets worldwide went to Helsinki, too. FCI World Dog Show officials positioned the tall silver trophy just so for the official photographs, which, in addition to the winning pooch, would also include a beautiful blonde in a long, red evening gown.

The FCI winner for 2014 turned out to be an Affenpinscher nicknamed Tricky Ricky. He took top honors in Helsinki after being bred in the United States. The dog is co-owned by Indonesia's Jongkie Budiman and Mieke Cooijmans of the Netherlands.

Yes, that Mieke Cooijmans, the same person who co-owns Tricky Ricky's father, Banana Joe.

CHAPTER EIGHT

INDUSTRY WASTE

"What's dangerous is not to evolve."

—Jeff Bezos

O leg Deripaska recognized the problem long before the broadcasters arrived and revealed it to the world. Multibillionaires have a way of doing that, of seeing beyond what average people notice and discerning a smarter way forward. The only thing Deripaska didn't realize, so early on, was that he'd have to be the one to build the actual road to the future that would save the dogs.

It was several years before the 2014 Olympic Games in Sochi, and the Russian tycoon was walking around the sites where about fifty thousand of his workers were building everything from the athletes' village to the seaport to the revamped airport. He was forty-four years old at the time and a dog lover since childhood, when his first best friend was a stray who would walk with him to the post office. He remains a fan of pups today and has no fewer than nine of his own, which is why he couldn't help but feel a connection to the increasing number of dogs roaming around with the Sochi construction workers. At first, he saw one or two at a time, but as the Games approached and workers began to return home to other parts of Russia, Deripaska was seeing the dogs in packs. The workers, he realized, had been feeding them as pets and now were abandoning them, creating what would become an international spectacle of strays.

About six months before the opening ceremonies, local government officials were ignoring his requests for help and announcing plans to exterminate the dogs ahead of the international attention that the Olympic Games would bring. A mass cull would be unthinkable if it were done to purebred show dogs—like the ones expected to flood by the thousands into Moscow for the FCI World Dog Show in 2016—but for the friendly, healthy strays living as pets in Sochi just a few years earlier, the plan, to Russian officials, made perfect sense. That realization is why Deripaska had his teams develop a rural area of government land just beyond Sochi's borders into an animal shelter called Povodog. He gave $15,000 to construct the initial site, and he pledged about $50,000 to run it for the upcoming year. By the time reporters descended on Sochi to cover the world's best bobsledders, skiers, and figure skaters in February 2014, Povodog was feeding and vaccinating about eighty dogs, including about a dozen puppies, with plans in the works to shelter hundreds at a time.

Deripaska was far from alone in his personal outrage about the government plan to kill the dogs; reports surfaced of everyday Russians like Vlada Provotorova, a dentist who rescued Sochi strays using a makeshift shelter, and Igor Ayrapetyan, who drove about a thousand miles from Moscow to rescue eleven Sochi strays and bring them back to his home. But Deripaska, as one of the world's richest men, was a magnet for major news organizations. He's married to the daughter of Valentin Yumashev, who served as Boris Yeltsin's chief of staff, and he has been said at various times to be even wealthier than fellow Russian tycoon Roman Abramovich, who owns several of the world's largest superyachts and a personal Boeing 767. Deripaska's mere existence as a character in the homeless dogs' story got the attention of news producers around the globe who normally wouldn't care about any dogs besides the ones who win at Westminster, Crufts, and the FCI World Dog Show. Even Yahoo Sports ran an article titled "How to Adopt a Sochi Stray Dog" after the storyline eclipsed the gold medal counts in daily news reports from the Olympic Village.

It was arguably the only time in modern history that global media came together to promote the world's throwaway dogs with the same force and attention so often given to dogs considered the purebred elite. And the kicker was that the entire fuss was made over about four thousand pooches, give or take a few. It's a number so small that it usually fails to register in many of the nations whose top networks covered the Sochi strays, nations where far more homeless dogs, purebreds and mutts alike, are killed en masse on a regular basis.

Sochi's dogs represented a fraction of the number abandoned every summer in Spain, Italy, and France, where in the last country alone, an estimated one hundred thousand domestic pets are left behind when their owners take off on annual vacations during July and August. The problem has become so acute in the land of Liberté, Égalité, and Fraternité that the French SPCA runs an annual campaign, putting up posters in Paris transit stations to implore people, "Don't leave your pet this year."

The four thousand dogs in Sochi also were a statistical blip compared with the estimated sixty-five thousand pooches—one for every thirty people—living on the streets of Bucharest, Romania. Those dogs became what are known as *roamers*, or strays people consider pets, feeding them and providing them shelter at night, after the government ordered houses demolished and replaced with smaller, pet-unfriendly flats. In early 2013, a four-year-old boy died in an attack by roaming dogs, and the government in

Romania came up with a solution similar to the one envisioned in Russia: round up the dogs and kill them. Photos soon emerged of people clinging to beloved dogs, including one woman grimacing and pleading as she threw her body between men with cages and her dog, who was trapped beneath a net. "On many locations dog-catching teams capture each and every dog they see on the street," says Ruud Tombrock, the Netherlands-based European director of World Animal Protection. "Owners then have fourteen days to find their dog in one of the many crowded and sometimes distant animal shelters. In the shelters I visited in Bucharest, I saw many dogs that clearly belonged to someone, but that no one was collecting. Hard to tell if their owners were even aware that their dog was captured and had started a search."

Sochi's four thousand strays also were nothing compared with the estimated two million dogs killed for food every year in South Korea, where officials were already worrying in 2014 about how their nation's dog-meat restaurants would fare in 2018 during international news reports from the scheduled Olympic Games in Pyeongchang. The restaurants were banned in Seoul ahead of the 1988 Summer Olympics there, but enforcement is lax and elderly residents in particular keep up demand for the dog meat, especially in restaurants near hospitals, because they believe it gives people stamina and energy. Truly old-school restaurateurs inflict pain and suffering before cooking the dogs, thinking the meat tastes better if the dogs have high adrenaline levels at the moment they're killed. Reports about beatings and immolations up the road from the Olympic hockey venue are not what Korean officials want to see at the top of the ESPN *SportsCenter* ticker.

In Japan, the government-sanctioned killing is done behind closed doors in animal control facilities, where an estimated five hundred dogs and cats are killed every day. Even if only half of them are dogs, Japan is killing—every two weeks or so—the same number of homeless dogs the world cried out to save in Sochi. A lot of times, the dogs die in gas chambers sanctioned by the Department of Public Health. They call them "dream boxes" because, well, it sounds nicer than asphyxiation boxes. Time will tell if those dogs make the news the way the Sochi dogs did when Tokyo hosts the Summer Olympics in 2020, but the odds are not good. When the killing is taken behind closed doors, not only do the cameras tend to ignore it, but even local citizens often fail to recognize its scope.

That is the case in the United States, the most dog-loving nation on Earth. As in Japan, gas chambers are used across America—they're legal in about two dozen states—and the numbers of dogs being killed outside the public eye typically shocks those who learn the truth. Long gone are the days when dogcatchers would do things like round up dogs from the streets of New York City, herd them into an iron cage, and sink it into the East River, in full view and earshot of the public—who eventually demanded change. Today, with America's dog culling being kept behind closed doors, estimates suggest that taxpayer-funded facilities are killing as many as 38,000 dogs a week. That's some 5,500 dogs *every single day*, more than the entire population of Sochi strays, every twenty-four hours.

And it's not primarily because Americans are moving to smaller homes or have roamers crowding the city streets. US residents have zero affinity for dog meat on restaurant menus, and they are not known for abandoning their Spots and Rovers during summer vacations. It's also not because there are more dogs than people who want them in the United States. The notion that America's homeless dogs face an "overpopulation problem" does not match up against the available statistics. Supply is not exceeding demand. Americans want about eight million dogs a year as new pets, while only about four million dogs are entering the shelters. America kills about two million of those shelter dogs each year while US dog lovers get their new pets from other sources. If just half the Americans already getting a dog went the shelter route, then statistically speaking, every cage in US animal control facilities could be emptied. Right now. And the United States would still need another four million dogs each year to meet demand. Americans want more pups than any other nation on the planet. In the United States, there are no extra dogs in terms of quantity. There are instead millions of throwaway dogs in terms of perceived quality.

What makes America a pernicious leader in this sphere of the dog industry is its general beliefs about pups, beliefs that are, surprisingly, often more in line with the governments of Sochi and Bucharest than they are with those of dog lovers fighting to protect and save canines on the streets worldwide. A solid third of America's dog-buying citizens believe that the best way to get a pooch is to buy a purebred. Thirty-five percent of Americans say they want a purebred, and a slightly higher percentage say they won't adopt a dog from a shelter, or even consider doing so, because they believe it's impossible to know what you are going to get. In the United States, most of the homeless dogs who never make it out of animal-control facilities do not pose any actual problem. The vast majority of dogs being killed are healthy and friendly. Many are puppies, mixed breed and purebred alike. These dogs are dying because not enough Americans believe they are good enough to welcome into homes. The dogs face a stigma that, at its core, is a marketing problem tied to the way Americans understand the dog business.

Workers at Lee County Animal Shelter in Sanford, North Carolina, don't need to see any surveys to understand this aspect of the problem. Their shelter is typical of many in the United States. It doesn't charge an adoption fee for the dogs in its cages, and even still, it kills a lot of them because it can't find anybody to take them home, not even for free. A lot of people just can't see the value in them, people like the man who walked through the front door in early November 2013. He was the type of person who walks into facilities like Lee County's every day. He didn't have a vicious dog to surrender. He didn't have a sick dog or a troublesome dog or a dog who had ever exhibited any kind of a behavior problem at all.

Instead, he had an unspayed dog back at home who had gotten knocked up and produced the boxload of seven puppies he had in his arms.

The puppies were just two weeks old. According to a Lee County animal control officer who posted their photos on Facebook in a plea for help, the man was explicit in his reason for handing them over. They were useless, he said, because they were mixed breed.

That moment didn't make the news, of course. It was too run-of-the-mill in America to matter.

Even Sarah McLachlan reaches for the remote control when her commercials come on. "I change the channel. I can't take it," the singer told the Huffington Post. "I can't even look at it. It's just so depressing."

The Canadian singer's commercials for the ASPCA have become so ubiquitous since they began airing in 2007 that they now embody the images and soundtrack that countless Americans see in their minds of homeless dogs. The mood the spots set is certainly no national anthem being sung by the cast of *Jersey Boys* before a dog show. First, viewers hear the haunting opening notes of the Grammy Award–winner's tearful ballad "Angel." Then come the photos, one after the next, of dogs behind bars, their big weepy eyes pleading for help, their awful fates sealed unless viewers donate—and fast. Any dog lover who makes it through the first fifteen seconds is likely to end up in tears. Those who hang in until the end are so disturbed that they've sent checks and credit card digits totaling more than $30 million to date.

An estimated quarter of the dogs in US shelters are purebreds, but that's irrelevant to most buyers who care about pedigree papers; once a dog has the stink of a shelter on her, breed no longer matters even to the top breeders. AKC rules state outright that any dog found in a shelter cannot qualify for anything other than alternative listing. These dogs are welcome at performance and other events, just like mutts, but they are no longer acceptable in the primary rings at dog shows like Westminster. Simply having spent one night in an American shelter can turn a $3,500 puppy into a dog in need of a telethon to save her life.

Nobody with a shred of intellectual honesty would argue that breeders, even the most irresponsible ones, are causing all of the problems with homeless dogs worldwide, but at the same time, anyone with a hint of a conscience must acknowledge that the rise of the purebred industry as a whole has helped shift homeless dogs into the position of secondhand options, or even disposable goods, in nations all around the world. Two hundred years ago, a mutt who had come along, guarded the house, and been kind to the kids served just fine. But since the advent of dog shows and the globalization of the purebred message, nonbreeder dogs who are perfectly healthy and friendly have become so much less valued that, in some cases, they become government-sanctioned targets for culling by the millions.

It was inevitable that society would get to this point, given the chosen path. Once the world decided that it was okay to parade some dogs around on stages and televisions as the best that money can buy, then by definition, cheaper alternatives had to exist. And cheaper, in many minds, equates not only with less valuable, but also with less inherently worthy. It's an economic scale that, when taken to its logical end, terminates as throwaway garbage in any industry.

Prices matter psychologically. Premium pricing versus value brands, Ferraris and Lamborghinis versus Hyundais and Fiats— consumers have been conditioned to respond to the numbers as a measure of quality, even if the far less expensive Hyundai or Fiat will serve basic needs well for ten or fifteen years. As much as people love their dogs as members of their families, the reality today is that dogs are products, just like cars, ones that are advertised and packaged and bought and sold to the tune of about thirty million pooches a year worldwide from breeders, shelters, pet stores, and nonprofit rescue groups. The total market value is somewhere in the neighborhood of $11 billion, based on the average price paid per dog in the United States and typical pricing elsewhere. That's not money spent on puppy sweaters or orthopedic beds or veterinary care; it's only the cash plunked down to bring home the dogs in the first place. The people listing dogs for sale, obviously, want consumers to buy from them first, and pricing plays a role, just as it would in any other market. It's delusional to think otherwise, no matter how different people feel dogs are from other luxury and value-brand goods marked with a price tag.

In fact, fully half of Americans surveyed recently said dogs who come from shelters or rescue groups were low-priced options. That's a huge percentage of people with an ingrained belief about value—about the same level of market penetration, in terms of messaging, that Apple has in terms of sales with its iPads among all tablet computers. At the opposite end of the belief spectrum, fewer than one in ten Americans say dogs coming from breeders, pet stores, or even puppy mills are low-priced options. Those dogs are immediately thought of as the higher-quality items from the upper shelves. This message on pricing is firmly established in our culture, the value of different types of dogs is set, and it all plays right into the stereotypes about purebred champions and homeless mutts so often seen in the media.

On top of that, most people instinctually crank up the volume of their doubts about some dogs' quality. Psychologists call it negativity bias, and it refers to the fact that humans have a greater recall of unpleasant things than positive things. It's believed to be an evolutionary trait. The caveman who forgot that he once saw a certain type of tree had nothing to fear, while the caveman who failed to remember the danger posed by a saber-toothed cat was likely to become supper. The negative image had to be more memorable, to take precedence in the brain's filing system, so the next time the saber-toothed cat appeared, the caveman instinctively knew to run and hide without even thinking. The human mind is thus quicker to form—and to retain—bad impressions. It's better to assume the worst when seeking the best chance of staying alive, or at least of preventing arms from being chewed off in a bloody fight with a giant feline. This survival mechanism springs from a crucial time in human evolution and remains deeply embedded in the human psyche, even today, and it's one reason why people who are dog lovers in general can continue to see certain dogs as innately worse than others.

In a groundbreaking paper published about fifteen years ago titled "Bad Is Stronger than Good," researchers from the United States and the Netherlands showed how negativity bias affects countless decisions people make. The phenomenon is seen across cultures and throughout history, with hardly any exceptions. Whether it's bad emotions or bad feedback, the human mind processes bad inputs more thoroughly than anything good. The bad stuff gets more deeply ingrained, more wound up in the brain pathways than the pleasantries. Once someone believes something is bad, even if she's mislabeled a tree, she's going to react to it like it's a saber-toothed cat. It happens at an instinctual level. Negativity bias can be that strong of a force from within.

The things most people say they want in a dog—a healthy, friendly pet—can become nonfactors in their thinking once negativity bias takes over. If they've formed a bad impression of shelters or mutts, then they intuitively stop looking at who the dogs actually are and instead focus on the ingrained response to other factors like price and source. If the dog costs $200 and is from a shelter, then in many minds, she is by definition not as good as a dog who costs $2,000 and comes from a breeder—even if it's the same exact dog being marketed two different ways. Remember the study of Americans in which 35 percent said that with a homeless dog, it's impossible to know what you are going to get? There's actually no guarantee with any dog, including a purebred, that he'll grow up to be friendly, healthy, or long-lived.

And yet the belief persists that the shelter dogs are the more worrisome option, a belief that may be on the rise in America, despite years of educational outreach, with young adults now saying in one survey that they're more likely to buy a "more desirable" purebred than to adopt from a shelter.

One reason for the lingering power of stereotypes may be that today's forms of media exacerbate the beliefs that have been established during the past few generations, creating a feedback loop that is ingraining the messages more deeply. People forty or older can remember a time when the primary media advertising was on television, which they watched for an hour or two at night and saw a few ads here and there between favorite shows on the dozen or so channels that existed. Today, adding things like endless satellite channels and smartphones into the mix, many people spend more time with technology than they do sleeping. Britons average eight hours and forty-one minutes a day using devices. Americans spend eleven hours a day with electronic media. Those negative stereotypes—whether in Sarah McLachlan commercials or news reports out of Sochi—are coming far more often and being further and further reinforced, while the handful of messages promoting the opposite of ingrained beliefs are even more likely to get overlooked because of the constant media deluge.

"When you look at a Facebook feed, the average person has something on the order of 250 friends as well as businesses that they've liked, and so it becomes increasingly difficult now to stand out against all of this. Think about Twitter. It's like an avalanche coming at you," says Dr. Angela Hausman, an associate professor at Howard University in Washington, DC, specializing in Internet marketing and consumer behavior. "The cultural value for so long has been, 'Get this wonderful purebred dog because they're so gorgeous and yada, yada, yada.' We've become used to this, and we think this is normal because it's what we see."

Social media also has an aspect to it that makes people more likely to click on photos of sad puppies, which makes trying to get out the message of mutts even more likely to rely on the existing stereotypes. One of the things researchers have figured out is that social media posts with images get more people's attention, especially if the image is of somebody recognizable, Hausman says. People stop and look at celebrities and friends more often than they stop and look at strangers. And, it turns out, people also stop and look at animals, including puppies. Digital users recognize the emotions on the animals' faces and intuitively respond to them as something well known. Negativity bias is at work here, too, making people most likely to notice a sad puppy's face coming through their Facebook feed. Instead of turning these messages off, like a lot of people do with the sad television commercials, social media's properties make users more likely to stop and click on the message that shows shelter dogs as downtrodden, further reinforcing the belief.

"If you want somebody to donate money, negativity helps," Hausman says. "It's very tough to turn it around. Things like the ASPCA commercials are really counterproductive in a lot of ways because they reinforce the stereotype that these rescue animals are somehow undesirable."

Establishing and reinforcing beliefs about quality: that is how the low end of any market is created, how any product, including a perfectly wonderful, healthy, friendly puppy, can be made to seem less worthy than others or even unworthy of life itself, brought by the boxload into a shelter at two weeks old and handed over like garbage to be destroyed, or captured and killed in the streets by the millions, without so much as a second thought.

What people believe is about the dogs is not always about the dogs. What people say about dogs, and what people accept as truth about dogs, is often no more than what consumers have allowed sellers to convince them of—sellers with fat cows and new purebred styles and sad fundraising schemes who for several generations now have been tapping into innate thought processes that don't get questioned because they simply feel normal.

⁂

John Hibbing and Kevin Smith have been wondering something specific lately about dogs: do people with liberal political leanings see them as somewhat equal family members while conservatives see them more as loyal underlings?

It sounds like a loaded question, the kind that would land the purebred owners Barack Obama, Vladimir Putin, and Kim Jong-un in a political nightmare, but it's where research into things like negativity bias has led the two University of Nebraska–Lincoln political science professors in recent years. In 2013, with their colleague John Alford of Rice University, Smith and Hibbing published *Predisposed: Liberals, Conservatives and the Biology of Political Differences*. It contained more than three hundred pages of evidence from experiments across cultures documenting how people's political inclinations, like taste buds or athletic aptitudes, appear to be rooted not in intellect, but in biology. Humans are not so much hardwired to be liberal or conservative, they argue, but people are just as predisposed to political leanings as they are to, say, a love of spicy foods. Environment and experiences play a role in who each person becomes, but humans are not born as entirely clean slates, and those who are conservatives are more influenced by certain things, including negativity bias, than those who are liberals.

"Conservatives and liberals are different on tons of things other than politics," Smith says. "That is not a question. Our own research and the research of others shows it's everything from taste in food to taste in art to preference in different cars—tons of things. One of the things John and I have speculated on is difference in pets, that given liberal and conservative tendencies in other areas, would they be attracted to different types of pets, would they treat them differently, what would their relationship be with pets."

When asked to take an educated guess, Smith added, "My hypothesis would be that conservatives would be more likely to go with purebred dogs and liberals would be more likely to go with mutts from the pound."

It doesn't take a degree in political science to see that, around the world today, the mutt-versus-purebred proposition has become something of a tribal political marker, like abortion or immigration. Since about 2005 in America, nonprofit rescue groups have been transporting death-row dogs by the hundreds of thousands from the high-kill shelters in conservative Southern states up to eager adopters in the liberal Northeast. From London to Brussels to Amsterdam, liberals are now waving fingers and shouting with disgust about conservative-minded people from Eastern Europe, where purebred puppies are farmed while strays are slaughtered. One longtime purebred seller from a conservative region in the Midwestern United States has endured similar judgments from people in metropolitan areas who call their dogs, to his befuddlement, four-footed children. He responds by saying, "I don't have a problem with somebody in New York City or Boston being a vegetarian or not wanting to go hunting. I'm not saying we should shove our lifestyle down their throat. But they shouldn't do the same thing to us, either. And I don't like the term 'companion animal.' My companion is my wife. My dog is my pet. What he deserves from me is attention, love, socialization, vet care, a good food source, clean water. But he's not my companion. He doesn't own me. I own him."

These types of comments—not about taxes or military policies, but about *dogs*—are as politically charged as it gets, and when put into the framework of Smith and Hibbing's work, they seem to make absolute sense. The authors say that while dogs may be an issue of the moment, they're one of many things about which people take up sides, and those sides are based on how people feel about a few bedrock social dilemmas. Each person has core preferences for organization, structure, and the way society operates, and those core preferences frame the teams they join when arguing about issues of the day, be they gay marriage or marijuana legalization or which puppy is the best that money can buy. With pretty much everything, the authors say, human leanings boil down to bedrock dilemmas like maintaining tradition versus experimenting with new things, ensuring strength versus encouraging equality, and protecting oneself from outside groups versus being open to them. Conservatives on any issue of the day tend to lean toward the first option in each set, while liberals tend to lean toward the latter.

Additional studies show that conservatives are more prone to negativity bias—which affects all those bedrock dilemmas, too, and every issue of the day that arises, including dogs. Those who are conservative literally and physically experience the world differently than those who are liberal, the authors say. Conservatives have a physiological, more deeply ingrained response to anything that might pose a danger. And anyone who is more sensitive to threats—who has strong negativity bias—is more likely to stick with tradition and order. That person is more likely to want a strong leader who is clearly in charge. That person is more likely to be leery of outside groups with new ideas.

All of which lines up, quite naturally, with wanting a dog whose marketing label includes the word *pure*, whose breed is clearly defined in a book of accepted standards and judged by people in positions of authority, and who didn't come from a depressing shelter where who-knows-what might have been going on.

It is quite possible that all the purebred marketing, the organization and structure of dog shows, and the notion that breeders offer the best dogs because they're the highest-priced taps into an evolutionary need within the more conservative among the population to feel they are making the safest possible choice. It doesn't matter to some people which types of dogs might actually make the best pets for their lifestyle. Those who are conservative likely feel, in the marrow of their bones, that buying from the established purebred industry is just plain safer.

"It sounds very plausible to me," Hibbing says, with the caveat that no data yet exists on the question of liberals, conservatives, and dogs. "The one thing I would add, in addition to the tendency of conservatives to dislike not knowing what they're going to get, and not liking surprises, is also the concept of contamination and purity. People get nervous when you talk about this stuff, but there is evidence that indicates conservatives like things that are pristine."

Smith and Hibbing are quick to add that people fall into far more than two categories, and that it's unreasonable to paint all liberal-leaning people and all conservative-leaning people with just two brushes. (Gender may also play a strong role in choices. A PetSmart Charities study expected to be released in 2015 showed that an overwhelming number of women were open to the idea of getting a shelter dog compared with far fewer men.) Even so, the conservative–liberal tendencies are there in experiment after experiment done all around the world. Is it any surprise, really, that a conservative, authoritarian nation like Russia would come up with a plan to cull dogs in the streets of Sochi? Could anyone imagine that happening in, say, the liberal streets of San Francisco? Think about how, among their liberal friends, many people with purebreds are quick to explain, "Yes, my dog Cuddles is a purebred, but I got him from a rescue group, not from a breeder." Among their conservative friends, many people with mutts are likely to note, "Yes, I did adopt this shelter dog Snuggles, but only after he'd been in a foster home and been checked out for a few weeks, so I knew there would be no problems."

Such statements aren't about the dogs. Either of those comments could be made about exactly the same dog who originated at exactly the same source, such as a dog auction. Working with a breed rescue group signifies the liberal tendency to be okay with surprises and to care about all dogs being given an equal chance. Acknowledging that a dog was previously fostered indicates proper attention to potential threats and some kind of orderly process. What's being said with these comments is about the people and about what they've come to believe during the past two centuries about different types of dogs—that some are more worthy than others, depending on the worldview.

"These attitudes and orientations come from these really deeply embedded predispositions that are at least partially rooted in your biology, so they're awfully hard to change," Smith says. "It's not impossible, it's not deterministic. But these things are going to be more resistant to facts, to logical persuasion, because this is something that people almost literally feel in their gut. *This is the right thing. This is the truth.* People aren't completely irrational, but with those attitudes that are reflexive, those are tough to change."

In fact, what's going on around the world today with anti–puppy mill campaigns may just be the first global example of liberal dog lovers finally, if accidentally, learning to speak the language of conservative dog lovers through the media—and making a sizable dent in the purebred industry's pocketbook for the first time in at least a century.

CHAPTER NINE

THE UPSTART COMPETITOR

"Hell, there are no rules here. We're trying to
accomplish something."

—*Thomas Edison*

B ill Reiboldt is the kind of guy who can be counted on to wear
a plain tie. He carries himself as one might expect from a
Republican representing a conservative, agricultural district
in the Missouri State House of Representatives: dark suits, neatly
combed hair, and a frame that fits right in at American Legion
steak-and-potato suppers.

Reiboldt is as much of a homegrown local as people can be in
this part of Missouri, born in 1948 in Neosho, one of the communities he now represents in the southwest corner of the state.
Like a lot of his constituents, he's a farmer with years of experience in dairy, beef, and crops, and his farm today spans about five
hundred acres. Reiboldt is a husband, father, and grandfather. He

attends the local Hillcrest Church of Christ, and he signs off on his own website with "May God bless you." He's chairman of the committee on agriculture policy, whose work affects all kinds of farms, including those where dogs are bred in large quantities for sale. Part of his district is McDonald County, home to the Hunte puppy distribution company. If the community of Wheaton were a stone's throw west of its current borders, then Reiboldt would represent Southwest Auction Service, too.

Reiboldt won his first two-year term in 2010, the same year a lot of people who share his political leanings took a beating at the polls in the form of a statewide ballot initiative, one put before voters based on petition signatures instead of by lawmaker action. It was known as Proposition B, the Puppy Mill Cruelty Prevention Act, and this is how it was explained to voters:

> A "yes" vote will amend Missouri law to require large-scale dog breeding operations to provide each dog under their care with sufficient food, clean water, housing, and space; necessary veterinary care; regular exercise and adequate rest between breeding cycles. The amendment further prohibits any breeder from having more than fifty breeding dogs for the purpose of selling their puppies as pets. The amendment also creates a misdemeanor crime of "puppy mill cruelty" for any violations.

Quite a few of Reiboldt's constituents were outraged that the words "puppy mill" appeared in the ballot measure's title and the text. They would have preferred something more neutral, perhaps along the lines of "commercial breeding facility" or "large-scale kennel," which is how they describe the farms they run. After all, nobody calls the other farms in this region "cow mills" or "pig mills" or "chicken mills." Calling some farms "puppy mills," to them, seemed wholly biased, like a slur being made part of the official voting process.

Unfortunately for Reiboldt's fellow farmers, they were up against a trend in syntax that, by 2010, extended far beyond Missouri's borders. In just the two years before Proposition B made it onto the ballot, more than a dozen other US states had passed laws devised to crack down on large, substandard kennels, with headlines describing them as anti–puppy mill initiatives from coast to coast. In Britain, Europe, and beyond, the term is "puppy farm," but with the same effect. Ireland's newspapers reported the passage of an anti–puppy farm law in summer 2010, news that was similarly noted in other countries thanks to Ireland's nickname at the time: the Puppy Farm of Europe. Down under in 2010, RSPCA Australia issued a bulletin titled "End Puppy Farming." The folks on the farms in Missouri could be as offended as all get out, but the language had already made it into the global lexicon, and it had voters riled.

The image that *puppy mill* invokes in people's minds is one of the main reasons Proposition B passed in Missouri, earning votes from Republicans and Democrats alike. The arguably liberal voters who cared about dogs as family members didn't want them being treated like livestock, while the arguably conservative voters who cared about rules and order couldn't stand the visual of filthy stacked cages. That's the political magic of the term *puppy mill*. It offends just about everybody, even if for different reasons.

As far as Reiboldt was concerned, the phrasing of Proposition B was like a grenade being lobbed at the good people of farm country who had spent decades doing backbreaking chores in the kennels to satisfy consumer demand. He thought voters in his state had been at a minimum swayed, and more accurately swindled, by the people who worked hardest to get Proposition B on the ballot, people who didn't even live in Missouri: members of the Washington, DC–based HSUS. He said the group spent $4.85 million campaigning for Proposition B. Other sources put the figure closer to $2 million, but either way, it was a hefty sum compared with the $500,000 that Missouri's farm organizations had been able to muster in self-defense. In Reiboldt's opinion, HSUS had parachuted into Missouri and bought up a bunch of votes as part of a broader effort to destroy farms throughout the nation. "Not only is HSUS seeking to limit our state's legislative process and push themselves into our state's animal agriculture business," he wrote in *Kennel Spotlight*, "HSUS boasts of a $150 million budget to fund their agenda against animal agriculture in the entire United States."

The outcry from the farms was so profound that Proposition B, despite having won 51.6 percent of Missouri's vote, never became law. It took less than a year for Governor Jay Nixon, a Democrat, to succumb to lobbying from lawmakers in rural areas who said HSUS had hijacked the entire voting process by using the ballot petition initiative to foist a national agenda on them. The governor ultimately issued a statement saying both sides had worked out new language that protected both animals and the agriculture industry, and he signed into law a compromise version of Proposition B, one that was more favorable to the voters who lived in districts like Reiboldt's. It was dubbed "the Missouri Solution" and removed the fifty-dog limit along with specifics for exercise and rest between breeding cycles. The words *puppy mill* also were scratched altogether, replaced with "a dog residing in a large operation."

Even still, the close call on having to endure breeding restrictions flabbergasted a lot of Reiboldt's dog-raising constituents. He and other lawmakers set out to pass a "Right to Raise Livestock" amendment to the state's constitution, specifically prohibiting the ballot petition initiative from affecting the way animals are raised. The goal was to throw the future of large-scale dog breeders in with the lot of factory farms raising chickens and pigs on an industrial scale. That industry's financial muscle, along with some new legislative lines drawn, just might stop groups like HSUS from messing with the dog-breeding business in the Show-Me State ever again.

The puppy breeders may have seemed a bit unhinged to everyday dog lovers reading about the battle, but in reality, the farmers in Reiboldt's district saw the oncoming storm all too clearly. These longtime puppy producers had found themselves up against one of the most financially savvy, legislatively minded foes the dog-breeding industry has ever known—a group determined to reduce the market share of breeders operating worldwide, rural America's traditions be damned.

To be clear, animal welfare advocates are nothing new. In America, they predate even the Westminster Kennel Club Dog Show by eleven years. The beginning of the US animal welfare movement is often cited as April 19, 1866, which is the day the New York State Legislature granted a charter to a man named Henry Bergh to create the ASPCA. It was the nation's first humane society, and it came into existence forty-two years after the formation of the world's first animal welfare charity, which was Britain's SPCA.

The HSUS had a much later start, and it has been making up fast for lost time, like a teenager with a new hot rod putting the pedal to the floor and the screws to all rivals. HSUS has existed only since 1954, but it was able to bring financial muscle to Proposition B in Missouri because it has figured out how to harness and deploy charitable donations in an unprecedented, politically minded way. While many dog lovers mistakenly think the HSUS operates lots of shelters, it instead describes itself as the nation's leading advocate for legislation to regulate puppy mills, and it puts its money behind the lobbying effort in stacks and stacks that, if carried in cash, would require armored trucks to move through state capitals. In 2013, just fifty-nine years after being founded, the HSUS received more than $130 million in contributions, grants, and bequests, right behind the $140 million or so that the nearly 150-year-old ASPCA reported after a century-long head start on fund-raising. That's the kind of "new money" that can buy market share in any industry and get a term like *puppy mill* to become part of everyday language, everywhere.

And while HSUS has been amassing a powerful financial coffer to deploy in the world of politics, the most public defender of US breeders, the AKC, has been struggling to match the sheer dollar power. The same year HSUS brought in that $130 million in dona-tions, the AKC had consolidated total revenues of $64.6 million. The contrast was stark: AKC's supply of capital was almost exactly half of that at HSUS, putting breeders, for the first time on the historical arc since purebreds had become popular, in a position of being outfunded, outlegislated, and outmatched by the people trying to disrupt their business model.

The level of frustration this change of balance engenders in the dog business is matched only by the level of vitriol in comments like the ones Reiboldt penned after the Proposition B battle, calling out the "radical animal-rights extremists" at HSUS, criticizing "their attempt to handcuff the Missouri General Assembly," and adding—in language sure to get the attention of anyone who eats eggs and bacon with a glass of milk for breakfast—"Their long-range goal nationwide is to cripple and then destroy all animal agriculture by placing unrealistic regulations and restrictions on meat, milk, and egg industries. HSUS got its foot in the door in Missouri by attacking pet breeders."

What he didn't mention, but what his constituents intuitively knew and why they are now so scared, is that if global trends keep going the way they're going on anti–puppy mill laws, it's going to cut deeply into dog breeding's bottom line. They'll no longer be able to fund their way of life back at home on the farms, no matter how well they treat their puppies. The cam-paigns are arguably the most devastating salvo to hit breeders since the purebred business began its global rise in stature during the mid-1800s in Britain.

Remember the statement that America's shelters could be emp-tied if just two in four Americans already getting a dog today chose to rescue, instead of going to breeders? That shift in spending would mean more than just the saving of homeless dogs' lives. It would, without question, put more than a few breeders out of business. If the average price paid for a purebred puppy is, say, $600, then the shift of that many American dog buyers to shelters would mean a financial loss to breeders of about $1.2 million. If the average purebred price is $800, then breeders would lose about $1.6 billion. If it's $1,000 per purebred pup, then the hit to the breeders' pocketbooks would be a cool $2 billion.

Now that's an upstart competitor to watch.

Tracy Cotopolis can only dream about the kind of funding the HSUS has at its disposal. She thinks what HSUS does is important—somebody has to come at the problems affecting dogs by lobbying to tip the legislative scale—but she also sees the result of donation dollars being siphoned away from local shelters where she lives in Ohio. For eight years around the early 2000s, she volunteered at a progressive shelter that worked hard to find homes for dogs instead of killing them, and she did everything from cleaning the kennels to helping with fundraising to working at adoption events. "I thought everybody was doing that," she says today, almost incredulous about her early naïveté. "I was extremely fortunate. I didn't realize it at the time."

One day, a woman she knew said there was a dog in Pennsylvania who had been offered a home in Kentucky, and who needed a ride through Ohio. "I said, 'Okay, I can do that,'" Cotopolis recalls. "I had no dog crates. I had nothing. I knew nothing about it. There was this man and his partner, and they had rescue magnets all over their car, and they showed me how to tether a dog in a car using a seat belt."

Cotopolis had unwittingly become among the first members of what today is an interstate and sometimes international network of cars, trucks, and planes moving dogs from high-kill shelters to homes by the hundreds of thousands. Where shelters say they cannot get the job done, more and more nonprofit rescue groups are stepping up and proving it is possible; transporters include everyone from individuals like Cotopolis to major organizations like PetSmart Charities, whose Rescue Waggin' has transported more than seventy thousand dogs since 2004. Just as puppy distributors like the Hunte Corporation use the Internet to upload photos of their dogs so pet store owners nationwide can place orders, nonprofit rescue groups and shelters are using the Internet to upload photos of the dogs they have so everyday dog lovers can offer them a home well beyond any shelter's immediate neighborhood. Petfinder.com has become the hub of the click-to-adopt phenomenon in America, with about thirteen thousand adoption groups listing available animals and some five million unique page views a month. Petfinder is the modern-tech equivalent of newspaper classified ads: the place where more and more people look first when wanting to get a dog.

Often, all the dogs end up needing is a ride to their new homes, but Petfinder doesn't arrange the adoptions or the transports, which is how people like Cotopolis find themselves ferrying cars full of dogs from point A to point B in bucket-brigade style. She joined a Yahoo group called the Dog Rescue Railroad and began to drive dogs for a transport coordinator in Michigan whom Cotopolis felt was particularly on the ball—which is important, since she's heard all too many tales about well-intentioned rescuers piling vans full of dogs from multiple shelters in varying degrees of health, stacking crates one atop the next with no consideration of disease prevention, and semitrailer trucks creating filthy conditions. "They're not stopping for water breaks, they're not cleaning out the crates," Cotopolis says. "There are horror stories all over the Internet if you look."

In this sense, it's fair to say that nonprofit rescue groups today are sometimes operating similarly to the way many commercial breeders were operating in the 1980s, shipping dogs by hook or by crook to get an increasing number of deals done. There are well-organized rescue agencies, for sure, with serious protocols even more stringent than government regulations require, but generally speaking, the market for homeless dogs has grown faster than the infrastructure to move them into the homes of adopters.

Campaigns like the ones that urge dog lovers to "Adopt, Don't Shop" are shifting huge numbers of buyers away from pet stores and breeders, and pushing them toward shelters that, for generations, have operated more as animal control pounds than as adoption centers. The increasing popularity of rescue is shifting buyers toward new nonprofit groups that are mom-and-pop in nature and often working without a net. Volunteers like Cotopolis love the fact that so many dogs are being saved—animals who otherwise would be killed—but she also sees the growing pains of the process up close. When people like her choose to work with responsible fellow rescuers, the decision is often the only thing that helps the better rescue agencies grow and thrive. As with purebreds, so much of what happens to the dogs often boils down to a single person's character and decency.

Most of the dogs Cotopolis transfers have foster homes or permanent homes waiting at the end of the line, as opposed to dogs who are sometimes moved from shelter to shelter to buy them extra time in the system before they're killed. Cotopolis's dogs have health certificates from veterinarians, and some of them are already spayed or neutered. She moves about a hundred dogs a year, and after she transfers them to other volunteer drivers, they end up in places like New York, New Hampshire, and Canada. It's up to the coordinators to ensure that everything is in order before the dogs get into the vehicle-to-vehicle labyrinth, and Cotopolis looks for coordinators who approach the work the same way staff members did at the shelter where she once volunteered.

Generally speaking, she thinks the current, mostly self-regulated nonprofit rescue networks have about a seventy-thirty percentage split, with more than half the volunteers following sound protocols to ensure the dogs' health and safety, and to disclose the dogs' true nature and condition to adopters.

"One coordinator I drive for, she's a schoolteacher, and another one is an attorney," she says. "These are people volunteering. They have full-time jobs. The one I drive primarily for, she's hard-core. If the shelters don't have their act together, she'll turn the dogs away until they get it right."

Put another way, Cotopolis is talking about a private volunteer ensuring that a taxpayer-funded shelter is doing its job. Again, it's about a single individual setting standards—and it's hard not to see a similarity with, say, somebody like the large-scale distributor Andrew Hunte telling government-regulated breeders to treat the pooches better before he'll be willing to move them into the marketplace.

Most of the dogs Cotopolis transports sleep the entire way. They're not bouncing off their crate walls with stress, and they're not whining or barking with dismay. Mostly, she says, they seem relieved.

"They are universally accepting and friendly," she says. "Sometimes they're a little shy, but none of that spinning that you see in the mill dogs. They're very even-tempered. I'm shocked at the even temperament of these dogs."

Her favorite drive so far was on a bitterly cold January day when she found herself cruising into the snow-covered state of Ohio with a carload of Treeing Walker Coonhounds, Bluetick Coonhounds, Australian Shepherds, and Beagles who had been pulled out of shelters in balmy Alabama and Tennessee. She and her fellow volunteers followed the usual safety protocols, taking the dogs out of their crates on leashes so they could go potty in the grass, and the dogs did something unusual: they became eerily still. At first, she thought something might be wrong, but then they "stuck their noses in the snow and blew it up, and then four or five of them started playing and rolling in the snow. They'd never seen it before. There was this moment where they stopped being this fearful creature in the cage, and it becomes this confident, *I'm a dog.*"

It's the kind of moment that keeps people like Cotopolis going, doing more and more transports when she's not running her current project, SpayNeuterOhio.

"It was just beautiful to watch," she recalls, seeing the dogs realize there was no longer anything to fear. "We were all crying."

Dr. Scott Marshall wasn't the first to notice the trend. His predecessor in the job of Rhode Island state veterinarian coined the term *Underhound Railroad* in the mid-2000s after noticing an increasing number of everyday people transporting homeless dogs from the worst Southern US shelters up into New England for adoption. "He noticed it was happening," Marshall recalls, "but he didn't have a grasp of the magnitude."

Toward the end of 2011, the influx of small-scale rescuers moving dogs into Rhode Island could no longer be ignored because officials like Marshall were seeing the result of what people like Cotopolis would call the thirty percent of rescuers cutting corners, or simply not knowing any better, as they tried to save as many dogs as possible. Cases of canine parvovirus in Rhode Island started to increase beyond anything Marshall or his predecessor had ever seen. Parvo is highly contagious, swiftly debilitating, and expensive to treat, creating vomiting and diarrhea that almost always require veterinary hospitalization and intravenous fluids. It's also tough to kill the germs that linger wherever a puppy with parvo has been, which is how a single case can spread like a wildfire after a drought. If a single infected puppy is placed inside a car with a dozen healthy puppies and then driven eight or twelve hours in the close quarters, not only can all of those dogs be exposed, but so can the next batch of a dozen dogs who travel in the same car, and the next batch after that. Parvo has an incubation period, on average, of four to five days, which means the healthy puppies may look just fine when they arrive at the end of the line and get handed over to families. They can be put into homes where they play with other dogs, including more puppies who may not be fully vaccinated, with nobody even realizing that they carry the virus for the better part of a week.

At the end of 2011, Marshall says, parvo cases in Rhode Island shot to unprecedented levels. Calls flooded into his office from veterinarians. "We went from two or three cases a year to two or three cases a week," he says, "and every time we traced it, it was a rescue group."

That's why New England states including Rhode Island, Massachusetts, New Hampshire, and Connecticut have begun to pass emergency orders and regulations trying to standardize the way small-scale rescues operate. The effort is especially prevalent in the region because it's where so many of the rescued dogs end up right now in the United States—making New England the canary in the coal mine of the broader transport phenomenon. State animal health officials started to demand things like quarantine periods for every dog entering a given state, to ensure the pups coming in were disease-free, and nowadays are even working to institute regulations for temperament testing in Massachusetts, after officials there started receiving an increasing number of reports about newly adopted dogs who bit their owners after being advertised as friendly, without any type of behavior checks and balances in place.

In October 2013, New England lawmakers again went on high alert after a nine-week-old puppy from Georgia was transported to a rescue group in New York before being adopted by a family in Vermont, where the seemingly happy, healthy pooch quickly fell ill and died. The puppy had bitten her new owner the day before, so the law required a rabies test—which, to everyone's surprise, came back positive. The rescue group said it had mistakenly provided paperwork stating the puppy had been vaccinated, when in fact no rabies shot had been given. Vermont officials said it was the first case of rabies in a domestic dog since 1994, and as a result, at least fifteen people had to undergo precautionary rabies shots.

Despite such incidents—and in an ironic twist nearly on the level of a Shakespearean tragedy—a fair number of rescue advocates have reacted to every proposed New England rule in almost exactly the same way southwest Missouri's puppy farmers reacted to Proposition B. They're drawing hard lines and screaming that regulators are unfairly trying to put them out of business.

"It's as if they're saying purebred dogs carry less disease than mixed-breed. It's ridiculous. It's discriminatory," one rescue advocate told the *Warwick Beacon* in Rhode Island. "The barbarians are at the gate," one blogger writing under the byline Jim Crow Dogs warned of Rhode Island's efforts to oversee small-scale rescuers in 2012. That author might as well have been State Representative Bill Reiboldt of Missouri talking about HSUS.

And the tougher Rhode Island threatened to get, the more rescue groups from Providence to Newport began urging their supporters to call the state government and complain, so they could continue business as usual and save as many dogs as possible. The situation for people like Marshall in New England became stunningly similar to the one faced by officials trying to oversee breeders in the Midwest. He had to figure out a way to enact enforceable regulations without driving even more people dealing in dogs to take their operations wholly underground.

The noise surrounding small-scale rescuers, like the melee involving so-called puppy mills, is now becoming so cacophonous in some parts of America that the federal government is starting to take notice. In September 2013, the USDA closed what had become known as the "Internet loophole" in the federal Animal Welfare Act, which regulated breeders but not pet stores. Large-scale breeders had started selling pups over the Internet and arguing that they, like pet stores, were retail operations and thus should not have to endure federal inspections as breeders. Nothing had actually changed at the kennels; the only thing that was new was a website with a "click to buy" button. The 2013 rule put a stop to that end-around, at least on paper, to ensure that commercial breeders requiring inspections remained on the federal list.

As of this writing, the USDA hasn't yet instituted any rules that treat small-scale rescue groups the same way as breeders engaged in interstate commerce, but Marshall expects that to change because, generally speaking, the financial transaction now taking place between rescue groups and dog adopters is the same as what happens between breeders and dog buyers. A person goes online and agrees to buy a dog, and the dog is transported after money is exchanged.

"I think rescues, in their mind, they said it wasn't a sale," Marshall explains. "It was an adoption fee. Well, you can call it what you want, but you're not going to get that dog unless you pay a fee, so the USDA is starting to see it as a transaction."

For dog lovers who simply want to buy a pup from a responsible source, the distinctions among breeders and rescuers are becoming fuzzier as rescue groups gain a bigger and bigger piece of the industry pie. Laws are being passed in more and more US cities banning pet stores from selling purebreds, under the theory that those dogs start out in puppy mills, while allowing pet stores to sell dogs marketed by adoption groups, which, in some cases, may be operating with less regulatory oversight than the breeders.

"What's happening is a paradigm shift. People still want puppies. The brick-and-mortar pet store, at least in New England, is being replaced with the virtual pet store, which is Petfinder.com," Marshall says. "Rescues have created an us-versus-them mentality. They say, 'Get the dogs from us, not the pet stores, because they work with puppy mills.' I think those lines are very blurred, and now with the Internet, the middlemen are being eliminated. Dog breeders are going to end up selling to the rescues because it's more profitable for them both, and people are going to be getting their puppy mill puppies from the rescues."

That concept may sound totally down the rabbit hole, twisted up like some kind of *Alice in Wonderland* nightmare, but Marshall has the right idea—just the wrong verb tense. The scenario of rescuers buying from large-scale puppy farms is not coming in the future. It's happening now.

Remember the rescuers at the dog auction in Missouri paying to buy the dogs out of the system, with cuts of the money going to the dog auctioneer and the dog farmer alike? Those dogs are being transported from America's puppy mill capital for sale to eager families not far from Marshall's office in New England. They are marketed as having been rescued, in cash transactions called adoptions instead of sales. Dog lovers from Manhattan to Maine can't get enough of them.

If all shelters were actually shelters—places of refuge that helped and healed dogs, and found them new homes—there would be no need for nonprofit rescue groups. Put another way, some of the people taking tax dollars as salary and saying they're handling the problem are far too often choosing to solve it in slaughterhouse style. Many shelters are great, but in more than a few, the statistics can be truly shocking. In some taxpayer-funded facilities across America, the kill rates are as high as 95 percent unless the nonprofit rescue groups step in, with even friendly, healthy puppies killed, legally, inside of seventy-two hours in some states. The leading cause of death for healthy dogs in the United States is not car accidents or dogfighting, but instead shelter killing, a fact that, if it were about disease, would be treated as an epidemic.

The growing movement against shelter killing in America is being led by Nathan Winograd, a Stanford Law School graduate and former deputy district attorney who now levels prosecutorial cases against shelters and animal welfare groups alike if they fail to put dogs' lives first. He spent the early 2000s working as executive director of an SPCA in upstate New York, where he reduced killing by 75 percent, and disease and kennel deaths by more than 90 percent, and where he took the shelter's budget from a $124,000 annual deficit to a $23,000 surplus. In 2004, he founded the No Kill Advocacy Center, which gives shelters and nonprofit rescue groups the resources and education they need to follow the same plan he used, involving everything from spay/neuter initiatives to new ways of working with nonprofit groups and lawmakers. As of this writing, more than five hundred communities across America have achieved no-kill status, which means they're saving at least 90 percent of the dogs and, in some cases, up to 99 percent. *No-kill* does not mean *never kill*, but it does mean caring for and rehoming every dog who is truly savable, except for those with incurable disease or viciousness—what most dog lovers believe the definition of a shelter should be.

"Killing in the face of alternatives of which you are not aware, but should be, is unforgivable," Winograd wrote in the 2007 book *Redemption* (also the name of his 2014 documentary film). "It would be like a doctor who refuses to keep pace with the changing field of medicine, treating pneumonia with leeches instead of rest, antibiotics and fluid therapy. Killing in the face of alternatives you simply refuse to implement, or about which you remain willfully ignorant, is nothing short of obscene."

This same attitude, more and more often, is being embraced around the globe as dog lovers demand better for pooches of all stripes. With so many small-scale rescuers showing that homes can, indeed, be found for the vast majority of dogs, people are starting to realize that, yet again, they may have been duped by those in control of the marketing message, that the notion of "too many dogs" is nothing more than an excuse for failure inside taxpayer-funded facilities. By the late 1990s in India, the cities of Delhi, Chennai, and Jaipur had adopted no-kill strategies, and the entire country was working toward the goal as of 2005. Italy banned the killing of healthy, friendly dogs in 2001. In Catalonia, whose capital city is Barcelona, dogs used to have ten days until lethal injection and few made it out alive—until the region became Spain's first to ban killing as a method of animal control, in 2003. In Portugal, the Liga Portuguesa dos Direitos do Animal has a legal office and is trying to encourage no-kill principles. On the island of Kyushu in Japan, where the city of Kumamotu has a human population of nearly 750,000, the Kumamotu City Animal Welfare Center has been striving toward no-kill since 2001, when a new director took over. Between then and now, the killing has been reduced from hundreds of animals a year to fewer than ten.

In Monmouth County, New Jersey, which has a coastal edge and is best-known as having been walloped by Superstorm Sandy in 2012, the SPCA made the switch fifteen years ago and has since become a study in how to push the concept to new levels. MCSPCA was founded in 1945, and between then and the late 1990s, the practices were all too familiar. The current president and CEO, Jerry Rosenthal, doesn't like to talk about the number of pups who came in and never made it out, but it was high. "They were killing a lot of dogs," he says. "It was standard."

During the early 1990s, MCSPCA started holding spay/neuter clinics, being proactive about keeping unwanted puppies from being born and abandoned in the first place. That inspired a change of philosophy, which was officially put into effect in 1999. Today, MCSPCA is finding homes for about three thousand animals a year, about 750 of which are dogs (the rest are primarily cats and kittens). For dogs, the facility's save rate was 97 percent as of late 2014, with sixty-four staff members and about three hundred volunteers running the operation on an annual budget of $4.3 million, every last penny of it generated by private dona-tions and adoption fees, which range from about $180 for most dogs to about $400 for puppies younger than six months. There's no time limit for a dog's stay, and the only reason a dog would be euthanized is severe illness or behavioral problems that lead to biting, even after months of trying to resolve them. "We will have the 'tough sells' here for a year, and we can get them out," Rosenthal says. "It's a great thing we do, but it costs money, about six dollars a day for each dog."

Walking into the $6 million, 20,000-square-foot MCSPCA facility—also built without a single tax dollar, Rosenthal says—is like walking into a progressive preschool. It's light. It's bright. Ceilings are high, windows are huge, and sunlight is streaming inside. The walls are painted a perky shade of yellowy beige, and where a teacher might have letters of the alphabet bordering the ceiling, MCSPCA has happy messages from donors. Classical music plays in the background, just loudly enough to calm the dogs and the people alike without interfering in conversation. The place is a hive of activity with adults, kids, cats, and dogs in every direction. In lots of places, inspirational quotes are painted onto the fronts of counters, lines such as "Life is a voyage that is homeward bound," attributed to author Herman Melville.

Most dogs, even some of the smaller ones, are not kept in anything resembling enclosures or cages. There are enclosures for dogs in the veterinary area and some temporary transit rooms, but where the dogs live full time, the spaces are called "digs." Each dog gets his own dig, which is about three or four feet wide and another three or four feet long, with the same tall ceilings as the rest of the building, lots of glass to feel less confining, and individual air supplies to prevent the spread of airborne diseases. The digs are bigger than the largest crates most pet stores sell, and they contain floor beds or other soft places where the dogs can rest. The bottoms are solid, not wire or grated, much like a linoleum floor in a home kitchen. Walking through the digs on an average day in autumn 2014 was like walking through a clean, happy place full of smiling dogs and people alike. A few of the pups were barking, alert, and perhaps slightly stressed, but not a single one was cowering, shaking, or whimpering. Many were napping quietly, as content as could be.

Every dog gets at least two or three walks outside the digs per day, and the ones who are friendly with other dogs are invited to play groups once a day in Sweetie Park, which is a few steps outside the shelter's back door. It was donated by a supporter who thought the dogs should have a fresh-air space with artificial turf, agility equipment, fencing, and a roof for shade. Sweetie Park is also where adopters can bring their own dogs to meet potential new adoptees, and where the staff members and volunteers work with dogs on basic training and special needs.

"We designed the layout of the digs so that when we take a dog out to Sweetie Park, the dog goes past as few other dogs as possible," Rosenthal says. "We are trying not to cause the dogs stress from seeing other dogs go by. It's also good for reducing sickness."

Every dig has a label with the dog's name, estimated age, and breed, which MCSPCA lists as "looks like," since nobody ever knows for sure. Every dog six months or older is behavior tested so adopters will understand the dog's personality, and in difficult cases, the staff consults with experts at the University of Pennsylvania School of Veterinary Medicine to find training techniques that might work. "I'm on their board," Rosenthal says with a grin. "That makes getting help easier."

While shelters in Southern and Midwestern states are often filled with litters of unwanted puppies or with strays, in Mid-Atlantic Monmouth County, where spay/neuter rates are higher, the reason for drop-off is often a behavioral challenge, even if the people surrendering the dog claim something else. Rosenthal has learned to live with that reality, and his staff is trained in how to help most dogs work through whatever behaviors the original owners allowed to develop.

"I wish people would be more honest when they surrender the dogs," he says. "They're afraid if they tell the truth the dog won't get another home. It's usually behavior, and we figure it out in a week or two, but if they had told us from the start, we could've been working on it immediately." And again, based on the 97 percent save rate for dogs, the shelter is ultimately able to resolve most of the training issues.

For the truly challenging dogs, an "at risk" list is created and a meeting is held every Tuesday. Volunteers are allowed to attend and advocate on a dog's behalf, and at least five people, including Rosenthal, must agree there are no more options before a dog is euthanized. "It's a tough meeting," he says, "but unless we have unanimous agreement, we'll hold off. Somebody might get an idea. We've had a couple of cases where we stuck it out and the dog turned around. It doesn't happen every time, but it happens."

Not all of the dogs in the digs are from New Jersey. Some, especially the puppies, are from as far away as Puerto Rico, South Carolina, and Georgia, where spay/neuter rates are lower. The Puerto Rico dogs arrive via Newark Liberty International Airport, while the continental US dogs are brought in a converted Ford E-350 with a box truck enclosure on the back, funded half by donations and half by a grant from the ASPCA. Its colorful sides highlight the MCSPCA logo and the motto "Rescue, Relocate, Renew," and the inside looks almost identical to, if a bit smaller than, the inside of a semi-trailer transport truck from the Hunte puppy distribution company. There's a ventilation system, stainless-steel enclosures of various sizes, and lighting to help keep the dogs oriented. The MCSPCA truck can hold thirty dogs, and usually, it's full of puppies.

"We primarily bring in puppies because there aren't a lot of puppies around here," says Rosenthal, explaining how spay/neuter initiatives throughout the Northeast have all but eliminated unwanted litters being abandoned. "We can see the impact in the South. In Worth County, Georgia, their save rate was something like ten percent. Within a year of working with us and some others, they got it down to something like fifty percent."

The other truck MCSPCA owns is used to distribute dog food and supplies to low-income locals, a service that developed as an outgrowth of Superstorm Sandy. When the Jersey Shore was pummeled by one of the costliest hurricanes in US history, nobody save the National Guard troops was getting through to many of the shoreline communities. MCSPCA set up a dog food pantry, similar to human food pantries, where qualifying community members could get supplies for free—so they could keep their dogs even if there was no dog food in the stores. A truck delivering dog food to people in need also allows MCSPCA to have eyes in some of the lowest-income neighborhoods in the county, where dog owners can be told about low-cost spay/neuter clinics and other services the shelter offers.

Today, MCSPCA is about to break ground on an adjacent building that will be a full-time food pantry, taking this concept to new heights for whatever storms, big or little, dog owners may face in life. "People go through transitioning times," Rosenthal says, "and sometimes it comes down to a decision of surrendering their animal. The animal is going through enough turmoil, so we started it, and it's a permanent program now. We've helped about a thousand people. We talked to the food bank, and fifty percent of their clients have pets, so we kept our program. We figure we've kept about three hundred fifty dogs out of the shelter."

The other big form of community outreach at MCSPCA propels the concept of animal rescue full-throttle into the territory formerly dominated by breeders, an example of just how widely some rescue groups are cracking open the old business model of selling dogs. About a thirty-minute drive away from the MCSPCA building in Eatontown is Freehold Raceway Mall, an upscale shopping mecca with department stores such as Lord & Taylor, Macy's, and Nordstrom, and more than 1,600,000 square feet of leasable space. Like many shopping malls, Freehold used to have a pet store, but with the trend of not wanting to support so-called puppy mills, the mall's owner decided not to renew the pet store's lease during the early 2010s.

"A leasing manager at the mall, coincidentally, had just adopted from us," says Rosenthal, "so they rented us the space for the cost of utilities. We have puppies and kittens over there."

From the outside looking in, the Homeward Bound Adoption Center looks just like an old-school pet shop, right next to the Sears department store. Half the mall shop is retail supplies such as beds, bowls, and dog toys, while half has enclosures filled with puppies and kittens, about twenty of each, in two-tall, upper-and-lower stacks used as displays. On this particular day, all the puppies were from Puerto Rico—a fact clearly labeled for buyers to see. A few families with children browsed the cages just as they might look at clothes or toys at the mall, and some of the kids played with the puppies inside a movable gate in the center of the store while their moms talked with clerks about everything from the nature of rescue to whether their home might be right for bringing home a puppy.

The retail outlet is something of a startling sight in the Northeast, where messaging has long encouraged dog lovers never to buy from a pet store, and where pet stores selling puppies are an anomaly in most towns. But Rosenthal—who has an MBA from Columbia University and spent a quarter-century in the financial services industry before taking over the MCSPCA—says retail is rescue's business wave of the future. In fact, as of this writing, he was putting final touches on a deal to work with a local Petco to create a second 1,200-square-foot retail outlet for homeless pups in space that, a generation ago, might have been used to sell purebreds from breeders.

"For shelters," he says, "you have to be more creative. You have to go where the people are. I view it as, how do you impact the community and change people's thinking? We're front and center, right by Sears."

CHAPTER TEN

REPACKAGING AND REBRANDING

"To succeed in business, it is necessary to make others see things as you see them."

—*Aristotle Onassis*

Her face is pallid, probably not just in the black-and-white photograph, but also in real life. She's looking back over her right shoulder at the camera with eyes desperately wide and bloodshot. Nobody has to hear her speak to know she needs to be set free. "Chained to a desk with nothing but a mouse to entertain her," the flier's big type reads.

In another flier, it's a male, also pale-faced and hunched over. He looks as if the air all around has become so thick, so stagnant, that he can no longer bear to rise. The corners of his mouth are turned down, darn near weighted by jowls. "For nine hours a day, he is kept in a tiny box," it states. "And ignored."

These fliers aren't of dogs. They're of people—models photographed sitting in office conference rooms and in the glow of a cubicle's computer screen, wearing the dismayed expressions shared by so many nine-to-five prisoners of concrete jungles, all as part of a groundbreaking campaign called the Human Walking Program.

It sprang from the brain of Jake Barrow, a creative director in the Melbourne, Australia, office of GPY&R, a creative agency that is 600 people strong and part of a network of 186 global agencies. Barrow and his colleagues typically work on campaigns for big-ticket clients including the Virgin Australia Melbourne Fashion Festival and Australia's Defence Force, but he had an idea that had been in the back of his mind for a few years, and no matter how many times he tried to turn it off, it kept lighting him right back up.

"We were going through a busy period at work, and occasionally, I would walk a friend's dog just for fun," Barrow says. "And I thought, 'Oh, that could be a service for office workers, to go out and walk a dog, completely to benefit the human.' That was years and years ago, and I just remembered the feeling I got from walking that dog, and it was really good stress relief. It was completely selfish. I've been trained to recognize a good idea, and together with my copywriter at the time, we turned it into the Human Walking Program."

There was no client. No income was to be made. That didn't stop Barrow and his partner, who worked pro bono on the concept for six months and built it into a small presentation, sort of a miniature version of what they might do for a regular advertising customer. Then they asked one of the account salesmen at GPY&R to call the local shelter in Melbourne—which happens to be the Lost Dogs Home, founded in 1910 and today serving as Australia's largest shelter, caring for more than thirty-one thousand dogs and cats each year.

"I said, 'Hi, I'm Jake, this is Dan, we have this idea,'" Barrow recalls with a laugh. "They definitely saw the benefit of showing the dogs as the heroes instead of just sad. We did completely flip it around and say, 'It's about the humans getting out of *their* cages.'"

Shelter workers gave the GPY&R fliers to commuters from eight until nine A.M. in central business district train stations the week of the event and passed them around at all the buildings near the park where the walk would be held. Social media and radio stations were engaged as well, to spread the message that humans needed a break and a stroll—"to go walkies," as they say Down Under—perhaps even more than the dogs did.

When the day arrived, the weather was gorgeous. Barrow, like everyone else involved, found himself standing in a park, waiting with a rumbly stomach, wondering what the heck might happen next.

"We were quite nervous," he recalls. "Are we going to get the crowds we want? Is it going to be too big of a crowd? Is somebody going to get bitten by a dog? There were a lot of unknowns. You can only do so much planning for these things."

During the next few hours, his unease gave way to elation. More than five thousand office workers came outside to stand right alongside him, leaving behind their ergonomically accented desks for a much-needed meander the way nature intended. The Lost Dogs Home paired each participant with a homeless pooch so they could get to know one another in the fresh air, outside the shelter environment, in a way that would all but obliterate any ingrained ideas about the dogs and let them be seen as the happy, friendly pups they had always been inside their enclosures, where most of the people would have never seen them at all, or might have assumed there was something wrong with them.

"Their negative stereotype still exists, in our experience, because people do not realize that cats and dogs largely end up at shelters as a consequence of a human circumstance," says Martha Coro, a spokeswoman for the Lost Dogs Home. "The Human Walking Program was first and foremost a creative campaign that challenged people's intrinsic beliefs about lost and abandoned animals, [and] that also engaged a real-life event to tie it all together."

After the three-hour walk, amazing things happened. Every one of the dogs got adopted. Hits on the shelter's online adoption pages spiked 42 percent. A fund-raising appeal one month later became the shelter's highest-grossing in nearly a decade.

Barrow says it was one of the most satisfying days of his life—and even he failed to predict the impact his idea would have next.

"We did the event and the campaign, and whenever we do something more unusual than a television commercial, we create a case study, and we did that with this event and how successful it was," he says. "Somehow, the website Upworthy got hold of the case study, and the next thing you know, we had half a million hits on this case-study video, and we're getting calls from all over the world wanting to do a Human Walking Program in their own cities. We ended up saying we can't ignore it, so we set up a website that lets people create their own Human Walking Program. People can download all the ads and localize them to their area. It's a step-by-step guide. I know someone did one all the way over in the US. The calls were coming from everywhere."

What's so great about TheHumanWalkingProgram.org—in addition to the fact that it hands over, for free to the world, what Barrow estimates as an $80,000 to $100,000 creative campaign—is that it also makes clear how to copy the strategy as much as the actual walk.

"The creative rebranding of adoption dogs came first," Coro says, "which in a way [was] just as influential as the event." And she's right. What sets the Human Walking Program apart on a crucial level is its professional marketing approach. It was developed by seasoned pros, as an advertising initiative that helped people get to know the product—great dogs—instead of making a desperate plea for money to save their tragic little lives. Beliefs about homeless pooches are often so deep-seated that it takes a physical change of space or a professional advertising campaign to knock biases out of people's thought process, much like getting them to buy generic foods at the supermarket or new car brands off the lot.

"The ads with the sad dogs, I guess there was a time and a place for it, but as far as the general public goes, it gets squashed over now," Barrow says. "We need something else to wake us up and pay attention."

More and more shelters around the globe are coming to the same conclusion and partnering their efforts accordingly. Instead of begging people to see the wonderful pooches they know are inside the enclosures, they are looking to leaders in everything from creative design to architecture to retail sales to make new messaging work. It just might be the beginning of an unprecedented rebranding effort, potentially on the scale of what breeders did starting in the mid-1800s when convincing dog lovers that purebreds were the ideal pets in the first place.

The signs of change are worldwide. In Berlin, Germany, the animal protection society turned to the renowned architect and cat lover Dietrich Bangert to design its multimillion-dollar facility, one of Europe's largest at 163,000 square feet, about the size of the largest Target retail store on the US East Coast. The Berlin shelter holds about 1,400 animals at a time and cares for about twelve thousand animals a year. Bangert has serious drafting chops and is perhaps best known for his work on an art museum in Bonn and the German Maritime Museum in Bremerhaven; the result at the Berlin facility was a far different environment than most people imagine as an animal shelter, a modern study in concrete and water so futuristic that it was used as a set for the 2005 Charlize Theron film *Aeon Flux*, set in the year 2415.

Creating the architecturally inviting space gave potential dog owners a chance to breathe a bit easier when walking inside, so their brains would take precedence over any bad feelings created by more typical shelter buildings. They looked up instead of feeling down. They intuited that it was okay to relax, because nothing they were about to see would depress them. The professionally designed atmosphere allowed people's minds to focus not on what they thought a shelter might be like, but instead on what was actually before them: friendly, healthy dogs the volunteers had gone so far as to housetrain prior to sending them home, in the hopes of making each pairing more likely to stick.

Yet another example is in Costa Rica, where the Territorio de Zaguates shelter had nearly all mixed-breed dogs while adopters primarily wanted purebreds, so it worked with the San Jose–based creative agency Garnier BBDO to launch a marketing campaign around the idea of "unique breeds." Instead of calling the dogs mutts, they followed the same branding convention long used by breeders, labeling the dogs as things that sounded surprisingly like kennel club–recognized Dandie Dinmont Terriers and Finnish Laphunds: Chubby-Tailed German Dobernauzers, Fire-Tailed Border Cockers, Alaskan Collie Fluffyterriers, White-Chested Dachweilers, and Brown-Eyed Australian Dalmapointers. (Is it really any different from inventing a German Blabrador?) Watercolor artists painted renderings that mimicked the design of the purebred standard drawings, then added the unique breed names in a highfalutin, royal wedding–worthy typeface. The posters created a visual way for people to process the message that breed names, when it comes to choosing a pet, are often no more than a line of marketing copy.

By the end of the Territorio de Zaguates campaign—"When You Adopt a Mutt, You Adopt a Unique Breed"—the shelter's dogs had received more than $450,000 in news and public relations coverage. More than a half million people had discussed and shared the dogs on Facebook. Adoptions went up 1,400 percent, and the shelter got sponsors who now cover the whole of its operating expenses.

All in all, the teams in Costa Rica and Germany experienced the same thing organizers of the Human Walking Program saw in Australia: working with professional marketers and designers made a huge impact on people's perceptions about the dogs, who were suddenly in demand and welcomed into people's homes en masse—even though the pooches themselves hadn't changed at all.

"We have been inundated with interest from shelters from South Africa to the USA, which leads us to believe that shelters across the world generally share the same priority of changing the public's perception of shelter pets," Coro says from Melbourne, "and now there is a tried and tested plan that can help us all do that."

Mike Arms was lying in the street, somewhere between consciousness and death, when he had the first of two epiphanies that would save millions of dogs' lives.

Born and raised on a farm in Kentucky, Arms decided as a youth that he didn't want to work long hours in the fields for little money, so he got an accounting degree and headed off to New York City to make a life different from the one his father and grandfather had known. A recruiter told him about a number-cruncher opening at the ASPCA. At first, he thought the acronym stood for a business firm, something like IBM, and he figured he'd do just fine there earning a paycheck as an entry-level bean counter.

He barely survived seven months. What he saw inside the ASPCA facility several decades ago left him so shaken that he lost twenty-five pounds in half a year. He developed insomnia. He couldn't stand watching every type of dog imaginable, from eight-week-old mutts to purebred Golden Retrievers, being killed to the tune of 140,000 dogs a year, within twenty-four hours of entering the building, inside high-altitude decompression chambers that sucked the oxygen out of the dogs' lungs—a dozen or more dogs at a time.

Arms gave his two weeks' notice and was headed to a much more civilized office environment, with just six days left in his ASPCA tenure, when a call came in for a dog who had been hit by a car in the Bronx, a borough that, at the time, was riddled with gangs trying to prove which dude was the most macho. No drivers were available, so Arms took off his suit jacket, put on an ASPCA jacket, and drove the ambulance himself. When he got there, the hit-and-run driver was gone and the tan-and-black mutt was on the ground, bent almost backwards in half and quaking in pain.

Arms lifted the dog up to his chest. The terrified pup's gaze shot straight through to his soul.

That's when three guys came out from a nearby building and asked him what he thought he was doing. They had a bet going about how long it would take for the dog to die in the street, and Arms was screwing up their game.

Arms exchanged a few words with the thugs and then reached for the ambulance door handle to get the dog to safety. The guys jumped him from behind and stabbed him, leaving him to die in the street with the pup.

Dazed and in shock, lying on the ground, Arms made a promise to God: if he was allowed to live, he'd help the animals. He swore it. And he meant it.

Soon after, that dog died. Arms has since helped to save more than nine million others, and he's not even close to being finished.

His success is in large part due to the second epiphany, which Arms had while talking with a vacuum-cleaner inventor named Alexander Lewyt, whose claim to fame was that his machine, sold door to door after World War II, would not interfere with the reception housewives received on their big-box radios or black-and-white televisions. Lewyt had become involved with North Shore Animal League on Long Island, New York, in 1969, when his wife talked him into donating $100. He wanted to know how his money would be spent, so he visited the twenty-five-year-old shelter, which was closed more often than open, had one full-time employee, and barely had enough cash flow to keep the lights on. Lewyt, using his business acumen, worked with Publishers Clearing House and, in a single direct-mail campaign, raised the equivalent of about $67,000 today. The shelter's staff grew to twenty-five employees. Its hours of operation increased to every day of the year. "We have the same concept as bringing any product to the public," Lewyt told the *Wall Street Journal* in 1975. "We have our receivables, our inventories. And if a product doesn't move, we have a promotion."

He added, "Most animal shelters are run by well-intentioned people who don't know anything about fund-raising or running the place like a business. The only reason they don't go broke is that a little old lady dies every year and leaves them something."

Arms and Lewyt became friends, and Lewyt's wife, Elisabeth, kept bringing Arms all the homeless dogs she could find. "I would tell Babette I had room for five dogs," Arms recalls, "and she'd say, 'Okay, fine,' and come back with fifteen. I told Alex, 'I don't know how I'm going to do it.' He said, 'Don't look at me. You're just lucky she doesn't love whales.'"

Lewyt's ideas about marketing dogs differently, combined with Babette's incessant flow of dogs needing help, persuaded Arms to articulate a new way forward, something different than he'd seen inside the ASPCA, something that made sense to his accountant mentality. "When he was talking to me, it just clicked," Arms recalls. "It really is a business. If we want to save these lives, we can't do it from the heart. We have to do it from the head."

Arms started working for North Shore Animal League in 1977, increasing adoptions from 50 to 850 per week and generating an advertising budget of $1 million a year. He has since moved on, but the operation has flourished beyond what many dog lovers might think is even financially possible when it comes to dealing in homeless dogs. As of 2012, the organization had annual income of more than $36 million and its president earned nearly $350,000 per year. His salary was about the same as the one given to Wayne Pacelle, the president and CEO of the HSUS, and it was less than half of the $713,166 in annual salary and other compensation listed in the ASPCA's 2013 tax return for its president and CEO, Edwin Sayres. (In summer 2014, Sayres left the rescue segment of the dog business to become president and CEO of the Pet Industry Joint Advisory Council, whose board of directors includes Ryan Boyle from the Hunte Corporation as well as men affiliated with Petco and Petland pet stores.)

To put those dollar amounts into perspective, the annual salary of the president of the United States is $400,000, or $569,000 with travel and other expense accounts included. The similar six-figure lifestyles these leaders of the dog rescue community enjoy—while their nonprofit organizations continue to solicit donations from the public—has led to a new phrase, *retail rescue*, that breeding advocates hope to make as well known as *puppy mill* in the popular lexicon, casting some of the negative spotlight off themselves and onto their most financially successful competitors, including smaller nonprofits that typically operate with far less public scrutiny. "This year of 2014 has been horrendous with regards to total lack of sanity in the dog world," as one blog post on the Yankee Shelties website put it. "It has become acceptable for someone to call themselves a rescue, remain totally unregulated, and proceed to pillage and profit."

So far, attempts to rebrand financially successful rescuers have not stopped business-minded advocates like Mike Arms, who continues to save dogs without making any excuses for raising their value along with the professional value of the people working alongside him. Since 1999, he has been president of the Helen Woodward Animal Center in California, where he tripled adoption rates while charging some of the highest dog adoption fees in America and recruiting employees for their business and marketing savvy. (As of 2013, according to an independent auditor's report, the center's management salaries and benefits totaled $373,420. Arms's pay was not itemized.) Nobody can buy a dog from the center for less than $399. A couple of Labrador puppies sold recently for $500 apiece, and a six-month-old Goldendoodle went for $1,000 not long ago. Arms has no problem telling adopters they should pay fair market value because his dogs have just as much intrinsic value, and make just as fabulous pets, as the purebreds going for similar prices from breeders. "Why is it," he asks, "that somebody can go out and spend $2,000 or $3,000 on a pet and after thirty days realize it's not for them, and they take it to their local facility, and the minute it crosses that threshold, the value is gone?"

His approach leaves many shelter operators with mouths agape, especially the ones who can't even give their dogs away for free. Arms believes that their failure has nothing to do with the quality of the dogs, but instead with the quality of the dogs in people's minds, which he sees as the job of shelter directors to manage. The problem isn't the dogs. The problem is the marketing.

"I'm getting more and more frustrated with my peers as I get older," he says. "It just seems like they're going backwards in time now. They think the way to increase adoptions is to lower fees and come up with gimmicks. That doesn't increase adoptions at all. All that does is devalue the pets. How in the world can we change the public's perception of these beautiful pets if we're the one doing this?"

The root of the problem with homeless dogs and pricing, he says, goes back to the way many rescue organizations got started. It's usually a woman who finds a puppy in the street and gets him into a loving home. The woman likes the feeling of having done right by the pup, so she helps more dogs, and then more dogs, until she decides to form an organization along the lines of a humane society. "They weren't getting paid for it," Arms says. "They just liked doing it as a hobby. So they felt, 'If I'm not doing it for pay, nobody else should be doing it for pay.'"

Try telling a breeder she should care for all the dogs for free and give them away out of the goodness of her heart. Rescuers often have a completely different mentality, Arms says, one that devalues their own worth as well as the worth of the dogs.

Arms regularly finds himself standing on stage in front of a room filled with rescuers who fit that mold, most of them women, even today. He tells a particular story again and again, one that seems to make the message clear. It starts when he asks them what they would do if they were invited to a formal dinner banquet at a high-end restaurant. What is the very next thing you'd do, he asks, after you accepted the invitation?

To a person, they answer that they'd go out and buy a new dress. "Now, human nature is that a lot of people will put a budget on what they're going to spend on that outfit," he tells them. "You go out in the department store and start trying on outfits and none of them fit you right. The color's not right. You get depressed and you're going to walk out, and then on your way out you see a dress that's a hundred dollars more. And it fits. And you buy it. You're willing to spend three hundred or four hundred dollars on that dress that you're going to wear three or four times, but you're not willing to spend it on a dog. What are we teaching the public about value?"

Arms loves dogs just as much as the rescuers in the audience do, but he treats the pooches far more like products than most of his colleagues might—because he believes that's what gets them into homes. He's had courtesy shoppers from the department store Macy's come through his shelter to tell him what he can do better in terms of staffing and displays. He brought in BMW salesmen to train his staff. ("Nobody is a better salesman than a car salesman," he says.) As of this writing, Bruce Nordstrom, former chairman of the upscale retailer Nordstrom Inc., was scheduled to do training at the center, all because Arms believes the sales techniques in the dog rescue business need a swift reboot into the modern era of retail sales. He wants to be the BMW of the used pooch industry, the place where buyers can go and know they're getting a top-quality product worth every penny of the extra money, not unlike a pre-owned luxury sedan.

"They can call it adoptions or rehoming or whatever they want," Arms says of rescuers, "but they're in the business of selling used dogs. And they'd better be good at it, because those lives are on the line."

Arms has been invited to speak to shelter directors everywhere from British Columbia in Canada to multiple cities in New Zealand, preaching the philosophy that shelters should be run by the savviest marketing and sales people, raising their prices and preaching the overall value of every great pup. Shelter directors should have a heart for dogs, but first and foremost, a mind for business—because that's the only thing that breaks through stereotypes and helps dog lovers understand what they're really getting for their money.

"We have to change the public's perception," he says. "The public believes the pets in pet facilities are there because there's something wrong with the pet. We have to teach them that the pet is there because there's something wrong with the person who had the pet. That's the reality."

No less than the Westminster Kennel Club is starting to come around to this same idea, that if it wants to gain the business of all dog lovers in the world, it has to start doing a little repackaging and rebranding of the mutts, too—and maybe, just maybe, a little admitting that the dogs shouldn't have been singled out as different in the first place.

Instead of calling them Fire-Tailed Border Cockers or White-Chested Dachweilers, Westminster's organizers settled on the label All-American Dogs. Same marketing concept, different choice of words. The pooches were allowed to compete among the purebreds at the Westminster Kennel Club Dog Show in 2014, for the first time since the show began in the 1800s, as part of the inaugural Masters Agility Championship of running, jumping, and obedience skills.

Westminster's purebred experts heralded the event as welcoming the mongrels in a measured way, calling it "the opening act" of the long weekend's traditional show program. "Agility dogs are not designer dogs, or they don't have to be," the long-time breeder and Westminster show chairman Tom Bradley told reporters. "Westminster honors the diversity of the dog with the addition of agility, and therefore the diversity of all dogs," the Westminster media director, Karolynne McAteer, explained. "We're very excited about the fact that Westminster can play a leadership role in embracing, really, the sport of dogs," the Westminster president, Sean McCarthy, said. They also created a special award, Best All-American, either in keeping with the mentality of categorizing all dogs as purebred versus those ineligible for registration, or in keeping with the marketing plan to ensure a mutt with a ribbon would be available to the media even if the purebreds ran through the tunnels and jumped over the bars faster.

The agility competition featured sixteen mutts comprising 7 percent of the 228 agility entries (and about 0.5 percent of the more than 2,800 entries in the overall Westminster show that year). By all accounts, the atmosphere in the agility rings was festive and energetic, but that portion of Westminster was not shown on mainstream television channels during prime time like the two-day conformation event based on looks. Agility was instead shown on a Saturday on Fox Sports 1, a new twenty-four-hour network with a far smaller viewership. The winner turned out to be a purebred Border Collie named Kelso, while Best All-American went to a Husky mix named Roo. Both had their names prominently mentioned in the official postshow Westminster announcement.

Really, the mutts had been kept squarely in their place as fewer than one in ten dogs competing in a sideshow event, but it was hard to deny that public pressure had encouraged the purebred glitterati to reconsider the image the show was sending around the world, one that more and more often contradicts the increasingly savvy marketing on behalf of all types of dogs, including mixed breeds sitting in animal control facilities. Westminster's organizers are business-savvy people who know enough to trim the yacht sails a little differently when the wind direction shifts. The more dog lovers bring mutts into their homes, and the more time they spend getting to know them instead of the stereotypes, the more people are realizing that claims of the ideal dog are as ludicrous as any other form of segregation—a reality kennel clubs are going to have to figure out how to embrace in the long run if they want people to keep buying the message they're selling.

"By seeing the great worth in all dogs, perhaps the AKC will get its priorities on the right track," as the veterinarian Debora Lichtenberg put it in a column for PetAdviser (now Petful.com). "I mean, if this great country can embrace marriage equality, repeal 'Don't Ask, Don't Tell,' and continue to work on equal pay for equal work, maybe there's hope that dog snobbery and elitism can wear a more inclusive muzzle, too."

There is hope, if only an early flicker. Westminster remains an invitation-only organization, as private as the storied Augusta National Golf Club, and yes, mutts have been granted their first invitation to come inside, but with a big, bold asterisk.

Even still, the cracking open of the gilded doors came just two years after Westminster cut ties with dog food maker Pedigree, a longtime sponsor, in a spat about the inclusion of sad-looking homeless dogs in television advertisements that were scheduled to air during the show in 2012. At that time, Westminster spokespeople had a decidedly different attitude toward the mutts than they expressed when welcoming them just two years later. Back in 2012, David Frei told the Associated Press, "Show me an ad with a dog with a smile. Don't try to shame me." Melissa Martellotti, a brand manager for Pedigree parent company Mars Petcare US, told the *New York Times* that Westminster's position in 2012 was clear: "They've shared with us, when we parted ways, that they felt that our advertising was focused too much on the cause of adoption and that wasn't really a shared vision."

The attitude shift into accepting the mutts—in the span of just twenty-four months—no doubt shocked some sensibilities, and it was at least a sign that a handful of powerful folks who want to keep the purebred dog party going can hear the bandleader fumbling through his sheet music, looking for a more appropriate tune to keep paying guests from heading for the exits.

And perhaps the last laugh of all will go to Pedigree. Its competitor, Purina, took over as the sponsor of Westminster, but a recent report stated that Pedigree's parent company ranks number one among all pet food companies and its dog food still outsells any of the top Purina brands, thanks at least in part to Pedigree's continued advertising focus on helping homeless dogs. To be clear, Purina also invests in causes to help homeless dogs—the Nestle Purina PetCare Company has owned the adoption website Petfinder.com since 2013, and Purina makes dog food donations to shelters—but Pedigree is trying to align itself more prominently with the bigger-picture marketing shift going on among dog lovers worldwide, and people who buy dog food in leading markets like the US and UK are supporting the business move with their bucks.

Pedigree doubled down on the Westminster-kicked-us-to-the-curb news in 2012 by starting the Pedigree Feeding Program to provide free dog food to shelters, along with the Buy One, Feed Two program, which promised up to ten million bowls of dog food to shelters in exchange for customer purchases in retail stores. Anyone who goes to the Pedigree website as of this writing is greeted with the slogan, "When you buy Pedigree, you're helping dogs in need." It's spot-on in terms of trending public opinion.

Pedigree's support for homeless dogs is now in overdrive, but it actually began well before the 2012 Westminster kerfuffle, at least as early as 2008, just before the *Pedigree Dogs Exposed* documentary uproar in the UK. That's when the company created the Pedigree Adoption Drive Foundation to help get more abandoned pooches into homes. Research into the campaign in the UK showed that Brits donated nearly £500,000 (more than $800,000) for homeless dogs, increased purchases of Pedigree-brand food by 6 percent, and believed—to the tune of an eight-point rating increase—that Pedigree as a brand had the well-being of dogs at its heart. Brand trust went up six points. The number of people who believed "I have something in common with this brand" spiked by nine points, the kind of improvement pollsters usually see only in their dreams.

By spring 2010 in the US, Pedigree had started airing a television commercial called "Heroes" that showed mutts looking alone, but proud; abandoned, but worthy. It was a revolutionary advertising campaign, one of the few to capture the dog-loving public's consciousness on the level of, say, the "*Yo quiero* Taco Bell" spot in the 1990s, and it tapped into that same notion of sticking up for the dogs so often left behind. The narrator's words in the "Heroes" advertisement were anything but sad or downtrodden, spoken in earnest while dogs looked directly into the camera, eye-to-eye with viewers, as if simply wanting to be seen, for a change, with honesty:

> *Shelter dogs aren't broken. They've simply experienced more life.*
> *If they were human, we would call them wise.*
> *They would be the ones with tales to tell and stories to write,*
> *The ones dealt a bad hand who responded with courage.*
> *Do not pity a shelter dog.*
> *Adopt one.*

The creative team behind this commercial was TBWA/Chiat/Day, a big-time firm with offices in New York, Los Angeles, and beyond, whose work has included cultural-shift campaigns including the Orwellian "1984" spot that introduced Apple's Macintosh computers to the world with a woman hurling a hammer into an oversize black-and-white screen featuring a demagogue whose reign, and whose tired ideas, were about to come to an end.

TBWA/Chiat/Day is also the same company that cast Gidget the Chihuahua in the Taco Bell ads almost twenty years ago. The times are changing. Smart money, at least for now, is banking on the shelter pups.

CHAPTER ELEVEN

LEMONS VERSUS STEALS

"It takes character and control to be understanding and forgiving."

—*Dale Carnegie*

A steaming pile of trash was blocking the lane, so the driver stepped out of his air-conditioned car and into the blistering summer sun. Some thoughtless litterer had dumped a mess of stuff and then high-tailed it away, probably without even looking back, leaving this driver to be the Good Samaritan who cleared the roadway. Maybe the Samaritan was frustrated that he'd been forced to pull over. Maybe he was concerned about other drivers' safety. Whatever his reasons, he walked over to the heap—and then likely stopped short, a bit in shock.

"When they got closer, they realized the garbage was breathing," says Kathy Cain, recalling that day in 2010 on the Utah highway.

"And when they rolled him over, they realized his front right leg was really bad."

She's talking about Cassidy, the twenty-pound Shetland Sheepdog the Samaritan found buried in the assortment of filth. Cassidy was emaciated. His protruding ribs cast shadows across his fur, which was packed with foxtails, the pointed green fans sometimes called spear grass. He was five, maybe six years old, and wore a red collar without any identification tags. The collar had a piece of twine attached to it, indicating Cassidy had at one point been tied to something, but if he'd ever been a fan of humans, he wasn't showing it. He was terrified as the Samaritan approached, and clearly in a great deal of pain. Had a corner been available, Cassidy would have cowered into it. Instead, all he could do was lie there in the trash on the asphalt, deeply broken inside and out.

Somehow, the Samaritan got him up and rushed him to an animal hospital, where another unknown Good Samaritan donated the veterinary fees for the leg's amputation. When little Hopalong Cassidy was medically well enough to leave, the veterinarian checked around the region. Nobody was trying to find him.

Sheltie Rescue of Utah took in Cassidy on a Monday, right about the time Cain was realizing she couldn't keep Paxton, a Pit Bull she'd welcomed into her home as a foster dog. Paxton was a good boy, a sweetheart who got along well with Cain's two Shelties, Stitch and Jiggers. ("It's short for gigolo," she says. "That's a whole other story.") Alas, however, Paxton was too big and energetic for her small apartment. Feeding times were a serious challenge. Cain called her friend Barbara Edelberg at Sheltie Rescue, where she sometimes volunteered, and within two days, Edelberg had found Paxton a home. "I went to a Sheltie club meeting that night," Cain recalls, "and it was a tearful goodbye to Paxton, but I heard about this three-legged dog. I had told myself that when they helped find Paxton a home, I was going to adopt another dog."

By Friday, less than a week after Cassidy had left the vet's office, Edelberg handed him over to Cain, his new foster mom.

"But I realized it wasn't going to be a foster situation," as Cain remembers it. "The first time I laid eyes on him, I told her, 'He's never coming back here.'"

Cassidy's leg healed and he figured out how to walk on the remaining three, but he had emotional problems galore. He not only was frightened in general, but he couldn't seem to trust anyone. He was depressed, by Cain's estimation, and spent a lot of time trying to hide. When fireworks went off outside, he launched himself into his crate, seeking cover like a war veteran with posttraumatic stress disorder. Then he developed an abscess that required surgery near his carotid artery, and he had a near-fatal, 1-in-100,000 reaction to the subsequent medication. "I almost lost him again," Cain says with the worry still trembling a little in her voice, even now that several years have gone by.

There's more than the usual reason for her deep-rooted feelings. Instead of Cassidy dying at that time, Cain lost her mother, who died within about a year of Cain's best friend. Her father passed soon after that, too, one dear loss right after the next. Fate seemed determined to pound her down, blow by wicked blow.

Except, there was Cassidy. He started to get better and almost radiate light as his eyes opened and looked up in a new way at the world. Soon he wasn't just walking; he was running, romping, and playing. Within about a year, his nerves relaxed and he started to feel comfortable around people, including strangers. Cassidy proved easy to train. He listened and learned, eager for the chance to try new things. And he developed a habit that Cain, even with her own battered heart, couldn't help but smile when she saw: Cassidy would walk up to people, put his single front leg around their necks, and nuzzle them, almost like a human giving them a hug.

"I had suffered a lot of loss within three years," she recalls, "and I would look at him and say, 'You know what? I'm going to get through this.' Mine was emotional hurt. His was physical. He has bounced back and come so far."

A rehabilitation center is near Cain's home, and she got the idea that maybe Cassidy's one-legged hugs could help more people than just her. The center has short-term as well as long-term residents, many of them older and some of them recovering from serious surgery.

"The first time we went," Cain says, "this lady really loved dogs, so we placed Cassidy on her bed. He kind of sniffed around. She had recently had a leg amputated. He sniffed the stub and curled himself around it."

Everyone in the room took a deep breath, and Cain looked over at the patient, trying to gauge her feelings.

"She looked like the rest of us did," Cain remembers. "Our mouths just dropped. I'm sure I had tears running down my face."

Today, Cassidy makes the rounds at that rehab center about twice a month, work that helped him to earn the American Humane Association Hero Dog Award in 2013. At home, he's as happy as could be—and he sometimes outruns the four-legged Stitch and Jiggers at the park, where he makes a friend of pretty much everyone he meets. Cassidy is now working toward therapy-dog certification, which would allow him to go into more facilities and try to make more people smile. He sometimes joins Cain at the local library, too. They talk about pet care and how everybody has a purpose, even if they're a little different.

"One man's trash is another man's treasure," Cain says. "Sometimes you just need to have that extra patience. Give them a chance. They can teach you so much. They can be the greatest thing in your life. Look in their eyes. Just because a dog may cower or act like he's afraid, well, maybe he's the one that needs you. It's always the cute little puppies that jump up and down that attract most of the people. It's the ones who hurt, if they appear to be what some people would call 'defective'—I hate that word—but if they're blind, they're deaf, if they're missing a leg, don't just turn your back on them, because you could be missing out on a great, great member of the family."

⁘

The Pit Bull was just four weeks old when his owner decided to drown him. There was no reason, really, nothing at all wrong with the puppy, which is why the owner's roommate scooped him up and carried him, with great desperation, to Westminster Veterinary Group in Orange County, California. The roommate pleaded while handing over the pooch, who was so small and defenseless he would never have survived on his own. "Please!" the roommate begged the veterinary team. "Hide this dog!"

Not terribly far away was OC Animal Care, the region's public shelter, but the roommate had perhaps thought twice before bringing the Pittie there. A $2.5 million ongoing lawsuit brought against the facility in 2014 and not yet adjudicated alleged that OC Animal Care, as recently as 2010, was killing nearly half the animals entrusted to its care, including injured dogs, older dogs, and dogs nonprofit rescue groups were willing to take, with the killing sometimes happening before the legal hold period of four to seven days. The lawsuit's allegations had been whispered about, and the reputation of the place, right or wrong, had gotten around, which may be why the roommate instead entrusted the pooch to veterinarian Tia Greenberg and her staff. They did things the public facility likely never would have done, including bottle feeding the pup and helping him put on some weight, keeping him alive with as healthy a start in life as was humanly possible.

It was enough to save little Ri-Ri, as he's now known at home with Greenberg and her wife, Michelle Russillo, but it wasn't enough in general, at least not in Greenberg's mind. She'd saved plenty of dogs' lives since opening the veterinary office in 2000, but something about this dog's story and his lack of options moved her to want to do more. There should be an actual shelter, she thought, a place of refuge and care and hope. If the taxpayer-funded facility wasn't getting that job done, then she was going to do it herself.

In 2011, Greenberg founded WAGS, a shelter that is fully integrated with her veterinary practice to provide all the treatment a dog could possibly need. "We saved Ri-Ri and [Greenberg] said, 'My job as a veterinarian is to save pets and not dispose of them,'" says Russillo, who is now chief executive officer of WAGS Pet Adoption. "She founded it with a passion, and I took it over about six months later."

WAGS is a no-kill shelter on steroids thanks to the veterinary component of the organization. Animals brought into the city's animal control facility stay there five days, and then, by contract, become the legal property of WAGS. "With the previous shelter, five days was their life," Russillo says. "It was done."

Today—from the day WAGS opened its doors—almost all of the 2,200 or so pets who come through each year are getting homes. It's the same exact population of dogs, but they are being saved instead of killed thanks to a more progressive approach to sheltering. A recent bout of upper respiratory problems and pneumonia among kittens spiked the kill rate at WAGS to 9 percent, Russillo says, but that's an anomaly. Most months during the past three years, she says, the kill rate has been less than 3 percent, and often, it's lower than 1 percent. Well more than 90 percent of the dogs not only are being saved but are going on to thrive.

The terms *treatables* and *manageables* are part of the everyday lexicon at WAGS, just as they are within a growing number of forward-thinking shelters worldwide. Dogs that some public facilities would see as a waste of time, the WAGS team sees as savable. A needy puppy like Ri-Ri, as well as a three-legged dog like Hopalong Cassidy, would fall into the treatables and manageables categories at WAGS. Treatable means a medical condition that can be resolved, anything from parvovirus to a broken paw. Manageable means medical or behavioral conditions the WAGS team feels can be handled by adopters, such as a dog in need of insulin injections for diabetes or continued training for behavior.

"Some come in that are bright and shiny and cuddly with wagging tails, and nothing shows up on their entrance exam that is concerning to the doctor," Russillo says. "So upon that entrance exam, upon the first twenty minutes, we know how easy it's going to be to place that pet. On the flip side, in twenty minutes you can also tell you've got an abused dog, a malnourished dog, a dog full of fleas, rotten teeth, smelly ears."

Problems like bone fractures are easy, she says. They heal, and they're history. On treatable dogs, WAGS has a budget able to fix pretty much anything up to $3,000 in veterinary bills. As the coffers continue to grow along with the business, that figure will rise, Russillo says.

The tougher cases are the manageables, including the ones Russillo calls "fresh" who spend extra time learning manners with the shelter director, Cortney Dorney, who has twenty years of experience as a dog trainer. Dorney also spends extra time working with dogs who have emotional challenges so severe that some other shelters might not even give them a chance—and who, nine times out of ten, will be fine if given whatever time they need.

"It's truly case by case," Dorney says. "We have dogs that come in here that look to be emotionally destroyed, like there is no turning them around. They've completely given up. You can see the look in their face. They're not showing any desire for physical attention, for human contact, they won't eat, nothing. But if you give them five minutes, they completely flip around. Sometimes, it's a dog where we can't clean the cage without fear of getting injured, and in two days, it's gone. Sometimes it's three months before we feel the dog is adoptable and safe to put out in the public."

She adds, "We can't have therapy sessions with them. We can't ask them what the mental issue is. We have to work through the steps and read the body language and put them in situations and see how they respond, and figure out what they were never exposed to, whether it's men or people in sunglasses or people leaning over, because they've never been hugged."

Dorney says it's a mistake to believe that even the toughest-case dogs in shelters are permanently damaged, or that whatever behaviors they happen to be showing upon intake are behaviors they've either shown all their lives or will continue to express. (And plenty of people do believe that: a PetSmart Charities study expected to be released in 2015 showed the percentage of people who think a dog from a shelter may have behavioral problems jumped from 8 percent in 2009 to 13 percent today.) The reality, Dorney says, is different from that stereotype. She says a dog's challenging behaviors are often a function of rational, understandable, and even situational fear, and the behaviors usually improve to a manageable level or vanish entirely as the dog learns that new things can be safe.

"I hear so often, 'Oh, they must have been abused,'" she says. "Well, yes and no. Animal beating isn't as common as most people think. Really, where the abuse usually lies is lack of socialization. They're acquired and left in a back yard, never to experience anything. That's where you get aggression. It's not because they're born this way. It's because their owners made them this way. It's like a child: if you never take them anywhere, they're going to have socialization problems."

She adds, "The number one thing we see here are the dogs that sheerly lacked the socialization they needed in the first sixteen to eighteen weeks of life. That's when their window is open and they're not afraid of anything. They're spongy and adventurous and want to discover. Once they're four or four and a half months old, that window closes and they're afraid of everything, and you have to go backwards in time and show them that things aren't scary, instead of doing it right when they're babies. These dogs that people call lemons, it's really a lack of socialization."

As the 90-plus percent save rate at WAGS shows, almost all of them can be brought back around with time and training, but the handful of dogs WAGS kills does include the ones who, after making every effort, still cannot be trusted as manageable out in the community.

"We had one dog this year, Nina, a beautiful Pit Bull, and we worked with her for months," Russillo says. "She came in scared to death, we finally got her comfortable and we were doing the adoption to a family with kids, and they backed out, and another family came in to adopt her, and right when they were coming to pick her up, we started to notice that she'd been with us so long that we had lost verbal control of the prey drive. We had to make the hardest decision ever. We could not place her with a family where she would ever harm a child. We as a group sat and wept. It was the hardest thing."

Russillo knew, though, that it was the right thing for public safety. "We go to the farthest end, but if a dog is truly vicious, it's going to harm a child. That's the line I draw."

Half the battle in the city of Westminster, Russillo says, is that it contains the largest number of Vietnamese people beyond the borders of Vietnam. By some estimates, the culture encapsulates at least a third of the city's population, and older residents of Little Vietnam or Little Saigon, as it's known, are like their contemporaries in Southeast Asia when it comes to animals as pets: The concept is completely foreign. Spaying, neutering, training, socializing, microchipping, and keeping dogs indoors simply aren't ideas that enter the owners' thought process.

The result Russillo sees is a predictable rhythm of intake, with a flood of Chihuahuas and Pit Bulls (dogs of choice in that culture) showing up at WAGS every June, July, and August. Nearly all of them are intact and found running loose, producing more puppies and developing behavioral issues that make them challenging to place in homes without at least some basic training.

"Realistically, a pet needs to have rules," Russillo says. "It needs to know it's not the alpha dog, especially when it's a powerful dog. If people just throw it in their back yard and don't train it, there are problems. It's bored. It does have a tendency to want to go after small things. You have to have voice control. People are irresponsible owners. They don't spay and neuter them, and they don't train them."

Just two towns over, she says, owners do whatever it takes to find missing dogs. They're microchipped. They're searched for—intensely. With much of the population in her city, she says, people make a half-hearted effort, give up, and buy another dog. It's an education problem WAGS is starting to work on, and it's why no dog leaves WAGS without a microchip that notifies the authorities that the dog should be returned directly to WAGS if there's ever a problem in the future.

With the dogs who show up as manageables, either one time or repeatedly, the first adoptions aren't always successful, but WAGS keeps working on whatever challenges exist until the right home can be found.

"If we get a returned dog, the person really didn't think long and hard about what the needs are of that dog. We've had them come back: big ones, little ones, great ones," Russillo says. "I would guess it's a dog who had a management issue the person couldn't handle."

The treatables, on the other hand, are usually a breeze. WAGS has found homes for dogs with one eye. For dogs who need wheelchairs because their back legs are lame. For dogs like Hopalong Cassidy who have broken bodies but stellar souls.

"They may take longer, but there are people out there who want those special-needs dogs," she says. "There's a population of adopters who want to step in and do more. It's not everybody. Some people may not have the pocketbook to do it. But some people are more like special-ed teachers: They have the heart."

Twitter went live in 2006. Facebook has been online since 2004. Teri Goodman was well ahead of them both, putting the Senior Dogs Project out on the World Wide Web in 1997, the same year the domain name Google.com was registered. She, too, hoped to change how people understood the world, and maybe make it a better place for older dogs who were far too often considered unadoptable.

It was a time when the senior dogs not only would be among the first killed in shelters, but when they sometimes wouldn't even be allowed through the front doors. Everybody wanted puppies, and the aging pooches with gray muzzles were an adoption nightmare. They lingered in the cages. They missed their homes, grew confused, and became depressed. Some shelter directors where Goodman lives near San Francisco often couldn't even be bothered to try. They'd turn them away, to whatever other fate their owners decided.

The attitude offended Goodman to her core. She'd been in the dog biscuit business, which involved a lot of travel, so instead of having her own dog, she would watch over friends' dogs when they needed a sitter. A cousin with a ten-year-old Golden Retriever named Misty took her up on the offer, and Goodman and her husband ended up keeping Misty for the last four years of her life. Misty was just plain happier living with them, and they couldn't have asked for a better dog—one who was already house-trained, had manners, and was long past the urge to chew up everything in the house. Misty had been a wonderful find and had given back every ounce of love the Goodmans gave her.

All of which got Goodman to thinking about how silly it is that so many people pass by dogs like Misty when looking for a great pet to bring home. Senior dogs, to her thinking, are an awful lot like the treatables and manageables. Might they have some medical issues? Sure. Is longevity in the cards? Not always. But those things can also be true of a brand-new puppy—and with an older dog, a buyer really can see the finished product and know what she's getting before taking a dog home.

"My purpose is raising consciousness," Goodman says today. "I started with an idea to do a book on older dogs, just vignettes, and then I built the website. I did do some hands-on going to the shelters and pulling dogs, and there were many adoptions over the website. As the years went on, more and more shelters and agencies started websites themselves, so I figured I'd done my job, and now I link to them."

In her nearly twenty years of focusing on senior pooches, Goodman has seen more people than she cares to remember abandoning perfectly great dogs for surprisingly common reasons. A first baby is on the way, and though the dog would love to meet the kid, too, the parents decide there's no time for both dependents. A work schedule changes and it's too much hassle to hire a dog walker for a few months. The teenagers went off to college and the adults decided to travel. Dad likes to jog, and the dog can no longer keep up. It's just too much aggravation every night, carrying the aging dog up the stairs at bedtime because his hips are a little sore.

"This is a very materialistic society. If you buy something and then you don't want it, you throw it out," she says. "I was walking on the street with Misty one day, and there was a woman who said a woman up the block wanted to get rid of her older dog. I said, 'What's the problem? Is the dog unhealthy? Is there a problem with finances?' And the woman said she was selling her house and moving to an apartment, and she had a garden and could let the dog out, but at the apartment, she'd have to walk her. The dog was fourteen. She'd had her from a puppy. Now that I've been in this senior dog world for a while, that's not an uncommon story. People think of a dog as a commodity, that you can get rid of it if it's inconvenient. It's incredible that people will behave that way, but on the other hand, there are many people who will take these dogs and give them great homes."

One of Goodman's favorite people is Cari Broecker, who, along with a woman named Monica Rua, founded the Peace of Mind Dog Rescue to serve California's Monterey, Santa Cruz, and San Benito Counties. "We had both been doing rescue work, and we were both on the board of directors for Animal Friends Rescue Project," Broecker says. "We'd done that for twelve years, and we were taking a break from rescue, and an acquaintance of mine had a dog, and she was dying of emphysema. I would take her dog to hospice to go and visit her, and the doctors were clear with her that she had maybe a few weeks to live, and the main thing on her mind was what was going to happen to Savannah, her Sheltie mix. She knew Savannah had some socialization issues and she wasn't going to be easy to adopt out at nine years old, and the woman thought she might have to put her down. I left that visit and came up with the name: Peace of Mind rescue. We knew from Animal Friends that we were so focused on rescuing the shelter dogs on the euthanasia list that we couldn't even address these kinds of calls from the community. I knew it was a niche that needed to be filled."

After five years, Peace of Mind has developed a network of foster homes that allows the group to save sixty to sixty-five senior dogs at a time. They don't have a minimum age, per se; a five-year-old German Shepherd could be considered a senior dog, while a five-year-old Chihuahua would not, because the smaller dog can live as long as twenty years. "Most of our dogs are ten years and up, and we've taken in some that are seven or eight," Broecker says. "In the shelters, if you're over three, you don't get looked at very often. The puppies, the one-year-olds, the two-year-olds, they're everywhere, but with the five- or six-year-olds, it's hard to get them adopted."

Broecker and her team have done a great job of changing the fate of the senior dogs, in part because their nonprofit group is so narrowly focused. An older dog in a shelter, sitting surrounded by bouncy, energetic puppies, can look even worse than she actually is. She can be ignored altogether, which only compounds the emotional trauma that probably led her to the shelter, often because the person she trusted has died or become too ill to care for her. The dogs, having known human affection and companionship all their lives, become depressed. Some of them will no longer even lift their heads.

Many shelter directors see the correctable problem but lack the time or ability to handle it, which is why people like Broecker step in. When she gets the dogs out of the shelters and into foster homes, almost always, they turn right around. As she puts it, the dogs get younger. They're back to being treated the way they know they're supposed to be treated, and they respond by letting their personalities shine, often for quite a few more healthy years.

These are the stories for which Peace of Mind Rescue has become known. People going to Broecker's website to adopt don't see the older dogs as less worthy than puppies. They don't see puppies at all. They see a rescue agency trying to show senior dogs in their best possible light, doing serious health testing including blood work for things like common thyroid and liver problems in older dogs, fully disclosing any issues that are found so that buyers understand what they are getting, and prescreening buyers to ensure financial resources will be available to care for the dog as he or she ages. The senior pooches are sold for $100 to $300 apiece unless they have monthly ongoing expenses, such as thyroid medication, in which case Peace of Mind adopts them out for free.

"We did just bring a dog from Washington State. Someone had passed away, and the family contacted us," Broecker says. "It was a twelve-year-old dog, and the local rescue up there said it was impossible for him to get a home. He was a Papillon. We put him on our website, and within three days, we had an application for him. It *is* possible. People go to our website expecting to get an older dog, whereas up there, the rescue group was dealing with younger dogs, so this dog was being overlooked. It's about going to the right market."

Broecker believes the future is nothing but bright for senior dogs, especially as the overall population of US residents is aging. The market share for these dogs previously considered unadoptable, she thinks, is going to grow. It's partly because people are watching parents and grandparents live well into their eighties and nineties, and are understanding the needs of seniors plus all they contribute to a full life. It's also partly because, as specialty rescue groups like Peace of Mind become more prominent, quite a few dog lovers are realizing a puppy may not actually be the right choice for a pet in their home.

"People are starting to understand the benefits of getting an adult dog or a senior dog," she says. "They have less energy, which means shorter walks. They're mature. You know who they are, so there's no adolescence where the dog you thought you had as a puppy turns out to be another dog as an adult. They're usually pretty well trained. More and more people are starting to understand the value of taking in a senior dog, not just for their own benefit but for these dogs. If you're a ten-year-old dog, you weren't in a shelter for ten years. You were somebody's dog, and something happened. You were attached to people and some life situation lands you in this shelter, and you get depressed. Some of them completely shut down, they face the wall, and the shelter will say they think the dog is dying—but we get them out and into a home with proper care, and they get younger and younger. They're happy again. They're bouncing around. They turn around. We've seen it again and again and again."

Not everyone is willing to take in a "less than perfect" pooch, and though more and more shelters and nonprofit rescue groups are helping people see that dogs previously considered lemons are really fantastic steals of a deal, more and more lawmakers are responding to dissatisfied purebred puppy buyers by creating laws that relegate the dogs to the status of broken merchandise. It's the entirely opposite mentality, and it's fast becoming more prominent.

The idea that dogs can be akin to defective products has exploded in recent years with the passage of "pet lemon laws" in various US states. (In Britain, dog purchases are covered under the Sale of Goods Act, while in the European Union, laws vary on a nation-by-nation basis.) While "pet lemon laws" usually do not apply to shelters or nonprofit rescue groups, breeders and pet stores nowadays are being forced into financial accountability if something goes wrong with a puppy. Even if a veterinarian says a problem is a quirk of fate, totally unpredictable, the seller of the dog can be liable for thousands in cash. Some breeders build this liability into their sales predictions, considering it a basic cost of doing business.

In America, the laws began to appear in the early 1990s, and as of mid-2014, the American Veterinary Medical Association listed twenty-one states, nearly half the nation, with pet purchase protection laws. Interestingly, the laws are common in the Northeast, where demand for dogs as pets is high, while the laws are nearly absent in the Midwest and South, where many large-scale breeding operations are located.

All of the laws are consumer-protection statutes that give dog buyers legal recourse if a puppy from a breeder or pet store has "disease or defect." Buyers usually have one to three weeks to file a claim of illness, and sometimes as long as two years to file a claim of congenital or hereditary problem. Breeders and pet stores can be liable for everything from a refund to reimbursement of veterinary expenses up to a given amount, depending on the state, and they may be required to offer a replacement puppy, just like a manufacturer replacing a wristwatch that ticks a little too fast. In some states, including Florida, the law even applies to misrepresentation of breed. If somebody hands over big bucks for a purebred Norwegian Buhund and the dog turns out to have something else in her DNA, the breeder or pet store can be on the financial hook, held accountable in a court of law if he fails to make good.

The ultimate problem with these laws, of course, is that once a committed dog lover brings home a puppy and gets to know her, that person would no sooner return her like a broken toaster than he would chop off his own big toe—and the puppy will be nothing but confused and scared, being tossed aside after believing she had a loving home. Countless dog buyers have experienced this wrenching moment of decision, standing in their veterinarians' offices with their children in tears, fearing for the health of the newest member of their families. That's when the vet says: "Please take a seat. We need to discuss the cost of the surgery."

In 2008, when the *Los Angeles Times* ran an article about puppy lemon laws, the outpouring of reader mail was so overwhelming that a second article was published to feature stories from people who had endured huge financial loss and emotional trauma. One reader, Brenda Stang, had spent about $650 in six months on treatment for a congenital knee problem in her $1,500 Toy Fox Terrier, Dinkee. The law would let her return Dinkee and avoid the $5,000 surgery to correct the problem. "How could we possibly give her back?" Stang told the reporter. "What would we be telling our children? Dogs are disposable?"

Even John Grogan, the author of every Labrador lover's favorite book, *Marley and Me*, has been put in this position. When the movie based on the book was being filmed, his eleven-year-old daughter fell in love with a fifteen-week-old puppy cast as young Marley. He was a happy, playful boy, so Grogan brought him home, and the family named him Woodson. But in short time, Woodson started having trouble doing normal puppy things, like jumping up onto the couch, hopping up into the car, or making his way up the stairs. The culprit turned out to be a crippling birth defect: Woodson's rear hips had disconnected balls and sockets. The breeder offered to take Woodson back and give Grogan's family their pick of the next litter, a clean dog-for-dog exchange.

"I have to admit the offer was tempting, like turning in a lemon automobile for a gleaming new model," he wrote. "But dogs are not commodities to be discarded when they break, and I assumed that if Woodson were returned, he would be euthanized."

The puppy lemon laws are, in a way, an outgrowth of a practice that arguably responsible breeders have been undertaking for quite a long time. Many hobby breeders, in particular, advise buyers to bring the dog back because they want to know what the problem is, to try to breed it out in future litters as well as to ensure the dog will receive the care he needs if the owner will not provide it, or to end the dog's life in what they see as a compassionate way. The lemon laws are often instituted by lawmakers eager to hold less-responsible breeders to these same standards that many hobby breeders have argued, for years, should be considered the ethical business model.

Dorney, the director at WAGS who works with treatable and manageable dogs, says that's not necessarily illogical thinking. She'd like to see more accountability for certain breeders, too. She says she sees a clear abundance of socialization problems in dogs bought at pet stores versus purebreds from hobby breeders and mutts on the street, and when she's tried to go back to the pet store suppliers for help after families get overwhelmed and dump their dogs at the shelter, she gets radio silence in response.

"More toward the beginning of my career twenty years ago, the people would bring the dogs in with the papers from the breeders, and we'd call and say, 'Hey, you made this dog, come and get it,'" she says. "We've made the calls dozens of times, where I could look at the papers and hunt down the breeders. And there were two, in all those years, who came down and got the dog. One was a white German Shepherd, and one was a Poodle. That's where I think the wall gets put up of 'shelters don't like breeders,' and people say that if breeders would stop breeding, we wouldn't need shelters. Well, that's not true, but I do think breeders should do their fair share."

More and more people are starting to realize that, in this context, certain breeders are like big factories that, for generations, have spewed toxic waste into the air and waterways while leaving society, like taxpayer-funded shelters, to bear the financial and ecological burden of cleaning up the mess. Dog owners who fail to spay, neuter, and train their pets of course are part of the problem, too, but because dogs are legal products with which owners can do pretty much whatever they want, and because there are no laws requiring anyone to be a wholly responsible dog owner, the only course lawmakers can take is to go after the breeders when something goes wrong, by calling the pups defective and helping buyers get financial damages.

And now that the very idea of a defective dog is out there in the ether of the universe, it's sometimes consumers *demanding* a right to refunds or exchanges. The term *puppy lemon law* has become something entirely different than an attempt at forcing responsibility. It instead presumes that all dogs should be perfect, right out of the box and forever onward. Otherwise they're faulty, a product to be returned or refunded.

This mentality can stay with an owner for far longer than the few days it takes to schedule an initial checkup at the veterinarian. In one all-too-typical case, a Pennsylvania family adopted a mixed-breed puppy at about ten weeks old. The puppy had been in foster care with two others from his litter, had a sweet temperament, and was eager to learn. In fact, he already had a pretty good grasp of "sit," played well with his siblings as well as adult dogs, and was just about housebroken when they took him home. The family had never before owned a dog, and though they registered for a series of puppy kindergarten classes, they failed to teach him to walk nicely on a leash, which made it hard to give him exercise, which left him bouncing-off-the-walls cuckoo in their home. They never let him socialize with other dogs again, and they failed to break the common habit of puppy nipping, which, by the time the dog turned about six months old—and weighed at least sixty pounds—had become not-so-gentle biting at their children's bodies to get attention. Instead of working with trainers to resolve the adolescent dog's issues, the family returned him, handing over his leash in the original foster mom's driveway without even telling the dog goodbye. He was still wearing his puppy collar, which was practically choking his now much-larger neck.

That family believed—without question—that the dog they'd adopted was a lemon. They had gone to six or eight hours' worth of puppy-training classes, and the dog still turned out bad. It never occurred to them that they had failed in their responsibilities as owners. After they returned the dog to the nonprofit volunteer and saw the puppy's story explained online as part of a search for a new home, the wife scolded the volunteer by telephone, saying with disgust, "This is why people don't rescue."

"Kids go to kindergarten, grammar school, middle school, and so on," says Liz Palika, a dog trainer and author of more than fifty pet books. "Puppies need puppy kindergarten, adolescents need basic obedience, and adult dogs need a refresher course once in a while. Training keeps the communication open between dog and owner: a vital skill. Plus, a bored dog is going to get into trouble. A dog who plays scenting games, learns new tricks, and participates in other activities with his owner is far less likely to get into trouble."

Dogs who get into serious messes often end up being evaluated by a person like Nick Jones, a behaviorist in Britain who works with everyday people in their homes on dog behavior and who is regularly asked to testify as an expert witness in police cases that involve biting. He's worked with upward of a thousand dogs during his ten-year career, everywhere from London to the countryside, and he says that even people who have had dogs all their lives can encounter training issues that are new and seem insurmountable, but that really are more common than they think. After all, even people who have had dogs since childhood have likely known maybe three to five dogs in their homes overall. It's an awfully small sample size for anyone to believe they will have experienced every behavior a dog might present.

Jones, like Palika, says training issues during adolescence are a common, recurring theme. Even if owners have gone to puppy training classes, new issues crop up almost like clockwork as the dog ages.

"It's about people's expectations. They purchase a puppy that may not be right for them and their degree of experience, and then things aren't working out. Usually the dog gets to about six months before the owners feel they're really struggling," he says. "If I showed you my ten most recent inquiries, they will probably be for twelve- to eighteen-month-olds. The average dog I work with is about two years, and that's because the dogs are reaching peak adolescence or coming into adulthood. The owners may have struggled with their own trainers or looking up things on the Internet, and they're coming to me close to the breaking point, seeking help."

Jones's work has taught him—including with police cases where a dog has bitten a person—that the vast majority of dogs can be turned around. His success rate is similar to the one at progressive shelters like the MCSPCA or WAGS, often exceeding 90 percent. In his behavioral work in people's homes, he's surprised if more than one in one hundred dogs each year is unable to make progress that resolves the issue.

Again, it's often as much about expectations as it is about the actual dog. For instance, dog-on-dog aggression, such as one dog in a home snapping or biting at another, is a common problem Jones sees. The owner may want to see both dogs lolling about as best friends, but realistically, even if Jones can use training techniques to remove 50 percent or 75 percent of the problem, it's often more than enough to satisfy the owner and keep both dogs safe and happy.

Where Jones draws the line, just as with responsible rescue groups and shelters, is with biting that is likely to endanger people. "A recent case comes to my mind that was a little West Highland White Terrier owned by a mum and dad and a girl ten or eleven years of age," he says. "This dog was muzzled throughout my visit, but it attempted to bite me twenty-plus times. The dog was exceedingly possessive of the young girl in the family. If I tried to go near her at all, he would go mental. The mother in that family would have children come to the home for day care, so it was completely incompatible. The difficulty is, can we rehome the dog? No, not in this state. Can I take the dog? No, I'd have twenty dogs here already. The dog was very young, only six or seven months of age, and in my opinion wired incorrectly. There was something seriously wrong. We tried to give the dog the benefit of the doubt and a bit more time, but on my return visit we made the decision to put the dog down."

More than a few trainers, shelter directors, and nonprofit rescue volunteers say they wish there were some kind of a law that required buyers to train their dogs: to register for classes, to work with professionals, to identify problems early, and to be responsible for correcting them before they become bigger and get dumped at the doorstep of society. Instead of believing the dog is flawed, people would learn that, in many cases, the problem is at their end of the leash.

So far, lawmakers haven't been willing to take that step of requiring owners to train, but some leading animal law experts are starting to think about other laws that might force everyone to change their attitudes—and lawyers are pushing for legal changes harder than ever before in world history.

CHAPTER TWELVE

THE GENESIS AND THE FUTURE

"Every young man would do well to remember
that all successful business stands on the foundation of morality."

—*Henry Ward Beecher*

Kate Neiswender had fallen under the spell of Assisi. Who could blame her? The Italian town is pretty much in the heart of Italy, about halfway between Florence and Rome and as awash as any place can be in the architecture and artwork of medieval, Roman, and Christian history. The Basilica of San Francesco d'Assisi—mother church of the Franciscan Order that continues in Catholicism today—stands just as imposing and ornate as it did when it was completed in the 1200s. Much of the medieval castle called Rocca Maggiore still towers as a stone-walled backdrop over the entire settlement, with its tallest points now used for photo ops of Umbria's lush fields instead of as lookout posts where guards once scanned the horizon for invaders approaching on horseback. Nearby is the small Eremo delle Carceri monastery, where St. Francis of Assisi is said to have preached to birds about God's love for all creatures. He is remembered today as the patron saint of animals, having urged his followers not only to be kind to them but also to help them if they are in trouble.

Being in that place, surrounded by that particular history, Neiswender couldn't help but think about the way the earliest Christian teachings continue to affect the way humans treat dogs today. She felt the same breezes on her face that blew through the chapel where Francis used to admonish those who treated animals poorly, and she thought, with great sadness, about how much of what people do nowadays is about as far as anyone could get from the teachings of the venerated saint.

The way dogs are bought and sold and handled, really, all comes down to a single question in her mind, a question she is prepared to answer with a thumb in the eye of even the oldest and most celebrated religious doctrine, in Assisi or anywhere else: "Do we have a right, as a single species on a great big planet, to say every species is subordinate to us?" she asks. "My argument is we do not. No bloody way."

Neiswender is an attorney from California, where she specializes in land use and environmental law and works in the field of animal law. When she looks at the legal system, she sees that everything people do with dogs stems from the earliest Christian doctrine. There is a reason the first breeders in Victorian England believed it was okay to make dogs their genetic play-puzzles without stopping to think twice, and that people the world over think the same way today about creating ever more new types of dogs. There is a reason people from the US believe it is okay to auction dogs to the highest bidder along with other items they own, just as there is a reason dogs are bought and sold everywhere from pet stores to roadside parking lots as a matter of regular business today. There is a reason it's legal to kill homeless dogs en masse in public facilities, just as there is a reason shelters and rescue groups can legally give homeless dogs to families while collecting a fee. There is a reason people all across the world continue to believe it's all right to keep dogs as personal pets. There is a reason the global dog-selling industry came into being, and there is a reason so few people question that industry's right to exist.

The reason is because the foundations of society say that dogs are not individual beings with rights, but instead are legal property—the dominion of people—a belief rooted in a Bible passage that has permeated human existence for some five thousand to six thousand years:

> Genesis 1:26: And God said, Let us make man in our image, after our likeness: and let them have dominion over the fish of the sea, and over the fowl of the air, and over the cattle, and over all the earth, and over every creeping thing that creepeth upon the earth.

Neiswender sat in Assisi, thinking not about the gorgeous scenery but instead about that Bible passage. It was like a constant buzz in her brain. She wished she could jump into a time machine and erase Genesis 1:26 from existence. The lives of dogs today, she says, would be much better for it, along with lots of other lives, too.

"I think there would be a significant difference in the way the world works," she says. "Every time a Western race—the Conquistadors or the English or whoever—is conquering the world, they all go back to, 'This is God-ordained.' And why does God tell you [that] you have the right to slaughter other people? Because you have dominion over everything on earth."

The law as Western culture knows it today stems from the Law of the Twelve Tables in 449 BC. It established basic procedural rights for one Roman against another and created punishments for wrongs. Those laws evolved during the period from AD 529 to 565, when the Byzantine emperor Justinian I sponsored the creation of a legal system, or code, that brought all existing Roman rules into a single collection of law. He wanted everything written down so citizens could be held accountable for reading and knowing the basic rules of society. Even during these early times, one was either a person or property; women, children, and slaves, along with animals like dogs, at one point or another fell into the property category. Fast-forward to the Middle Ages, which continued into the 1400s, and the laws being developed stemmed from that Code of Justinian, only now with a twist. The Romans had been pagans, but the new people writing the laws were Christians. "They took the Justinian Code and then matched it to the Bible, and built it on that," Neiswender explains. "When you're talking about Roman law, really, honestly, everything was either owned or there was some sort of relationship between a property-owning male and everything else on the planet. Where you got the dominion over animals comes directly from Genesis. There's no waffling on that one."

The laws written in the Middle Ages became the basis for the laws that ultimately followed in the English courts, which in turn formed the foundation for the law in the modern United States and many other parts of the world today. The result is that current laws recognize two entities: people and property. There is we, the people, and then there is all the rest, including dogs, over which people have dominion to do as they please.

That's why, when people look at someone treating dogs badly and cry out, "There ought to be a law against that!" their personal sensibilities about their beloved pets are often at odds with legal realities. Whether dog lovers are outraged by auctions or conformation shows or high-kill shelters or irresponsible rescue groups or lousy owners or any other instance in which dogs are being treated in disturbing ways, the modern social mores are bumping up against thousands of years' worth of religious beliefs and regulatory statutes that define dogs as just another form of property.

In fact, in the history people and dogs, the distinct pursuit of animal law is but a footnote in a centuries-long story. It's true that some of Western society's greatest thinkers, including Charles Darwin, postulated that dogs had abilities such as abstract thought that made them different from other forms of property, but attempts to codify those beliefs into law is a much more recent phenomenon. As recently as 2001, only nine colleges and universities in the United States offered animal law courses, and they were the first of their kind. Today, more than a hundred exist in the United States, along with similar curricula in Canada, the United Kingdom, Austria, Spain, Australia, New Zealand, China, and Israel, countries where there is a thriving middle class who keep dogs as pets.

"In most countries I'm in touch with, the first thing that triggers social concern about animals is stray dogs," says David Favre, who is known in the United States as the father of animal law. "Having a middle class means having enough time and energy to notice what's around you. People notice that these dogs, who have been on the streets forever, are being mistreated by governments. You have to have a certain level of freedom and capacity before you can really talk about the dogs."

China, as an example, is undergoing this transformation right now. Dogs are still hunted in some cities in China because they carry rabies, which is a deadly public health concern. Dogs also are still used as food in some parts of China. But as the middle class is evolving from Beijing to Shanghai, a growing number of Chinese are bringing dogs into their homes as pets—just as the Victorians did in mid-1800s England and as the postwar generation did in the mid-1900s United States—and the Chinese of the early 2000s, too, are beginning to think of dogs as beloved members of their families. A generation or two from now, the landscape of animal welfare in China just might look similar to where it stands elsewhere today. "As the dogs become more and more prevalent as pets in the city," Favre says, "there's this social transformation about them as animals and enhancing their status."

Favre and his colleagues in the United States are leading the world's thinking on animal law not only because the field first emerged there, but also because of the nation's history of concern about individual rights. America was founded on the principle of religious freedom and the pursuit of individual happiness. Women, children, people of different skin color, people of different sexual orientation: all have earned rights in America they previously did not enjoy. "It's pretty meaningless to talk about animal rights in Africa when some people don't have rights," Favre says. But in the United States, it's a matter of being next in line, and in more and more homes today, that means being the family dog, who is often already treated like a human child.

Here's the rub, though: to change the way people treat dogs in America or anywhere else—even to say a dog should enjoy the same legal protections that a human toddler has—there needs to be a change in law, something that distinguishes dogs from other property. And that king of change, by definition, could affect the way *all* animals are treated under the law.

The unintended consequences are virtually limitless when attorneys talk about finding a legal path to stopping the worst abuses. The spectrum of what could happen by making, say, puppy mills illegal because dogs have certain rights as sentient beings could quickly lead to demands for ending the farming of all cows and pigs for food. Some legal scholars argue it could lead to the abolishment of dogs as pets altogether, depending on how far down the road of animal welfare and rights modern society wants to walk. Companies engaged in everything from biomedical research to the production of chicken nuggets are resisting this change with every lobbying dollar they have. Even the American Veterinary Medical Association is against the concept, fearing that if dogs are no longer property, a flood of malpractice lawsuits could become the norm for botched surgeries and procedures. If a dog is no longer worth his mere purchase price, but instead the far greater sums commonly awarded with punitive damages, then veterinarians could be driven out of business.

Right now, animal law leaders are testing various routes to upend the entire legal principle that ranks dogs in the same category as inanimate objects. These legal minds haven't yet figured out how to blow up the foundation of dogs-as-property law, but they're doing their level best to make some big cracks in it for the first time in human history—and some are taking a more radical approach than others.

There's Adam Karp in the Pacific Northwest of the United States, who regularly files lawsuits for people whose dogs have been harmed or killed. While the courts and insurance companies often seek settlements reflecting a dog's value on paper—how much he'd cost to replace, like a broken window—Karp fights for emotional distress awards like the ones given to parents whose children are harmed or killed. His work has led some courts to recognize the intrinsic value of a pet, forcing them, as he puts it, to "think outside that earlier box."

There's Massachusetts-based attorney Steven M. Wise, who founded the Nonhuman Rights Project in 2007, naming the group for the fact that humans, too, are animals, and that under current law humans are the only animals with legal rights. Wise and his team, which includes legendary British primatologist Jane Goodall, want to create new legal standing for species who show clear, scientific evidence of certain cognitive abilities. Currently, they say, that includes elephants, dolphins, and whales, and the four species of great apes. In late 2013, the Nonhuman Rights Project filed lawsuits in New York state seeking to free four chimpanzees from a life in cages under the language of legal personhood, and to have them released to a sanctuary. While the cases would not immediately affect dogs, and while motions thus far have been denied, they could, through appeals courts, crack open the door to new legal possibilities for all animals. "We'll take it to the Appellate Division and then the state Court of Appeals," Wise told the Associated Press. "We've been preparing for lawsuits for many years. These are the first in a long series of suits that will chip away at the legal thing-hood of such non-human animals as chimpanzees."

There's Gary L. Francione, the Nicholas deB. Katzenbach Scholar of Law and Philosophy at Rutgers School of Law in New Jersey. He advocates total veganism, an end to animal farming, and a legal distinction of nonhuman personhood for all sentient animals, and he teaches that the very action of owning a pet violates the animal's basic rights to be considered something other than property. If only two dogs were left on Earth, he says, he wouldn't breed them to create more pets. "It's morally wrong," he says, "to bring any domesticated animals into existence for human purposes."

And then there's Favre, who comes down somewhere in the middle of the spectrum with his work as the Nancy Heathcote Professor of Property and Animal Law at Michigan State University. His idea is to create a bridge between people and property under the law: a new category called *living property*. He got the idea during the 1990s, when he heard animal rights activists comparing the ownership of pets to having slaves. "I'm looking at my dogs and thinking, 'I'm sorry, but this just is not slavery,'" he says today. "I don't accept that, so I had to cast about and see what I think of as a step forward. Where we are is not acceptable, but we need to add a category. I came up with the term *living property* as a place for the law to think about this other set of beings and the relationship we want to have with them."

Favre thinks a good place to start talking about living property is not in terms of all animals, but in terms of vertebrates, because those are the creatures whom animal cruelty laws typically protect. Most lawmakers accept that animal cruelty laws exist because vertebrates can feel pain, so it's a good place, in Favre's mind, to begin the conversation about how to redefine the legal status of favored vertebrates like canines. Most dog lovers are already on board with the notion that a pooch is special compared with other animals, such as frogs or wasps. Once people believe dogs are unique, all that remains is for political leaders and judges to get the law in line with public sentiment.

"Our society is already there, conceptually," Favre says. "It's a matter of the law catching up with society, at least in regard to pets."

Opposition, Favre knows, will be strong; the slippery slope of logic turns many minds immediately to food supplies and billions of dollars at stake for everyone from dog breeders to pharmaceutical companies using dogs in research (about seventy thousand Beagles alone are used in US laboratories each year). There's also the daunting fact that creating a new category like living property would, to some people, be akin to going against the very teachings of God.

And yet the law evolves along with society, and society is changing its opinion about dogs. In the early 1900s, the law didn't recognize pets the way it does today. Just one century ago, when many of today's grandparents were born, it wasn't a crime to steal a dog because society, through its laws, hadn't yet made the dog something of value. "At the moment, we [Americans] don't perceive dogs the same way we did a hundred years ago, or the way they're perceived in other countries now," Favre says. "You're living in a world that has come into existence in the past fifty years or so."

For now, with attorneys attacking on multiple fronts, what's happening in the courts often provides the greatest insight into where we may be headed next, and one recent case hints that dogs may be considered individuals sooner rather than later.

Most dog lovers already know this case well, and many have strong feelings about it, even if they don't realize its significance in the history of animal law. Ironically, it came about not because anyone sought to change the legal status of dogs as it has been known since biblical times, but instead because a professional athlete was forced to endure a come-to-Jesus moment before a federal judge in the United States of America.

At first, Michael Vick denied knowing anything about the dogs.

A year after the Atlanta Falcons star became the first National Football League quarterback ever to rush for more than one thousand yards in a single season, and at a time when his public reputation and financial prospects were soaring skyward, a federal grand jury in Virginia indicted Vick and several others on accusations of dogfighting. According to the summary of the facts issued by a US District Court in Virginia, Vick and his associates spent six years sponsoring and participating in dogfights, buying and training dogs to fight in multiple states, and killing dogs who didn't work out as part of the business plan. The details were gruesome and involved things like electric-shock execution along with a "rape stand" that may have turned at least one female dog irreparably vicious. Headlines fast appeared around the world and continued to dominate news reports for the latter half of 2007, and a lucrative market sprang up for hawking fake-blood-splattered T-shirts calling for the athlete's ouster from professional sports. Vick claimed ignorance of the dogfighting operation at a home he owned, saying he was hardly ever there, but testimony quickly mounted to the contrary.

In the end, he was sentenced to twenty-three months in prison, but his temporary removal from the sports highlight reels wasn't enough to quell public outrage. In December 2008, a full year after Vick's conviction, *Sports Illustrated* ran a cover photograph of a dog to promote a feature article about the surviving Vick pooches. The magazine received more letters and emails about the story than any other it had published the entire year prior, and in 2010, the article's author expanded the tale into the book *The Lost Dogs*, which became a *New York Times* bestseller. As recently as 2014, when the New York Jets signed Vick as their new quarterback, reports fast topped the news about longtime fans selling their season tickets in disgust. "He electrocuted dogs in a bathtub for fun," one fan wrote on the Jets' Facebook page. "I'm supposed to root for this guy?"

The involvement of such a high-profile athlete made the story sensational for the general public, but Rebecca Huss didn't bother paying much attention, at least in the beginning. She teaches animal law at Valparaiso University in Indiana, and she knew how dogfighting convictions usually turned out. Somebody might go to jail, and a lot of dogs would end up dead. The whole thing was just plain sad. Both the HSUS and PETA had called for the Vick dogs to be killed en masse, as had usually been done in cases involving dogfighting seizures. It was always assumed that dogs raised to fight were so badly damaged psychologically that they could not be brought back. Huss had no reason to think anything would be different this time.

That is, until her phone rang. She was asked to accept appointment as guardian/special master for the nearly fifty dogs who had become the legal property of the US government following their seizure from Vick's house. Nearly $1 million of Vick's fortune, a startling sum, had been earmarked for their care and treatment. Experts had been evaluating the dogs individually—a rare if not unique occurrence in a dogfighting bust—and had told the court that at least some of the dogs might be able to be saved. Media from around the world were watching, and the federal court needed to figure out what to do. Huss was the person asked to give official recommendations on handling the dogs and the money.

"When I got the initial call, the language used was *guardian,* and I thought, 'Wow, the animal people would love that,'" she recalls. Appointment of a guardian implies not property, but a victim, like a child caught between two parents in a custody battle. Guardians for dogs had been appointed in estate planning by people who wanted their pets cared for after the last family member's death, but never had a court appointed a guardian to oversee the care of seized dogs. Doing so would have been similar to a judge appointing a guardian to oversee the care of any other property, say, a furnace. The mere act would have been a watershed in the field of animal law.

"The reason why this worked and they could appoint me as a guardian is that the federal government at the time owned the dogs," Huss explains today. "Not only had they seized the dogs, but they had gone through the civil asset forfeiture procedure. The person who actually owned the dogs wanted to appoint me as guardian/special master."

Even though the legal action was technically narrow, its effects were substantial in advancing the cause of treating dogs as individual beings. While dog lovers around the world were focused on demonizing Vick, animal law experts were watching the legal machinations of the case with rapt attention.

One of the first things Huss did was travel to meet each dog in person, and she gave names to the ones who didn't already have them. "I wanted to look at them as individuals, and from a practical perspective, it's more compelling to say Haley or Halley or whatever you want to call the dog, Nigel, versus Hanover two-thirty-five," she says. "It's not sweet. It's necessary if we're going to treat them as individuals."

She walked through the shelters where the dogs were housed, and it was there that she realized how unusual her presence was in a legal sense. Her job was to visit several dozen dogs in particular, but she saw the faces of hundreds more who were homeless. Their gazes through the cage links weighed on her conscience.

"I was walking past all these other dogs that were not part of the case, that don't have a guardian/master, that don't have someone advocating for them," she says. "The shelters do what they can, but these [Vick] dogs, because of who they were, one of the criticisms was that they had a better shot of making it out of the system because of where they came from. It's just like the dogs after [Hurricane] Katrina. You had people walking into shelters saying 'I want a Katrina dog' and ignoring the dogs that had been there for a year."

Plenty of people contacted Huss asking to foster or adopt the Vick dogs. Others sent her emails of general support, encouraging her to do what she could for as many dogs as possible. Those emails, she loved to receive.

On the flip side were the emails saying she was evil if she didn't ensure all the dogs would die, presumably sent by people afraid that dogfighting refugees—dogs widely and falsely stereotyped as vicious Pit Bulls, at that—would ultimately bite or kill a person if she recommended that they be allowed to live.

"It was pretty intense," she recalls. "I was getting calls in the middle of the night from people, and people are very passionate about this, and rightly so. These are sentient beings that deserve a chance."

In the end, working with help from other evaluators, Huss recommended moving forty-seven of the forty-nine dogs into places where they could recover. Today, some are therapy dogs working in nursing homes and hospitals. Only two had to be put down, one for temperament and one for illness.

The million or so dollars earmarked for the dogs' care was given to the humans who took legal possession of them as property. It wasn't technically restitution being paid to the dogs as victims, but it was a whole lot more than had ever been done for dogs in similar situations, and the repercussions of that court action continue today. In dogfighting busts since the Vick case, groups including the HSUS and the ASPCA have sought to treat seized dogs as individual beings. The fact that the federal government allowed as much with the Vick dogs now gives the advocacy groups legal precedent to cite.

In August 2014, lawmakers began pushing for more, tying the cause of animal abuse to the cause of domestic violence and citing at least one study that shows 71 percent of women entering domestic violence shelters say their abuser also threatened, harmed, or killed their pets, making the dogs additional victims instead of just property. US Representative Katherine Clark, a Democrat from Massachusetts, and US Representative Ileana Ros-Lehtinen, a Republican from Florida, introduced federal legislation that would, in cases of domestic violence, add veterinary care to the list of restitution costs able to be recovered and that would, for the first time, recommend that all states extend legal protections to include pets in court-issued protective orders. (Twenty-seven states do today, along with the District of Columbia and Puerto Rico.) That legislation was recently reintroduced as the Pets and Women Safety (PAWS) Act of 2015—with forty-nine original cosponsors on board.

Also significant is what public reaction to the Vick case indicates about how future legal changes might be received. Each person who thought, "Good, make Michael Vick pay whatever it costs to help those poor, suffering dogs he abused," believes in the idea that dogs deserve to be treated as more than property. New York Jets fans canceling their 2014 season tickets because Vick is now on the team roster is no small thing, either. It's everyday people doing what they can to let the world know that they stand on the side of the dogs. These are the types of feelings to keep in mind when large-scale breeders talk about "animal rights extremists." Any dog lover who agrees that pups should have a legal status of victims, enjoy similar protections to human toddlers, and be financially compensated for harm more accurately described as a moderate animal rights advocate.

Many people, at the time of the Vick case, wanted to say Huss was a guardian for victims instead of property, and some media misinterpreted her position that way. She is still not ready to make that legal leap today, because the dogs always remained property in the context of the law, but she does believe the Vick case shows the law may be tipping toward change.

"I think as a society we're closer, because we didn't treat them like other types of property," she says. "That means something. It means that we recognize them as sentient beings. That's a huge thing in property law. Forty years ago, most of society would've just killed the dogs."

Joan Schaffner is thinking about presidential debates. It's not that she ever expects to find herself on the dais as a candidate; yes, she works in Washington, DC, but it's not as a congresswoman or senator. Instead, Schaffner directs the animal law program at George Washington University, just a few strides from the infamous Watergate building. On any given day, she's breathing the same oxygen as people aspiring to be the top boss in the White House, and she's wondering when they might be forced to articulate their stance on how we treat dogs and other animals before they are allowed to become the leader of the free world.

In her mind's-eye, Schaffner imagines sitting in front of the television like so many other citizens, watching presidential candidates field questions from a moderator. If she tunes her vision back, say, fifty years, the moderator isn't asking anything about the environment. It's not even on the public's radar. If she adjusts her vision to the present, the moderator is asking not only about green energy options, but also about same-sex marriage. The public's priorities have changed. And when she expands her vision to the future, the moderator is asking something that, to this day, has never been put to a presidential candidate in a debate, something along the lines of "Do you believe all publicly funded shelters should be forced to take a no-kill approach and save every treatable or manageable dog?"

"If that could actually be a question during a presidential debate . . ." she says, the sentence trailing off as she gasps at the thought of it happening during her lifetime. "Or, 'What do you think about the right of a Georgia aquarium to import eighteen Beluga whales from Russia?' That would be *huge*. It would be phenomenal."

Politics and the law go hand in hand, and it's possible, Schaffner says, for citizens to force a change in the law regarding dogs before the lawyers do. She's not as optimistic as Favre and others who believe change will come in the next few decades, at least not fundamental change to the status of dogs as property, unless elected lawmakers act before the judges do. Politicians being held accountable by voters can force legal change much faster, a fact

Schaffner knows in part because of what she has seen happen in the gay community in recent years. In addition to teaching animal law, she also is a faculty advisor to her university's gay-lesbian-bisexual-transgender organization, and she believes changing social attitudes are the reason laws in that area are evolving so quickly after centuries of discrimination.

"If you had asked me twenty or thirty years ago, did I think we'd see same-sex marriage in our lifetime, I would have said no," she says. "I am absolutely shocked at how fast the LGBT movement has changed our society, at least as a matter of law. The states are just dropping like flies on same-sex marriage. That's incredible to me, how fast that changed around."

Neiswender also cites civil rights changes as an indicator that animal law could have its breakthrough cases in the near future—especially because the speed of ideas spreading digitally is a new tool that can be hard for entrenched institutions to combat. Humans no longer live in the age of information traveling on horseback from castle to castle across the Italian countryside. Same-minded people from Assisi to Alaska not only can communicate instantly, but also can get organized and lobby for legal change, fast.

"We talk about environmental rights today as a given. It's part of every election. That did not exist forty years ago," she says. "Ask any gay guy around forty years ago if he could've envisioned what's happening today, and he'd tell you no. With social media, it's old before you've written it. If you had told a guy walking in Selma [Alabama] in 1963 that we'd have a black man in the White House in 2008, he'd have called you crazy. Things move fast now, and we can do it for dogs, too."

Favre believes the first nation to change the status of dogs from property will be the United States—but he'd take a side bet on Switzerland making the first real progress, too, because the Swiss have already created a place in their law that says animals are not things. "As a society and as a legal system, they're thinking about the word *dignity*, and that animals have dignity," he says. Whether that will translate into something more is yet to be seen.

Yolanda Eisenstein, an animal law attorney in Dallas, Texas, and author of the American Bar Association's 2014 book *Legal Guide for Dog Owners*, believes dogs are likely to remain property for the near future, but the inroads lawyers are making are substantial, even if they're piecemeal. If the current legal efforts weren't likely to succeed, she says, there wouldn't be commercial-scale dog breeders and agricultural businesses fighting back so hard in the legal courts as well as in the court of public opinion.

Eisenstein also says the way people are choosing to live their lives bodes well for laws changing even further in favor of dogs everywhere.

"I think that society needs their companion animals more than they ever have," she says. "We have more people living alone, people living to be older and their spouses die—dogs and cats have become family members in a sense that they weren't before. Unless that changes drastically, dogs are always going to have a very special place in our lives, and the law will have to follow. It's going to have to change."

For her part, Neiswender understands that change takes time. She looked at the buildings in Assisi and realized how long they took to create, how long they have stood for Western society's moral center, and how likely they are to stand well into the future. Their time on the world stage has been long, far longer than that of the birds to whom St. Francis used to preach.

Even still, all seasons do change, and for dogs and other sentient animals, the time for a new spring may be now. In April 2015—for the first time in world history—a judge in Manhattan Supreme Court issued an order to show cause and writ of habeas corpus on behalf of two chimpanzees, Herculus and Leo, who are being used for biomedical experimentation on Long Island, New York. Only a "legal person" may have an order to show cause and writ of habeas corpus on his behalf. In essence, the ruling meant the court believed the chimpanzees could be legal persons, and the case was continuing as of this writing, according to the Nonhuman Rights Project.

Neisweinder says it's likely that even more significant rulings are yet to come.

"You have to choose your battles, but eventually, somebody is going to file a lawsuit that gives chimps the right to exist in peace," she says. "Some judge is going to do that in the next few years, and the minute that happens, it's going to be just like gay rights. You'll watch the dominoes fall."

CHAPTER THIRTEEN

SMART SHOPPING

"Mindless habitual behavior is the enemy of
innovation."
                              —*Rosabeth Moss Kanter*

W e, the dog lovers, would be silly to wait for the lawyers
to sort all this out. Or the politicians. Or, for that matter,
the people who now stand at the top of the dog business,
from the auction houses to the distribution companies to the massive nonprofits to the most successful shelters. While many good
things can be said about the leaders on all sides of today's global
dog industry, and while the past few decades have included great
strides toward ensuring more pooches have better lives, the fact
remains that nobody has yet figured out how to resolve the root
problems. We still have regular, horrific animal cruelty busts. We
still have dogs exterminated by the thousands in the streets as a
matter of everyday business. We still have pups being killed by

the millions, behind closed doors, at taxpayer expense, often for no reason beyond human convenience.

Making sure dogs are treated the way they should be treated is like trying to organize a giant puzzle of irreparably mismatched pieces. It involves uprooting a global industry built on history, tradition, religion, culture, politics, gender, societal obligations, and personal responsibility—all the stuff of humanity's greatest world wars. Almost every individual interviewed for this book said he or she was a person who loves dogs, and almost everyone meant it in a different way. People who grew up believing dogs are outside animals who need only dry kibble every day are never going to understand people who let dogs sleep in their beds and eat home-made organic treats. People who believe a dog's life is incomplete without a daily walk in the park are never going to understand people who believe it's okay for a dog to live her entire life in a pen. People who have spent their lifetimes believing they can improve a certain style of dog more than nature itself are never going to understand people who feel they've gotten an awesome deal when buying a mutt for a thousand dollars.

Trying to fit the mismatched puzzle pieces together is about as likely to work as uniting conservatives and liberals, Christians and atheists, men and women. Instead, we dog lovers must use our collective power to speak the only language everyone in the dog industry understands: the language of money. More of us good-hearted people are out there in the world than bad guys trying to make cash by treating dogs badly. We dog lovers need to embrace our potentially game-changing role in the marketplace, because we're the only ones who can ultimately put the worst players out of business.

For more than a century, dog lovers have left this job up to others, and the results have been mixed at best. Groups like the AKC, Britain's Kennel Club, and FCI may imply that they have the breeders under control, but that's untrue because plenty of lousy breeders make as much, if not more, money selling dogs as their responsible competitors. Government agencies from the USDA to the European Union can institute all the laws they want to protect dogs, but it's not enough if there's still money to be made in treating them badly, as evidenced by regular puppy mill busts. Humane societies and nonprofit rescue groups can collect hundreds of millions of dollars, euros, and pounds sterling, and they can do a great job of finding homes for more dogs than in the past, but they cannot ultimately resolve the root challenges because they're up against a global industry with an ever growing supply of consumers.

Because it all starts with us dog buyers, it can only be resolved in large part by us, too. Every cent and pence that is made, every dog whose life is affected or ended, all of it comes back to regular people and how we choose to spend our money from the start. As long as enough of us keep feeding the worst parts of the system with our cash, the system as a whole will remain unchanged. It really is that simple.

The thirty million or so dogs brought into homes every year have to come from somewhere. Pointing fingers at breeders or rescuers is not the answer. Neither side is going anywhere. When all the arguing is done, there will still be breeders, there will still be shelters, and there will still be for-profit and nonprofit middlemen working the market in between. All of them are necessary to satisfy customer demand. That's the marketplace we've created.

The fastest way to create change for dogs today, therefore, is not ethical, legal, or political. It is financial.

Our pooches, no matter how much we love them as members of our families, are legal products for sale. Whether we're signing a contract that says "sale" or "adoption," and whether we are standing in an auction house or a shelter, we are handing over cash to fund not just one segment of the $11 billion industry but also an individual seller. The good news is that almost everyone dealing in dogs is a mom-and-pop business, or slightly larger at best. Nobody, not even the biggest pet store chains and nonprofits, has cornered the global market on dog sales like a multinational Walmart or Tyson Foods. Dog lovers are not buying into a system that is beyond the scope of change. We're buying into a system that is still evolving worldwide, and that will reshape itself depending on where we allow the most money to be made.

The biggest challenge, really, involves not what most breeders and rescuers are doing, but instead what we, ourselves, are thinking and feeling. Many of us love our dogs so much that contemplating their existence as products feels unconscionable. One recent study showed that more than 80 percent of us believe our pups are members of our families, equal in status to children, and that more than half of us call ourselves pet parents instead of pet owners. A 2014 headline in the *New York Post,* citing data on childbirth and dog buying trends, read, "More Young Women Choosing Dogs over Motherhood." Feeling this depth of love for our pups is a wonderful thing—but it's blinding us to the action that will solve their problems in the broader world today. If we want to change things for the better for all dogs, then we have to approach this issue not as pet parents, but instead as smart buyers. It's not heartfelt desire but cash flow that is the eternal counterforce to shady sellers. The role of the dog lover is to be a conscious consumer. As things stand today, money is the best leverage our beloved dogs have.

Once we understand and accept this reality, we can put our $11 billion a year to use with more savvy than any dog-buying generation in history. We can be the first truly conscious consumers of dogs. It starts with understanding the scope of the industry, and it continues with using that knowledge to see through the sales pitches the next time we decide to buy a dog—to ensure we truly are giving our money to a seller for the right reasons.

When Harold Herzog talks about social contagion, he's not talking about Ebola or the flu. He's instead talking about one of the many underlying forces that persuade us to hand over our money to one dog seller versus another, one of the forces we must learn to understand if we're going to be conscious consumers the next time we go shopping for a pup.

Herzog, a psychology professor at Western Carolina University, worked with colleagues at University College London and the University of California–Davis to study trends in AKC dog registrations between 1946 and 2001. The data set, taken from what is believed to be the world's largest registry of purebred dogs, included more than forty-two million pooches. And it showed that, decade after decade, decisions about which dogs to buy had less to do with the dogs themselves than many of us might believe. Consumer choices instead have followed a classic power-law distribution curve, or what in recent years has become known in business circles as a "long tail curve" (a most fortunate nickname when discussing dogs). It's basically a fancy way of saying that dog buying is often no more than a culture-wide popularity contest, or a series of fads.

The nickname *long tail* comes from the shape of the graph that a power-law distribution has when it's plotted on a standard X axis and Y axis. There's a huge spike where the line starts up in the top left corner, and then the line has a precipitous drop that flattens out and goes on and on forever to the right. That's the long tail.

In buying and selling, the power-law distribution curve is the stuff of blockbuster movies, platinum records, and bestselling books. Whatever it is that lots of people are buying creates that huge spike in the line at the top left, while the less-popular content exists on the long, thin tail, selling just a few copies apiece. Nowadays, Labrador Retriever sales would be up in the top left spike while sales of Cesky Terriers, Otterhounds, and Canaan Dogs would be at the far end of the tail. Everything that is for sale, eventually, becomes part of the long tail as its popularity wanes, but every seller's goal is to keep a product up in the top left corner. That's where the money is to be made, in being the most popular product for as long as possible.

Knowing the magic mix that gets a product into that top left corner is what makes legendary marketing careers, but researchers have shown it often includes hidden drivers, like social contagion, that most people never notice. The idea of social contagion is that we have a tendency to copy what we see others doing, whether or not we've even met the other people. It's why top-ten lists are everywhere: Consumers seem to have an innate desire to follow other people's buying instincts and choices. We do it when picking baby names. We do it when deciding whether or not to take up the habit of smoking. Researchers have proved that people are copycats with all kinds of things, including, according to Herzog and his colleagues, deciding which dog to buy.

"Over the past five decades, shifts in preferences for some types of dogs show the boom-bust patterns that are hallmarks of fads," he writes. "Fluctuations of this magnitude suggest that social contagion is a major factor in the choices people make for their animal companions. In this regard, pets are no different from popular music, athletic shoes, and clothing styles. In short, dog breeds have become a form of fashion."

Herzog also determined, in looking at AKC registration data, that the average time any breed spends in the top popularity spot is fourteen years. Each of the popular breeds has had a boom-bust cycle no different than any other fad in our culture, be it bell-bottom jeans during the 1970s or Madonna albums during the 1980s or Harry Potter books during the 2000s. Dog lovers make one style of purebred the favorite for a while, and then tire of it and bring in a new blockbuster, right on cue.

Rin Tin Tin is a great example. His run of popularity starting in the 1920s was approximately thirteen years, from the date of his first starring movie role until the German Shepherd breed was replaced in the number-one purebred popularity slot—by the Cocker Spaniel, which held sway for more than a decade as well. The current favorite, Labrador Retriever, has enjoyed a reign of ten to fifteen years, depending on how one judges the statistics. Odds are good there will be a new favorite soon, no matter how many people claim today that Labs are the best dogs in the world. Arguably, today's trends in buying mutts may include a social-contagion factor. "Rescue is my favorite breed" T-shirts and magnets are now becoming as ubiquitous in some places as "I love my Labrador" merchandise was in its heyday.

This phenomenon of social contagion is what underpins comments made at the core of the dog market by people like Chadd Hughes, who said, back in chapter 1, while coaxing breeders to invest in underpriced dogs at the auction house: "Anybody in the dog business knows that if you have *the dog* when the trend hits, that's when you make your money." The phenomenon is also a reminder of what happens when a whole lot of consumers jump on the bandwagon and rescuers end up inundated with Dalmatians or Jack Russell Terriers. "Fads may also be a factor in euthanasia of unwanted pets," Herzog writes. "Individuals who choose a puppy on the basis of unconscious social contagion may find that the now-grown dog is not suited to their living situation."

Understanding the impact of forces like social contagion, and knowing what a big business dogs are, should prompt all dog lovers to think far more carefully about why we're choosing a particular dog the next time we go shopping. If we're buying a certain type of dog because we think it's a cool idea, then we're not asking ourselves, or the sellers, serious questions. Too many of us buyers are letting our subconscious rule, and we're likely falling prey to marketing tricks or fads, and giving money to the worst sellers out there.

Another sneaky tactic for which buyers tend to fall is the pixie dust phenomenon. A certain level of magic comes with being unattainable. Celebrities have it. So do kings and queens. When they endorse something, it's as if they sprinkle their pixie dust on it—and they work hard to make sure they never lose their pixie dust supply. Consumers may know the celebrities' names, and the biggest stars let the average folk see just enough of their world to maintain adoration, but hardly anyone knows anything real and true about these people. That's the way they want it, because the more normal they become to consumers, the more their pixie dust fades. "Not many people know this," writes Martin Lindstrom in *Brandwashed*, "but the reason many royals wear those long gloves isn't just for elegance; it's to create an intentional psychological distance from members of the public."

Think about the pageantry of purebred dogs. The crowning of champions. The tales of historic bloodlines. The gold-colored rope placed as a barrier around the winner of the Westminster Kennel Club Dog Show. The fact that everyone can see the world's most expensive dogs on television, but that trying to buy one, to an everyday person, is the equivalent of gaining access to Prince William and Kate Middleton's youngest child for a play date. It's all a way of ensuring that certain dogs possess pixie dust. It's a way of increasing perceived value. If Affenpinschers were available in shelters on every corner, a dog like Banana Joe would look a lot less special standing in a winner's circle. In fact, he'd seem totally out of context, and his value would plummet.

Fear-based advertising is another common sales ploy in the world of dogs, a tactic that has worked with tons of products for generations. Everyone dousing her hands in sanitizers nowadays is the modern incarnation of Listerine customers in the 1920s. Back then, everybody had bad breath, and Listerine's marketing team coined the scary-sounding term "chronic halitosis" to describe it. Suddenly, the public lived in fear of having chronic halitosis and started buying Listerine, to solve a problem that previously bothered few except the accountants calculating the mouthwash maker's profits.

Savvy marketers have long known that people want what is safe and clean, which is why dog marketing pitches like this one, from auctioneer Bob Hughes, hit home with so many people who decide to buy a purebred puppy: "If you've got a family and two children, and you go to the local shelter to get a pet, you have no history of where that dog came from. Let's say that dog ate out of a Dumpster and a restaurant owner wore a red apron while chasing that dog away. Then your kid goes out in a red T-shirt and the dog bites your kid in the throat, because it's been conditioned."

Note the lack of any sales pitch *for* the purebred puppy. He's not talking about how what he's selling is good; he's talking about the fact that if we choose something else, we could be making a fatal mistake. That's fear-based advertising. It often has nothing to do with the reality of the temperament of a dog in question, and feelings of fear often prevent us from even asking for other sides of the argument, be they temperament testing of puppies or considering an adult shelter dog whose personality is already well formed. As Julie Sanders of Four Paws in Britain puts it: "Some people say they don't want a rescue dog because they don't know its history. Well that's fine, but go get a rescue puppy. It can start out with you." There is always at least one other side to any sales pitch, and it's our job as conscious consumers to find it.

Fear-based advertising meshes perfectly with human desire to purchase products that are healthy. This is sort of the flip side of getting people to buy based on worry, only instead of scaring us, the seller offers a positive alternative that is perceived as healthier. For instance, many people believe that if they eat the fancy-brand protein bar instead of the average cupcake, they'll be healthier, even though plenty of people who eat an occasional cupcake live perfectly long lives. Some people believe that if they drink water instead of wine, they're doing something healthier, even though recent studies show a little red wine now and then can be a good thing. This same type of thinking leads us to believe that if we buy one type of dog instead of another, we will have the best chance of her being healthy, too.

Advertisements for purebreds have long hinted that they are the healthier choice, but more and more research is proving this notion false, exposing it as nothing more than a marketing ploy. There is a reasonable argument to be made that a dog in a shelter may have different behavioral challenges than a purebred puppy—and that purebred puppies from different types of sellers may have their own variations of behavioral issues—but a dog's health is a different issue. Documentaries like Jemima Harrison's *Pedigree Dogs Exposed* are showing that modern breeding practices can actually make dogs less healthy, and research by people like *The Genius of Dogs* co-author Vanessa Woods is backing up what quite a few veterinarians have long said privately: dogs are individual living creatures, much like humans, and no matter where they originate, some of them are going to have more health problems in life than others. "It's a DNA crapshoot, this game of genetics," as veterinarian Patty Khuly wrote for Vetstreet. "Some win, some lose."

A sales trick that lends yet another note to this same song is what Lindstrom calls perceived justification symbols. These are things like certificates of authenticity that come with an athlete's autographed baseball or an artist's signed print, some type of "marketing moment" that reassures the buyer he has made the right purchase. Is there really any other reason to have a certificate of authenticity from a kennel club verifying a dog's official registration? The paperwork that comes with some pooches has nothing to do with temperament, health, training, or anything else that makes a dog a great member of a family. If the buyer is not planning to breed more dogs, all the certificate usually means is that a premium has been paid for the pup, and that a piece of paper somehow justifies the extended outlay of cash.

The notion of a certain purebred being "the best" can affect dog buyers for years, because once we decide a brand is worth paying for, we tend to stick with it. In *Born to Buy*, Juliet Schor writes that children who can recognize logos by eighteen months old—not even age two—grow up to prefer those brands. If a child is raised eating at McDonald's, she will likely prefer it to Burger King all her life, and then she'll take her own children to McDonald's, furthering the brand relationship again. If we grow up in a family of Yale University graduates, we will forever cheer against Harvard

University teams. And anyone who spends his youth playing with a Golden Retriever in the family living room is likely to buy a Golden Retriever when he gets his own dog as an adult, instead of even considering a Plott Hound or a mutt.

"Look at the rise of designer fashions for the very young," says Schor, who is a professor of sociology at Boston College. "You have six-, seven-, and eight-year-olds needing to have the 'big' names like Armani, Burberry, and Gucci." Why would kids think of expensive purebred dogs as anything different? Adults sometimes have to work hard, as when shopping for a pooch, to recognize these types of beliefs as something that dates back to childhood.

Dog buyers also have to work a bit extra as adult shoppers to get past another habit ingrained in us as kids, when we're taught to believe what people in positions of authority say. As adults, people seem to apply a similar thought process with those considered experts—to the point that part of our cognitive process actually shuts down and we stop thinking for ourselves when a so-called expert offers buying advice.

Such expert dependence was shown to be true in 2009 research led by neuroeconomics and psychiatry professor Gregory Berns at the Emory University School of Medicine in Atlanta, Georgia. He and his team used brain-scanning technology to see what happens inside human skulls when people are asked to choose for themselves versus when they are asked to choose with the benefit of expert advice. "This study indicates that the brain relinquishes responsibility when a trusted authority provides expertise," Berns states. "The problem with this tendency is that it can work to a person's detriment if the trusted source turns out to be incompetent or corrupt."

Whom are dog lovers most likely to see as a person of authority? A breeder who commands $3,500 per puppy, perhaps? Or maybe someone like Westminster Kennel Club Dog Show spokesman David Frei, featured on the news year after year as the man with one dog who is better than all the rest? How might buyers perceive information about dogs coming from, say, a rescuer who fosters homeless puppies in her living room? Might we fail to challenge the big-money breeder and Westminster spokesman with the same types of questions we ask of the rescuer?

The list of marketing and psychological traps that dog buyers face is far longer than most people imagine. We could spend our entire lives trying to spot them all, and we'd fail. The better approach for conscious consumers is to be aware that, even if a choice seems well researched, sometimes it is not—and to seek far more information from dog sellers than we ever have in the past, to try to break through the most common sales pitches that have maintained the status quo in the dog business for so long.

"You can buy a purebred-registered, USDA-licensed-kennel puppy from the best breeder in the country, and the puppy can still have a problem. You can do the very best research possible, but the dog may not be perfect. Have you ever adopted a child? It's never going to be perfect. You're never going to genetically breed a perfect dog."

It may be surprising that those words were spoken not by a rescue advocate, but instead by dog auctioneer Bob Hughes, whose family has likely made more money buying and selling dogs than most other families in world history. Honest breeders, when asked, often say similar things, and they offer evidence of how they stand by the dogs if something goes wrong. Colleen Nicholson, for instance, selling show-quality Dobermans, raises the point about potential problems before buyers even question her, and she offers references from previous clients as proof of her commitment for the long term, along with stacks of paperwork documenting everything she can about every puppy she sells.

Elizabeth Brinkley, the Sheltie breeder who stands up for breeding rights in her work with lawmakers, outright urges buyers to walk away from any breeder who is making a glowing sales pitch that seems too good to be true. "Get smart. Realize you are not always being told the truth—breeders *and* rescues," Brinkley says. "Ask enough questions that you get a feel for the person as much as the dog. If the person showing you these dogs is pushing really hard and you're getting bad vibes, don't buy the dog. Use common sense. Don't feel bad and think you have to get the dog out. All you're doing is just keeping that guy in business."

Stefano Paolantoni, the breeder of Lhasa Apsos, Maltese, and Toy Poodles in Italy, says he would never advise buying a purebred dog from anyone who is selling them without any connections to other breeders. "In my opinion, a potential client should never buy from a breeder who is not showing his stock. A good breeder is the one who goes to shows and who wants to have comparison with other breeders," he says. "And in my opinion, it is always better to go to visit the breeder and to see with your own eyes the conditions where the dogs are living."

Dave Miller, the commercial breeder of Newfoundlands, Beagles, Shiba Inus, Corgis, and Puggles, agrees with Paolantoni on the latter point: buyers should go and see the truth for themselves. As an example, he's proud to show clients the amount of land on his farm that is devoted to each of his pooches. "Frankly, that's one reason we raise Newfoundlands," Miller says. "Not everybody is equipped to raise these big dogs."

Doing research before buying a dog does not mean looking at a website. It does not mean reading a book, or a catalog, of different purebred styles. To research something means to investigate it systematically. It means attempting to verify *everything*. It requires more effort than shopping for a new sweater. It demands that the buyer asks smart questions and listens hard to the answers, instead of hearing whatever it is she wants to hear.

One of the best things to do in terms of research is arrive at the breeder's kennel, the shelter's facility, or the nonprofit's foster home with printed-out questions in hand. Make a list. Write everything in advance. Everyone knows that the minute we see the dogs, our heartstrings start draining the blood flow away from our brains. If we go in prepared with open-ended questions that force the seller to fill in the blanks, we're going to do a much better job of actually researching the source.

Asking open-ended questions is key. They cannot be answered with a yes or no. They usually start with "how" or "why" or "please tell me about," and they are designed to elicit the most information possible. There is a difference between asking, "Does this dog have a good temperament?" (of course the seller will answer yes) and asking, "How do you, Mr. Seller, know this dog has a good temperament?" The open-ended question will require the seller to explain why he thinks the dog is friendly—which can mean everything from relying on breed stereotypes (a red flag) to discussing temperament testing (better) to explaining how the dog has been living for the past month with three kids, two dogs, and a cat without any problems (ideal).

The same practice of asking open-ended questions applies to, say, ensuring that every type of dog from a purebred puppy to a senior shelter mutt is free of socialization issues. The question "Have you socialized the dog properly?" is going to elicit a yes, while rephrasing the question as "Please explain what you have done to socialize the dog" is going to give buyers far more information, not only about the particular dog they're thinking about buying but also about the seller's beliefs on how dogs should be socialized in the first place.

Asking open-ended questions almost always leads to more questions, because the more information the consumer can get, the more she is able to understand and think through the reality. That is how to do serious research—about a dog *and* his seller.

Here are some additional questions that should be on every buyer's list:

When may I visit your kennel, shelter, or foster home?
An outright *never* should be a big, flashing warning

sign. Some breeders don't want strangers inside their kennels because the adult dogs may get scared and puppies could get hurt, but responsible breeders will show us, at least from a distance, the conditions in which the dogs are being raised.

How would you feel about the veterinarian or trainer of my choice coming with me to assess your dogs—not just the puppy I want, but his parents, too? The second part of this obviously applies to breeders instead of shelters, but it can also be enlightening to have a veterinarian or trainer by our side when we walk through a shelter or meet with a nonprofit rescuer. Any seller who refuses an independent examination of a dog (at our expense, not his) should raise serious questions in our minds.

What protocols do you follow for making sure the dog is healthy and friendly? Good answers include things like health certificates and vaccine records from veterinarians, high-quality food, toys or activities, and socialization with adults, children, and other dogs. Ask for proof. Demand to see a stack of documents, as well as videos and photographs when available. Anyone buying a dog for the first time can call a veterinarian and ask what health papers should be provided with a puppy, to be sure the seller's answer is a good one.

What references can you provide from previous buyers? Having no references is a huge warning sign for breeders, shelters, and nonprofit rescuers alike. Who would eat at a restaurant without any good reviews, or hire a handyman, let alone buy a dog who is going to become a part of our lives for more than a decade?

How are you registered as a charity? This obviously applies to rescue groups and shelters. While it does not guarantee anything about the health or temperament of a dog, it does show that the organization is not fly-by-night, and that it is likely to be a known entity with the appropriate oversight agencies.

What paperwork do you have on this dog's history? Breeders should be able to offer paperwork not only about the dog in question, but also about the dog's parents and perhaps several prior generations. Rescuers and shelters may be able to provide paperwork from other locations where the dog may have originated, or from a veterinarian who has seen the dog elsewhere, which lets buyers contact those people to see if they have any additional information about the dog.

What do you know about the dog's parents or siblings? Even rescuers sometimes know something about at least one of the dog's parents. Not all dogs in shelters are strays or singles. Entire litters of puppies are taken to shelters, sometimes with the mother dog right alongside. Buyers might be able to meet the mother or at least talk to whoever adopted the other puppies in the litter, to get a sense of their health and temperament. When adopting a puppy, ask if the mother dog, too, is available for adoption. Even if we don't want the older dog ourselves, we want to know the rescue organization is working to help more than just the fast-selling puppies.

How many breeding females do you have, and how is your kennel licensed or inspected? In most parts of the world, a number greater than four to six females on the first question usually means we are dealing with a commercial breeder versus a hobby breeder. Knowing the truth helps to determine whether state and federal inspection records may exist (in the case of commercial breeders). Those records are usually available online, free of charge, from government agencies. Beware anyone breeding more than four to six females who says he is not licensed or inspected in any way.

Please tell me the dog's price and how the money will be used. Better breeders will respond by talking about everything from the quality of dog food to the cost of genetic health tests. Better shelters and nonprofit rescuers will respond by discussing basic vaccinations, temperament testing, foster care, and things like transport expenses. Do not feel squirmy about asking a seller to defend the price of a dog. Someone charging a premium price should be able to explain why he believes he has a premium product.

What breed is the dog? This is a great question to ask even if we're not shopping by breed, because asking it can reveal as much about the seller as about the dog. Unless a blood or saliva test has been done, or a kennel club has registered the dog, there is no way to answer this question for sure. Study after study shows that judging a dog's breed by his looks is rarely accurate—a recent study showed that more than 87 percent of dogs adopted out by shelters were mislabeled, with more than twenty-five types of dogs commonly mislabeled as Pit Bulls—and yet plenty of sellers try to market dogs as purebreds or mixed breeds without actually knowing anything about their genetic heritage. An honest answer to this question, without papers or blood tests, is something along the lines of, "We're not sure, but he looks sort of like this and that, and let us tell you about his personality instead." Also, never trust the breed mixes on adoption websites like Petfinder.com; the site's input form forces rescuers to list breeds even if the rescuers have no idea what they are.

What is your system for handling dogs whose sales do not work out? Everyone dealing in dogs has had at least a few dogs returned. It happens to breeders, shelters, and nonprofit rescuers alike. The job of the conscious consumer is not only to listen to the seller's answer to this question, but also to ask to speak with any references who can verify the truth. We want to know more than what happens to us, and our money, if we return the dog. We also want to know what happens to the dog, because that tells us a great deal about the type of person doing the selling. Don't ask only about policies. Ask to hear actual stories, and get the names of other people in those stories. Contact them, too.

Why do you think this dog is a good choice for my family? People who truly care about dogs want every single one to enjoy a wonderful life, and they should be assessing us as buyers just as much as we are assessing them as sellers. The answer to this question should include information about the particular puppy's traits and how they match our own lifestyle—not "Well, he's a Schnauzer, and all Schnauzers are great," but instead, "You mentioned you like to jog, and this pup is the most active dog in the bunch. He has plenty of energy and will be able to keep up with you, and he's a good size for jogging the distance you described." The second answer shows that the seller is trying to match the right personalities, human and canine alike.

What is your live-release rate, and has it been going up or down during the past year? This is a key question to ask inside any shelter. If a shelter is killing more dogs than it saves, and if that has been the case for a number of years, then our money is likely paying the salary of a shelter director whose beliefs do not match our own. Our first call should not be to that shelter's adoption coordinator; it should instead be to the shelter director's boss, be it the city council or the mayor, demanding that he be replaced with someone who does share our belief in the worth of all dogs. A controversial, tough-love approach in this scenario is to forgo buying a dog directly from such shelters and to instead give our money to nonprofit rescue groups that are showing the community a better model for saving dogs' lives. If we see a dog we want inside a high-kill shelter, we can call a local nonprofit rescue group and ask them to help us get the dog out in a responsible way—while still demanding that the shelter director be replaced with someone who shares our commitment to all dogs.

The last, and perhaps most important, question everyone must ask before acquiring any dog is whether she fully understands what she is getting into, not just in terms of the industry but also in terms of her responsibilities as a buyer. As Donald McCaig, the defender of traditional Border Collies, puts it about people shopping for pooches, "They should ask themselves who they are and what they are willing to do for a satisfactory relation with a nonhuman animal who will live with them for more than a decade. If the answer is 'not much,' get a cat."

Everyone interviewed for this book from the rescue perspective— the people who see the result of mismatched dogs and buyers every single day—says the most important questions to ask are of oneself. All too often, the "problem dogs" are the ones who simply fail to meet unrealistic expectations, or misjudgments based on poor research and marketing hype. Some buyers think that if they spend enough money, a dog will turn out great even if he's given no training, no exercise, and an hour's worth of attention a day. That is just as crazy as believing the same would be true of a two-year-old child, which, according to some studies, has cognitive functions at a level similar to dogs.

Dog buyers must ask themselves, especially if choosing a puppy, whether they are truly ready to welcome a toddler-level, attention-demanding, sentient being with feelings into their lives. Dogs take work. Dogs cost money. Dogs need attention. Dogs require schooling. Dogs demand time that owners need to be ready to give, no matter what type of pooch they buy.

"Know what you can realistically handle with your lifestyle," says Cortney Dorney, the trainer and shelter director at WAGS in California. "Know what kind of household you have. What is your activity level? Are there kids? Is there a park where you can take the dog to play off-leash? All of our caretakers, the first question after they greet the people is, 'What are you looking for?' If somebody comes in and says, 'I'm looking for a dog I can take running, I have kids, and I have cats,' well we're going through all the dogs we have in mind. You can say you want a Beagle or a Chihuahua, but don't come in wanting the look of XYZ. Those are always the dogs that get returned. Before you even step foot in a shelter or with a breeder, think about your lifestyle."

Michelle Russillo at WAGS asks buyers to think about their lifestyle with as much detail as possible.

"What size house do you have, and what is your level of energy?" she asks. "Allergies are the second thing we think about so we don't have the dog coming back. It's tolerance to [the buyer's] lifestyle that's more important than them thinking they know the right dog for them. The other piece is: Do they understand the level of commitment in owning a dog? It takes a minimum of $500 to $1,000 a year to take care of a dog properly. Are they willing to do that instead of upping their cellphone plan? They're cute, but they're going to need medical care just like kids do."

Janis Bradley, who synthesizes dog research for the National Canine Research Council in the United States, says more and more studies are showing that the buyer's nature is ultimately more important than most dogs' nature at the time of purchase. Buyers are right to evaluate dogs and their sellers, but buyers also have to evaluate themselves with the same degree of skepticism and honesty.

"Most of what figures into whether or not the relationship is going to be successful, the lion's share of it falls on how you live with the dog," she says. "The single biggest watershed we're finding in dog behavior right now is, does the dog live as a family dog—in the house, with the people, with multiple opportunities for interaction every day—or does it just kind of live as a resident on the property? If you want a dog that's going to be happy and fit in with your family, then you'd better figure out how to integrate it into your family life. Most of the time, most of the dogs take care of the rest."

Mike Arms of the Helen Woodward Animal Center says finding the right dog is akin to finding a spouse. The decision, when made well, happens in a similar way.

"I see it all the time," he says of buyers. "They go in with something in mind because that's what they think they should have, and then they look into the eyes of some dog that wasn't even on their list, and those are always the best adoptions. In our lifetime, why is it we meet thousands of people but there's one that all of the sudden it clicks, they become our mate for life? It just happens. Let that happen when you want to get a pet, and keep in mind that this is a fifteen- or sixteen-year commitment. This is not something to play with today and discard tomorrow. Don't even go looking for a pet unless you're willing make that commitment. Then just let it happen."

CHAPTER FOURTEEN

CONSUMER INTELLIGENCE

"There is only one boss: the customer. And he can fire everybody in the company from the chairman on down, simply by spending his money somewhere else."

—*Sam Walton*

Bill Reiboldt, the Republican state lawmaker who battled against Proposition B in Missouri, took a break in March 2015 from writing about puppy farms and uploaded an article to his website titled "Condemning California Egg Regulations." It stated, "Production and marketing of eggs is big business, but now egg-producing farmers with new technologies and practices are coming under attack by animal rights activists, led in part by the well-funded, radical Humane Society of the United States."

It may have seemed odd to some of his constituents that he was focusing on a legislative battle taking place nearly two thousand miles away, but the people who own the puppy farms in Missouri cared quite a bit. If California were to succeed in passing stricter standards for how egg-laying hens must be treated, then its state law could lead to a new national standard that would force Missouri's farmers to change, too. Hens, like puppies, had become animals to which the public responded on a political scale—and had already caused a shift in business that dog breeders didn't want to see on their own farms, a shift that continues to affect some of the biggest brand names on the planet. This business reality makes the story of eggs a tale worth knowing for anyone interested in seeing life change for dogs.

In 2007, celebrity chef Wolfgang Puck committed to buying eggs from cage-free hens. His switch came at least a decade into animal welfare group efforts to raise consciousness about the stresses of industrial henhouses, with everyone from the HSUS to RSPCA Australia and various groups in Britain and Europe educating consumers about the way many egg-laying hens go through life, including living in cages so tiny the birds cannot even spread their wings (a practice called battery farming in most parts of the world). Puck made the switch to buying cage-free eggs about six months after the Ben and Jerry's ice cream brand had done the same thing. And while the move was a public relations boon for the culinary star, the problem that Puck immediately faced—and that all of the major food players who came onboard afterward would also encounter—was that there just weren't enough cage-free eggs to go around.

"It's not easy to find all the eggs you're looking for," Rob Michalak, a spokesman for Ben and Jerry's, told the *New York Times* soon after Puck's announcement. "The marketplace is one where the supply needs to increase with the demand."

At the time in America, cage-free eggs cost an extra sixty cents per dozen wholesale. Chicken farmers, who had long raised hens in cages, figured the cage-free craze might be a fad. They weren't about to toss out their cages—which they saw as a capital investment in equipment, similar to dog kennel enclosures—nor were they interested in paying for infrastructure improvements like ventilation systems to house hens cage-free without spreading disease. They hoped the cage-free trend would be a passing fad.

Fast forward to 2014, just seven years later, and the companies joining Puck and Ben and Jerry's in demanding cage-free options included McDonalds in Australia, the United Kingdom, and Europe; Burger King, Denny's, Red Robin, Subway, Dunkin' Donuts, Au Bon Pain, Whataburger, IHOP, and Sonic restaurants; Walmart, Safeway, Marks & Spencer, and many other grocery chains; Hellman's mayonnaise; Sara Lee desserts, Otis Spunkmeyer cookies, and Barilla pasta; Kraft Foods, ConAgra, Aramark, Nestle, and General Mills food manufacturing giants; Royal Caribbean and Carnival cruise lines; Virgin America Airlines; and Hyatt and Marriott hotels. These multinational businesses are not making the switch to cage-free eggs out of the goodness of their hearts. Their choices are about money. They've figured out that getting consumers to keep paying for their products means treating the egg-laying hens with respect.

As a result of this consumer-driven push for animal welfare, the percentage of hens living cage-free lives has more than doubled from 3 percent to 7 percent across America, and it's still going up. For some egg farmers in America, cage-free has grown to comprise 10 or 12 percent of their annual business. In the United Kingdom, free-range and organic eggs are now outselling eggs from caged hens altogether, having garnered 51 percent of the British market as of 2012. Though cage-free eggs still cost more, conscious consumers are continuing to show that we will buy them in greater and greater quantities. We are willing to pay an extra buck or two if we believe the hen who laid the eggs will have a better life. We are putting our money behind our values, and we are moving the market.

"This is a massive step forward for animal welfare, especially when you consider in 1995 that more than eight out of ten eggs [in Britain] were laid by hens kept in cruel barren battery cages," Alice Clark of the RSPCA told the *Daily Mail.* "Shoppers who buy cage-free eggs deserve a heartfelt thank you."

That type of continuing market shift worldwide is the only thing that could get the attention of farmers like Greg Satrum, who is the egg industry's equivalent of some large-scale puppy farmers in places like southwestern Missouri. Satrum is the third-generation co-owner of Willamette Egg Farms, Oregon's largest egg producer. In early 2013, Willamette announced it was doubling its cage-free production and building two new henhouses that would hold a total of eighty thousand birds. Not only would the new hen-houses be cage-free, but they also would be more energy efficient with features such as LED lighting.

"Building the new housing and increasing our cage-free flock to this degree is a significant investment," Satrum told the *Oregonian.* "We wanted to be proactive and get ahead of the curve, to be able to meet both the industrial and consumer demand in the years ahead."

Listen to what he's saying: His business made the switch because of consumer demand. He would never have said it, and none of the other businesses would have done it, if not for the egg buyers. Every stitch of progress started with producers and sellers wanting to keep customers happy.

Conscious consumers can next make it our business to see all sellers of dogs and puppies, all around the world, treating the dogs with the respect we demand. We already know we can do it, in part, through our individual purchases. We are proving it with the hens.

Here are two ideas for how we can all work together to get every seller's attention when it comes to our pooches.

It's a great time to be a buyer of anything in this world, because crowdsourcing is the most powerful force of consumer information the planet has ever known. From Amazon.com to Hotels.com, we sit at our computers in Boston and Bonn and Brisbane, and we share what we know with one another, for the good of us all. *This product worked as-advertised. That customer service was great. This refrigerator repeatedly breaks down, so don't waste your money. That hotel room is convenient but could use a quieter air-conditioning system.* Gathering our opinions into a usable, helpful format on this scale was impossible in decades past, but today, thanks to technology, we rate everything from products to plumbers online. We give them one to five stars, we explain our experiences, and, as a whole, the system separates the wheat from the chaff.

Companies that continually earn just one or two stars don't stay in business for long. Suppliers of everything from lawnmowers to honeymoon suites are being forced to improve their offerings as well as their policies for ensuring customer satisfaction. If they don't, we'll let their other potential customers know and business will dry up fast.

At the same time, we consumers are able to be far smarter shoppers because the information at our disposal is exponentially greater than ever in human history. If we choose to be diligent in our research, we really can spend our money in ways that support our values thanks to our fellow consumers worldwide who share their experiences online, too.

All of which makes it so hard to understand, with so many of us dog lovers out there, why we have not yet applied this crowdsourcing concept to pooches. They're a multibillion-dollar global business, with breeders and rescuers alike operating across state and national boundaries. What is stopping us from using the same approach to sharing what we know and putting the worst sellers out of business everywhere?

Perhaps we've not thought to crowdsource what we know about the sellers of dogs because, in our hearts, we don't think of our pets as products. It feels weird to rate them, or where they originated, the same way we'd rate the durability of their beds or the adjustability of their collars or the nutritional content of their food. It honestly doesn't occur to many of us to do it.

Perhaps we haven't crowdsourced our knowledge because some keepers of breed standards don't want us sharing what we know on a global level and have encouraged us to do other types of limited "research" instead. Until now, they've been able to carve us up into controlled markets. Many kennel clubs have not been willing to release public lists of problem breeders, even the ones they know are the worst. It doesn't take a doctoral degree to see that if the AKC or Britain's Kennel Club distributed a public-access ranking of the worst offenders, other breeders would likely pull their financial support for the groups, which are supposed to be defenders, not exposers, of the people offering purebreds for sale.

Perhaps we haven't crowdsourced our knowledge because the directors of some shelters aren't interested in our learning how they really spend our tax dollars, because if enough of us exposed the truth about the level of killing still going on in some places, the outrage would put the directors out of their jobs and pensions. Instead, they teach us to think "Adopt, Don't Shop," which is an admirable sentiment, but also one that keeps us from looking any deeper into what's really happening in the worst shelters today. It's the easy, uncomplicated way to make us feel like we've done our part without doing any actual research.

Perhaps the reason we haven't crowdsourced our information is polarization, the "us versus them" mentality that chokes us when it comes to breeder dogs versus rescue dogs in more and more nations. Groups like the HSUS put out lists of puppy mills, but there's no list of the worst shelters coming from advocacy groups. They keep that information quiet. Nobody relying on donations to support his rescue-based job wants to be seen as failing to solve the problems on his own side of the fence, and a website telling the truth about all sides—that there is good and bad happening everywhere—would be wildly off-message for most of today's dog industry leaders.

Luckily for us, we don't need any of them to make this happen. We can do it ourselves, for free, with just a few minutes of our time. It starts today.

This book is being published in conjunction with the launch of a website, DogMerchants.com, where all of us can share our knowledge through ratings. We can promote the best breeders and rescuers, and we can put their irresponsible counterparts out of business through honest, product-style reviews. Please log on and take a look. Our combined clicks will take minimal time and will have maximum impact for the health and welfare of dogs all around the world.

Think about all we'd know if we simply compiled the knowledge in one place. Just as we dog lovers are the biggest financial force for pups around the globe, we also are the biggest repository of information about pooches and the people who sell them. Some thirty million of us buy dogs every year. If the average pooch's lifespan is a decade, then the equivalent of the entire population of the United States of America is currently a dog owner somewhere on planet Earth. Collectively, we dog lovers are an encyclopedic force of information that has yet to be harnessed and deployed for the greater good. If even 10 percent of us are willing to answer a few quick questions on DogMerchants.com to rate the place where our dog originated and tell other buyers how our dog is doing over time, then the site will fast become the biggest international database of information about dogs the world has ever known, available for every dog buyer to see, every minute of every day, for free.

DogMerchants.com is an important tool for several reasons beyond the obvious shopping advantage. The first reason is that, no matter how loudly we scream from the skies that it's a huge mistake to buy dogs via the Internet, some people are still going to do it. It's going to happen with rescue dogs and breeder dogs alike, and the trend is only likely to amplify as the "digital native" generations become adults. The click-to-buy habit stuns even the biggest sellers of dogs today, including the team at the Hunte puppy distribution company, where vice president Ryan Boyle admits, "Mr. Hunte says his one big miscalculation in all these years is that he never thought someone would buy a puppy without seeing it and holding it in his arms." Abby Anderson, who co-owns the commercial Sugarfork Kennels in Missouri, says she, too, is continually astounded that people will put a thousand or two thousand dollars on a credit card to buy a puppy sight unseen. "We live in the age of convenience," she says of buyers. "They want it online and sent to them." Even if we can't get it through our heads to stop buying puppies this way—because it gives the worst offenders a way to hide the truth about how they treat their dogs—we can at least have online reviews easily accessible to encourage click-to-buy consumers to spend their money in the right places.

The second reason DogMerchants.com is an important tool is because even those of us who are local to a breeder, shelter, or rescue group and go in person to examine the property and people as well as the dog for sale can't possibly figure out everything on our own. While some sellers are honest, we all know we live in a world where others are not, and some people are pretty darn savvy about pulling the wool over our eyes. The bad guys often look just like the good guys. It's their superpower. Their kryptonite is our talking with one another and exposing their shenanigans. Some of us are going to think of things, and notice things, that others among us don't. Even if we are neighbors on the same street, we can often communicate more clearly by having our information organized digitally. If just two of us visit the same seller and upload what we know, then all of us will have twice as much information ahead of the next sale to help us decide whether or not to hand over our money.

The third reason DogMerchants.com is an important tool is that over time, we have seen that the biggest controllers of the dog industry rely on databases for their internal advantages in shaping the marketplace. Dogs are no longer a small, fancier affair. The notion that we buyers should be researching them in a small, personal way is at best quaint and at worst naïve. Everyone from the kennel clubs to the shelters are keeping global databases, figuring out what we're buying, where to get the best supply of those types of dogs, and how to market them to us. We need to put the database concept to work for us—and for *all* the dogs—instead of only for the good of business interests trying to control market share.

DogMerchants.com has been designed as a quick, click-the-box solution that lets users register and then rate the place where they got their dog. Users can upload photos as well as videos, and can talk about whatever they feel is important for other buyers to know. Comments can include information about the dog's health and temperament, as well as the source's honesty and business practices. Users also can leave a simple one-to-five star rating and move on with no further comment, an effort that takes perhaps one minute at most and could help countless other buyers avoid a untrustworthy seller.

If all of us dog lovers combine our knowledge about sellers in this single place, DogMerchants.com, then we will quickly create the world's largest-ever database of information on the subject. We'll no longer have to take anyone's word for the truth. We'll no longer have to trust the sales pitch. We'll have the data ourselves.

This isn't hard. This is business—the business of the conscious consumer who loves dogs.

The other big thing that must change on a global scale is the mass media's tendency to promote some dogs as better than others simply because of the way they look. This notion is the biggest marketing asset for the least-responsible breeders everywhere. It's also the most insidious stereotype that keeps so many homeless dogs' lives in jeopardy. Hobby breeders can continue to hold conformation dog shows—that's their right under the law, for now—but when those shows are put on prime-time television and the winners are paraded around the morning news, the result is thousands upon thousands of dogs being produced in copycat fashion and sold by some truly unscrupulous people. What is happening inside some breeders' homes may, in fact, be a hobby, but when it is shown on television, it becomes a financial bonanza for a global industry.

Calling for a boycott of beauty pageant shows like Crufts and Westminster won't change the current reality; we saw as much in Britain, after the *Pedigree Dogs Exposed* blowup, when the most pressure that frustrated dog lovers could bring to bear was a brief moratorium on the show's television presence. We also can't click a Delete key and make these types of dog shows go away. They make too much money for the networks that air them.

Instead, from a purely business perspective, the smartest option is to replace these shows, and the income they generate, with an alternative for the financial interests that rely on them—and then vote with our viewership to have advertisers follow us, in support of all dogs instead of just some.

Here's one way we could do it: Think about the *Idols* television show concept, which is known as *SuperStar* in some parts of the world. It's a singing competition that started in 2001 in Britain as *Pop Idol*, and it has grown into versions called *American Idol, Canadian Idol, Bangladeshi Idol, Nigerian Idol, Pakistan Idol,* and so on, with about fifty world regions watching in some one hundred and fifty countries and an estimated six billion or more viewers. It's the same format in nation after nation, tweaked just a bit for cultural sensibilities. It works, and it gets huge ratings.

Now think about replacing the singers with pooches in a series of next-generation dog shows called *Best Dog America, Best Dog Australia, Best Dog France,* and so forth, featuring all the best dogs in every nation judged not by their looks but instead in terms of health, temperament, and skills.

The *Best Dog* shows could be managed by a combination of an *Idols*-type producer and an X Games–type producer, updating the tone and style of the old-school dog show into something more exciting and modern, similar to the way the *Idols* series updated the age-old talent show and the X Games modernized the Olympics with new events. Sexy graphics, great music, and innovative camera angles with slow-motion replays of dogs doing fantastic tricks and stunts would snap our brains out of the tired routine of pageantry-style dog shows and wake us up to the fact that there is, in fact, a different way to attract a huge dog-loving audience to mass media during prime-time viewing hours. Yes, some agility-based shows are already on television, but dogs doing sports moves and other tricks needn't be relegated to Saturday-afternoon programming if television producers take a state-of-the-art approach. We can, and should, demand an annual show that is at least as polished as the one put on by the Westminster Kennel Club.

In terms of scheduling, the *Best Dog* shows could air every time there is a Westminster-, Crufts-, or FCI–sanctioned show held anywhere in the world, in the exact same time slot, on the exact same days. Advertisements would encourage us to "vote by remote" for which show we want to watch, and we'd show business interests worldwide where we really stand on the treatment of dogs when we're given a fair choice in the matter. Television networks could keep the old-school dog shows on the air, of course, but quite a lot of us will have changed the channel. We don't have to protest, and we don't have to scream. The networks, and their advertisers, will hear the deafening silence of us tuning our attention elsewhere, and the change we want will happen. Again, it's just good business.

Imagine it: Dogs competing in the *Best Dog* shows could be any breed or mix of breeds, since they would not compete in breed classes. They would do things like agility, obedience tricks, and demonstrations of being respected members of their communities— things that actually matter to us when we bring a dog into our lives. The format, like the *Idols* format, could be tweaked a bit here and there for cultural norms. For example, in America, where Pit Bulls currently face enormously unfair stereotypes, there could be a category for Best Pit Bull and Child Trainer Team. In South America, where more people than anywhere else list "breed for commercial gain" as a primary reason to own a dog, there could be a category that features the Healthiest Purebreds from Brazil to Chile—rewarding breeders who put dogs' health before profit. In the Middle East, where dogs traditionally have not been pets but more and more people are now buying them for protection, categories could include Most Responsible Training of a Guard Dog. And so forth, all around the globe.

We'd of course need big names to kick off the inaugural event, just as the *Idols* series regularly features singing stars mixed in among the contestants to get us to watch. Here are just a few possibilities we could hear coming over the loudspeaker in the voice of an announcer as practiced as Westminster's Michael LaFave, if some dog-loving celebrities were willing to participate:

> *Before the dogs take the ring, film stars Jake Gyllenhaal and Bradley Cooper will demonstrate the agility jumps in a short race.*
>
> *Who will run faster in response to the command "come," our dogs or movie heartthrob Orlando Bloom?*
>
> *Let's see if former television host Jon Stewart can catch more flying discs than our last-place dogs in that event.*
>
> *Camera 1, let's check in over at the Sit and Stay competition. Amazing! It's been ten minutes and Fido is still sitting while Broadway star Bernadette Peters sings and dances around him!*
>
> *Film actor Ryan Reynolds will now try to outmatch our best dock-diving dog in a twenty-five-meter pool race.*
>
> *Here to demonstrate the Most Sits and Downs in Sixty Seconds competition is comedian Ricky Gervais.*
>
> *Country singer Miranda Lambert will now present the award for Healthy Dogs Who Live the Longest.*

Who will respond faster to the command "go lie in your bed," our dogs or television host Ellen DeGeneres?

Who can catch more tennis balls in sixty seconds, our dogs or comedian Kathy Griffin?

Celebrity chef Jet Tila will now try to sniff out the hidden piece of sausage faster than our nosework-trained dogs.

Which contestant can do the best dance routine in three minutes, our dogs or singer Justin Bieber?

Film star Katherine Heigl will now judge our Best Display of Affection by a So-Called Dangerous Breed.

Singer Sarah McLachlan will now present the award for the happiest, most effective animal welfare commercial.

It takes precious little imagination for most dog lovers to embrace a concept like this, to see how giving awards for ability, responsibility, and inner qualities differs from judging dogs by their looks. Such a concept has never evolved from the old-school dog shows for two reasons: because no television producers have been willing to stand up and acknowledge that the dog shows are really about the business of setting the top-dollar dog market prices, and because we consumers haven't yet proved that we are going to put our money behind the alternative. We're still giving big television ratings to shows like Westminster and Crufts, which means we're still buying into what they're selling. Too many business interests are protecting their livelihoods, and too much money is at stake for one of the most sought-after products in the world.

Ultimate change on a mass-media scale has to come from us, the conscious consumers, demanding a new option. We have to show breeders and shelter directors and media advertisers alike that we will no longer pay to support the global market as it exists today. Offer us a better option, one that makes all dogs' lives better, and we'll take it every time. We'll give you our billions of dollars' worth of business, with pleasure. We'll tune in with television ratings that decimate previous records.

Perhaps the first television commercial might look something like this:

> *A shiny, "champion" dog is sitting on a dock at a Southampton summer house. He's being pampered by a well-dressed trainer attaching a blue ribbon to his collar.*
>
> *The dog looks downright bored.*
>
> *Along comes a flurry of running and playing dogs who are catching flying discs, doing dock diving, and nailing incredible agility moves. Some are purebreds, some are mutts. Their ears are flapping. Their lips are blowing in the breeze. They are as filled with life and fun as a dog could possibly be.*
>
> *The champion looks around, still sitting pretty, but confused. The trainer seems annoyed. She scowls at the ruffians making such a ruckus.*
>
> *Suddenly, a dock-diving dog makes a big splash in the lake. Water washes over the trainer's head. She crinkles her face like a schoolteacher who has just been hit by a water balloon, soaked from her hairdo to her sensible shoes.*
>
> *A voiceover comes up in a deep male baritone, the kind we all associate with a professional sports event: "Who are you going to root for, dog lovers? The so-called champions, or the real players?"*
>
> *The text fades in: Best Dog America, Best Dog Britain, Best Dog Canada, Best Dog everywhere.*
>
> *Because all kinds of dogs are the best, and all kinds of dogs deserve to be cheered.*

A NOTE ABOUT SPAY/NEUTER

My previous dog book, *Little Boy Blue,* included extensive reporting about the importance of spaying and neutering dogs, and about the positive impacts the surgery can have on the financial burdens and killing levels in shelters. No matter what type of dog you buy, please get your dog spayed or neutered. If you are uncertain about the concept, then look at it from a financial perspective, knowing everything you've just read about the complexities of the global dog industry. Unwanted litters of puppies only contribute to the existing problems, creating expenses and heartache that can easily be avoided.

ACKNOWLEDGMENTS

Countless people involved with dogs worldwide helped to make this book possible. Breeders, rescuers, government officials, attorneys, researchers, and everyday dog lovers often have wildly disparate opinions about what is in the best interest of dogs, and many of these people entrusted me with the stories of dogs from their perspectives, even if they knew I might personally disagree with them. I am grateful for their insights and their openness, for the sake of dogs everywhere.

Gwen Moran, Salley Shannon, Cheryl Alkon, and Mary South encouraged me to get the best possible representation for this book, and I was thrilled to land Scott Mendel of Mendel Media Group as my literary agent. His assistant, Elizabeth Dabbelt, flagged my proposal. Scott believed in this book from the start, helped strengthen my original proposal, and shepherded the final manuscript through easy and trying times alike, always with grace and skill. Jan Constantine, general counsel for The Author's Guild, and attorney John R. Firestone at Pavia & Harcourt LLP provided invaluable advice when challenges arose. Members of the ASJA Contracts & Conflicts Committee were always close by with smart ideas about contract negotiations.

Jessica Case and Claiborne Hancock at Pegasus Books championed this book not only because they appreciated the journalism that went into the manuscript, but also because, as fellow dog lovers who believe in animal welfare, they are keen to make the world a safer and better place for pups everywhere. Also at Pegasus, Michael Fusco put great thought into creating a smart jacket design, Maria Fernandez contributed her eagle eyes to page proofs and typesetting, and Phil Gaskill scoured the pages for every last typo during proofreading. Iris Blasi in marketing offered smart ideas for helping the book get traction in the marketplace.

Special thanks to copy editor Noelle Barrick at Sunflower Editorial Services for her smart edits and overall support for the project, and to attorney Alan J. Kaufman, who reviewed the manuscript and gave sage advice on how to report key sections.

Also deserving of special thanks is Eric Lowenhar at Barron's Educational Services, who continued to offer ideas that will benefit not only this book, but also my previous dog book, *Little Boy Blue*. Angela Tartaro, the editor of *Little Boy Blue*, also continues to champion my work and is a source of great support and friendship.

Fellow dog lover Debbie McManus at Book Expo America helped me see the bigger marketplace so my book can stand out in the crowd. Dave Sheingold is the most talented data geek I know and was a huge help with everything from Excel spreadsheets to big-picture editing. Gina Lamb is one of the sharpest line editors I've ever met and not only lent her careful eye to the first-draft manuscript, but also helped in selecting a title and cover concept.

Dan Merton at LS Media helped me envision the website Dog-Merchants.com, and Nicole Zeno and her team at Z2 Media made my vision a reality. I appreciate their attention to detail as well as their help with big-picture ideas.

Jennine Semanchik and Stacy Weiss constantly encourage me and are always available to help me relax with a glass of wine after a long week of writing. Jo Coudert, who died during the final editing stages of this book, was an exceptional writer and friend whose wisdom will remain with me for the rest of my life. Luisa Matarazzo trades insights from her own writing life to help make mine even more fulfilling. Mary Turkus is also a good friend and offers great insight into the world of bookstores.

Jeanne Craig and Lara-Jo Houghting made smart observations about everything from titles to early marketing videos. The Atomic Engineers are a great source of support, with special thanks to Gwen Moran, Amy Hill Hearth, Jen Miller, Kris Baird Rattini, and Lillian Africano for their feedback on early marketing concepts; to Caren Chesler, Pat Olsen, and Frances Benson for suggestions about getting cover blurbs; and to Leah Ingram for ideas about perfecting my promotional materials.

Marine magazine colleague Patrick Sciacca was helpful in selecting a cover concept, and he along with Dan Harding, Jake Lamb, Kenny Wooton, and Andrew Parkinson were endlessly generous about deadlines when I needed to take my focus off boats and place it wholly onto helping dogs. Eric Powell shared his expert knowledge of stock art, which helped me make polished promotional videos and more.

My parents, Marc and Donna Kavin, and my sister, Michelle Kavin, are my biggest fans, even when we argue at the dinner table about whose pups are best. I love them—and their purebred dogs—dearly.

Last but not least, my mutts Blue and Ginger watch me type until precisely four o'clock every afternoon, when they sit, stare, and bark at me until I step away from the computer. They then insist on a spirited walk along one of our many wooded local trails, and also a swim in a river or lake whenever possible. I may have saved their lives by choosing to bring them into my home, but they save me from myself every day. They are survivors whose hearts are filled with courage, honesty, and joy, and they are forever my inspiration.

BIBLIOGRAPHY

NEWSPAPERS, MAGAZINES, JOURNALS
All Animals Magazine
Art Das Kunstmagazin
The Atlantic
The Bark
Battle Creek Enquirer
The Believer
Best in Show Daily
Beton
Bloomberg Business
The Boston College Chronicle
The Boston Globe Magazine
Centre Daily Times
Chattanooga Times Free Press
The Chicago Tribune
The Christian Science-Monitor
Citations
The Columbian
Country Life
The Daily Mail
DogWorld
Forbes
Issaquah Press
Japan Today

Kennel Spotlight
Las Vegas Review-Journal
Livingston County Daily Press and Argus
Los Angeles Times
The Marietta Daily Journal
Metropolitan Barcelona
New York Post
The New York Times
The New Yorker
Orange County Register
The Oregonian
Orlando Sentinel
People
The Pet Press
Philadelphia Business Journal
Psychology Today
Radio Times
St. Louis Magazine
The Seattle Post-Intelligencer
The Seattle Times
The Sun Chronicle
Time
USA Today
USA Weekend
U-T San Diego
The Wall Street Journal
The Warwick Beacon

BOOKS

Anderson, Chris. *The Long Tail: Why the Future of Business is Selling Less of More*. New York: Hyperion, 2006.

Brandow, Michael. *A Matter of Breeding: A Biting History of Pedigree Dogs and How the Quest for Status Has Harmed Man's Best Friend*. Boston: Beacon Press, 2015.

Christakis, Nicholas A., and James H. Fowler. *Connected: The Surprising Power of Our Social Networks and How They Shape Our Lives—How Your Friends' Friends' Friends Affect Everything You Think, Feel and Do*. New York: Back Bay Books, 2011.

Dean, Josh. *Show Dog: The Charmed Life and Trying Times of a Near-Perfect Purebred*. New York: It Books, 2012.

Derr, Mark. *A Dog's History of America: How Our Best Friend Explored, Conquered, and Settled a Continent*. New York: North Point Press, 2004.

Duhigg, Charles. *The Power of Habit: Why We Do What We Do in Life and Business.* New York: Random House, 2012.

Gorant, Jim. *The Lost Dogs: Michael Vick's Dogs and Their Tale of Rescue and Redemption.* New York: Gotham, 2011.

Grimm, David. *Citizen Canine: Our Evolving Relationship with Cats and Dogs.* New York: PublicAffairs, 2014.

Hare, Brian, and Vanessa Woods. *The Genius of Dogs: How Dogs Are Smarter Than You Think.* New York: Dutton, 2013.

Hibbing, John R., and Kevin B. Smith. *Predisposed: Liberals, Conservatives, and the Biology of Political Differences.* New York and London: Routledge, 2013.

Kavin, Kim. *Little Boy Blue: A Puppy's Rescue from Death Row and His Owner's Journey for Truth.* Happauge, NY: Barron's Educational Services, 2012.

Kerpen, Dave, and Theresa Braun. *Likeable Business: Why Today's Consumers Demand More and How Leaders Can Deliver.* New York: McGraw-Hill, 2012.

Leonard, Christopher. *The Meat Racket: The Secret Takeover of America's Food Business.* New York: Simon and Schuster, 2014.

Lindstrom, Martin. *Brandwashed: Tricks Companies Use to Manipulate Our Minds and Persuade Us to Buy.* New York: Crown Business, 2011.

McCaig, Donald. *The Dog Wars: How the Border Collie Battled the American Kennel Club.* Hillsborough, NJ: Outrun Press, 2007.

Pacelle, Wayne. *The Bond: Our Kinship with Animals, Our Call to Defend Them.* New York: HarperCollins, 2011.

Rhyne, Teresa J. *The Dogs Were Rescued (and So Was I).* Naperville, IL: Sourcebooks, 2014.

Ritvo, Harriet. *The Animal Estate: The English and Other Creatures in the Victorian Age.* Cambridge, MA: Harvard University Press, 1987.

Underhill, Paco. *Why We Buy: The Science of Shopping.* New York: Simon and Schuster, 2008.

Winograd, Nathan. *Redemption: The Myth of Pet Overpopulation and the No Kill Revolution in America.* Brea, CA: Almaden Books, 2009.

NEWS ORGANIZATIONS AND WEBSITES

ABC News
The Associated Press
Ballotpedia
BBC News
Boston.com
Dogster
The Huffington Post

Mashable
National Geographic News
News.com.au
Newsmax
PetPlace
Philly.com
PoliticMO
RocketNews24
Science Daily
Seattlepi
Slate
Today
Vetstreet
VoiceofOC
WBIW
WCAX
WDRB
WebMD
WLKY
WRCB
Yahoo Sports

PRINT AND ONLINE ARTICLES

"About 350 Dogs Rescued from 'Deplorable' Kennel." *Marietta Daily Journal,* July 17, 2014.

Abraham, Marc. "Puppies to Parliament after 100,000 Sign Online Petition." Vetclick, November 26, 2013.

Allen, Lindsay. "Poodles Rescued from Paoli House Covered in Feces and Maggots." WDRB, May 14, 15, and 19, 2014.

Antenucci, Antonio, and David K. Li. "More Young Women Choosing Dogs over Motherhood." *New York Post,* April 10, 2014.

"Banana Joe Meets the Press." *Sun Chronicle,* June 2, 2014.

Bates, Doug. "Breeders Howling at Oregon AKC Judge." *Oregonian,* April 2, 2009.

Bradley, Theresa, and Ritchie King. "The Dog Economy Is Global—But What Is the World's True Canine Capital?" *Atlantic,* November 13, 2012.

Brekke, Kira. "Sarah McLachlan: 'I Change the Channel' When My ASPCA Commercials Come On." Huffington Post, May 5, 2014.

Briquelet, Kate. "Jets Fans Trash New Quarterback Michael Vick." *New York Post,* March 23, 2014.

Brown, Abram. "Sochi Olympics: Russian Billionaire Is Trying to Save the Stray Dogs." *Forbes,* February 6, 2014.

Busbee, Jay. "How to Adopt a Sochi Stray Dog." Yahoo Sports, February 8, 2014.

"Canine Parvovirus." WebMD, 2007.

Carroll, Matt. "Championship Dog Breeder Sues Over Lost Sperm Samples." *Centre Daily Times*, October 11, 2012.

Clegg, Cara. "500 Cats and Dogs Legally Killed in Japan Each Day, but One Organization Says No More." *Japan Today*, August 1, 2013.

Cohen, Ben. "Banana Joe's Westminster Show Win Set Off a Frenzy for Affenpinschers." *Wall Street Journal*, February 11, 2014.

Colker, David. "An Outpouring from Readers over Tales of Puppy Problems." *Los Angeles Times*, April 20, 2008.

Cooper, Rob. "Free Range Eggs Outsell Those from Caged Hens for the First Time." *Daily Mail*, February 17, 2012.

Coren, Stanley. "Do We Treat Dogs the Same Way as Children in Our Modern Families?" *Psychology Today*, May 2, 2011.

———. "How Many Dogs Are There in the World?" *Psychology Today*, September 19, 2012.

Couloumbis, Angela. "Chihuahuas Get Big: Taco Bell Dog Spurs Revolution." Philly.com, August 3, 1998.

"Court Docket: Sentencing Today for Alleged Puppy Mill Operator." *Battle Creek Enquirer*, July 17, 2014.

"Crufts Attendance and Viewing Figures Soar This Year." *DogWorld*, March 11, 2014.

Cuddy, Beverley. "Controversy over BBC's Purebred Dog Breeding Documentary." *The Bark*, September–October 2009.

Dean, Josh. "How to Win the Westminster Dog Show." Slate, February 10, 2012.

Dockterman, Eliana. "Finally, Mutts Can Compete in Westminster Dog Show." *Time*, January 16, 2014.

Dodd, Johnny. "Meet the Billionaire Saving Sochi's Strays." *People*, February 28, 2014.

"Dog Semen Lawsuit: Linda Blackie, Miriam Thomas Sue Vet Over Destroyed Poodle Samples." Huffington Post, October 12, 2012.

"Dogs' Intelligence on Par with Two-Year-Old Human, Canine Researcher Says." *Science Daily*, August 10, 2009.

"Dotty about Dalmatians." *Country Life*, April 26, 2014.

Eccles, Louise. "Crammed into Filthy Cages on Squalid Polish Puppy Farms, the Dogs Destined to Be Sold in Britain at a Huge Profit." *Daily Mail*, April 4, 2014.

Fackler, Martin. "Japan, Home of the Cute and Inbred Dog." *New York Times*, December 28, 2006.

"Financial Advice Causes Off-Loading in the Brain." *Science Daily*, March 27, 2009.

Gale, Alastair. "Dog Meat Issue to Hound 2018 Winter Olympics." *Wall Street Journal* Asia, February 10, 2014.

Garrick, David. "Has San Diego Pet Store Ban Built Momentum Against Puppy Mills?" *U-T San Diego*, July 12, 2014.

"A Generation Born to Buy?" *Boston College Chronicle*, November 5, 2004.

Gillet, Kit. "Bucharest to Start Killing Stray Dogs." *Columbian*, September 10, 2013.

Gillham, Omer. "Hunte Opens Doors to Huge Facility." *Tulsa World*, November 18, 2007.

Golden, Lori. "Behind the Scenes with TV's Top Dog: From Troubled Terrier to Canine Comedian." *Pet Press*, November 2002.

Good, Dan. "Meet America's Top Dog, Sky, the Wire Fox Terrier." ABC News, February 11, 2014.

Grier, Peter. "Westminster Dog Show 2011: Can My Dog Join Westminster Kennel Club?" *Christian Science Monitor*, February 15, 2011.

Grogan, John. "Woodson and Me." *USA Weekend*, December 21, 2008.

Hageman, William. "Mixed Reactions to Shelter Mutts." *Chicago Tribune*, July 1, 2013.

Hall, Chris. "Greed and Power are Behind the Stray Dog Extermination in Sochi." *Dogster*, February 7, 2014.

Hartley, Eric. "Lawsuit Challenges Euthanasia Practices at O.C. Animal Shelter." *Orange County Register*, August 21, 2014.

Hartmann, Ray. "Puppy-Mill Fiasco Shows the True Colors of the Missouri Legislature." *St. Louis Magazine*, June 21, 2011.

Hebert, Steve. "Old Foes Square Off over Issue of Puppies." *New York Times*, October 30, 2010.

Hilario, Francis. "165,000-square-foot Target Coming to King of Prussia." *Philadelphia Business Journal*, July 23, 2014.

"Homer Tops TV Favourites Poll." BBC News, June 12, 2003.

Hughes, Clyde. "Westminster Adding Mongrels, but Forget about Best-in-Show Mutt." Newsmax, January 16, 2014.

Judd, Ron. "Pet Attorney Is Raising the Bar on What Beloved Pets Are Worth." *Seattle Times*, January 24, 2014.

Kagarise, Warren. "Shelters Join Forces to Find Homes for Chihuahuas Seized in Issaquah." *Issaquah Press*, June 8, 2012.

Kedmey, Dan. "Burger King and Tim Hortons Tie the Knot." *Time*, August 26, 2014.

"A Kennel with Comfort." *Art Das Kunstmagazin*, August 2002.

Kirk, John. "Android's Penetration vs. Apple's Skimming Marketing Strategies." Tech.pinions, March 21, 2013.

Khuly, Patty. "The Great Debate: Are Mutts Healthier Than Purebreds?" Vetstreet, January 6, 2012.

Leach, Paul. "Filthy Kennels Described as 'Petri Dishes' as Breeder Arrested, Charged with Animal Cruelty." *Chattanooga Times Free Press*, June 14, 2014.

Lennon, Vince. "Puppy Mill Owner Charged with One Count of Animal Cruelty." WRCB News, June 12 and 13, 2014.

Lieber, Jill. "Pekingese Looks to End Career with Westminster Prize." *USA Today*, February 13, 2006.

"Louisville Woman Faces Charges after Filthy, Malnourished Dogs Discovered." WLKY News, May 19, 2014.

Mathewson, William. "With Right Tactics, It's Easy to Market a Three-Legged Cat." *Wall Street Journal*, March 6, 1970.

Mayo, Keenan. "Want a Dog Like Banana Joe? There Are 7 for Sale in America." *Bloomberg Business*, February 13, 2013.

McDonald, Christi. "Landmark Decision Sets Precedent for the Dog World." *Best in Show Daily*, undated, retrieved September 26, 2014.

"McDonalds Australia Announces Move towards Using Cage-free Eggs by 2017." News.com.au, September 13, 2014.

McGlensey, Melissa. "These Shelter Dogs 'Rescue' Office Workers from Their Sad, Lonely Cubicles for Lunchtime Walks." Huffington Post, June 20, 2014.

Mead, Nick. "Left Behind: Barcelona's Strays." *Metropolitan Barcelona*, August 26, 2010.

Midura, Kyle. "15 Treated after Vermont Puppy Tests Positive for Rabies." WCAX News, October 23, 2013.

Miller, Joe. "Britons Spend More Time on Tech Than Asleep, Study Suggests." BBC News, August 7, 2014.

"Missouri Dog Breeding Legislation: Proposition B (2010)." Ballotpedia, undated, retrieved August 26, 2014.

"More Than 350 Dogs Seized from Suspected Puppy Mill." *USA Today*, July 18, 2014.

Mortenson, Eric. "Cage-free Eggs Find a Perch in a Changing Market." *Oregonian*, February 27, 2013.

Mott, Maryann. "Sick Puppies Smuggled from Mexico for Sale in U.S." *National Geographic News*, January 30, 2006.

Neiswender, Kate. "Imagining a World without Dominion: Part I." *Citations*, May 2013.

Nir, Sarah Maslin. "Tired of Sad Ads, Kennel Club Takes 'Dog with Smile' Tack." *New York Times*, February 11, 2012.

Orlean, Susan. "The Dog Star: Rin Tin Tin and the Making of Warner Brothers." *New Yorker*, August 29, 2011.

"Pakistan Idol Talent Show Is Broadcast for First Time." BBC News Asia, December 6, 2013.

Palma, Kristi. "Attleboro's William Truesdale talks about his Westminster Best in Show Winner Banana Joe." Boston.com, February 13, 2013.

Petronzio, Matt. "U.S. Adults Spend 11 Hours a Day with Digital Media." Mashable, March 5, 2014.

Pulkkinen, Levi. "Animal Cruelty Charges Filed against Issaquah Dog Breeder." *Seattle Post-Intelligencer,* May 7, 2012.

Regan, Helen. "In Argentina, a Court Grants Sandra the Orangutan Basic Rights." *Time,* December 21, 2014.

Robins, Sandy. "First Mutt Census Reveals Strong DNA Trends." *Today,* April 4, 2011.

Rodrigues, Jen. "Advocates at Odds over Dog Quarantine." *Warwick Beacon,* April 3, 2014.

Roose-Church, Lisa. "Dogs Taken from Livingston Puppy Mill Settle into New Homes." *Livingston County Daily Press and Argus,* June 16, 2014.

Rossen, Jeff, and Patel, Avni. "AKC-Registered Breeders Raising Dogs in Miserable Conditions." *Today,* May 1, 2013.

Sandomir, Richard. "No Ordinary Affenpinscher, Banana Joe Is Named Best in Show." *New York Times,* February 13, 2013.

Severson, Kim. "Suddenly, the Hunt is On for Cage-Free Eggs." *New York Times,* August 12, 2007.

"Shelter in Berlin-Falkenberg." Beton.com, undated, retrieved September 11, 2014.

Shrieves, Linda. "Eddie, the Dog on 'Frasier,' Is a Star and a Handful." *Orlando Sentinel,* December 16, 1993.

Smith, Stephen. "60 Puppies Killed in Truck Fire." Associated Press, August 15, 2006.

Strom, Stephanie. "Ad Featuring Singer Proves Bonanza for the ASPCA." *New York Times,* December 25, 2008.

———. "Nestle Moves toward Humane Treatment of Animals at Its Suppliers." *New York Times,* August 20, 2014.

Stutz, Howard. "Baccarat Helps Drive Nevada Gaming Revenue to $11 Billion in 2013." *Las Vegas Review-Journal,* January 31, 2014.

Susman, Tina. "Mixed Breeds (a.k.a. Mutts) Take the Field at Westminster Dog Show." *Los Angeles Times,* February 8, 2014.

Thomas, Chloe. "Dog Lover Fogle Who 'Couldn't Stop Crying' When His Labrador Died Backs BBC for Axing Crufts Show Because of Over-Breeding." *Daily Mail,* October 18, 2012.

Trebay, Guy. "From Woof to Warp." *New York Times,* April 6, 2003.

Unferth, Deb Olin. "Gary Francione." *Believer,* February 2011.

Venning, Annabel. "The First Top Dog in Hollywood: Cited in a Divorce Case, He Had 40 Million Fans and Drank Milk from a Champagne Glass." *Daily Mail,* January 21, 2012.

Vo, Thy. "County Faces $2.5 Million Animal Abuse Suit." Voice of OC, August 21, 2014.

Vranica, Suzanne, and Jens Hansegard. "IKEA Discloses an $11 Billion Secret." *Wall Street Journal*, August 9, 2012.
Warrick, Pamela. "Frasier's Best Friend 'Eddie' Dies." *People*, June 26, 2006.
Williams, Laura. "Animal Shelters Fear Rise in Homeless Dalmatians after '102 Dalmatians.'" PetPlace, undated, retrieved February 15, 2014.
"Woman Arrested in Paoli Animal Abuse Case." WBIW News, May 19, 2014.
"The Woman Who Brought Crufts to Heel." *Radio Times*, February 27, 2012.
Yokley, Eli. "Should There Be a Constitutional Right to Farm? Missouri Voters Will Decide in August." PoliticMO, July 9, 2014.

GOVERNMENT AND INDUSTRY REPORTS, PRIVATE LAWSUITS, AND RESEARCH STUDIES

Ads of the World. "Territorio de Zaguates: Unique Breeds." February 2013.
Advocates for Animals. "The Price of a Pedigree." 2006.
American Pet Products Association. "2011–12 National Pet Owners Survey." 2012.
———. "2013–2014 APPA National Pet Owners Survey." 2014.
American Veterinary Medical Association. "Pet Purchase Protection Laws." June 2014.
Baumeister, Roy, E. Bratskavsky, C. Finkenauer, and K. D. Vohs. "Bad Is Stronger Than Good." *Review of General Psychology*, 2001.
Better Business Bureau. "The Puppy Industry in Missouri: A Study of the Buyers, Sellers, Breeders and Enforcement of the Laws." March 2010.
Calboli, Federico C.F., Jeff Sampson, Neale Fretwell, and David. J. Balding. "Population Structure and Inbreeding from Pedigree Analysis of Pure-bred Dogs." *Genetics*, March 1, 2008.
Considine and Considine Certified Public Accountants. Independent Auditor's Report, Helen Woodward Animal Center, 2012–2013.
Euromonitor International. "Pet Care in India." September 2014.
———. "Pet Care in the Philippines." January 2014.
The European Pet Food Industry. "Facts and Figures: Statistics Underline the Importance of Pets in Animal Society." 2012.
Gureckis, Todd M., and Robert L. Goldstone. "How You Named Your Child: Understanding the Relationship between Individual Decision Making and Collective Outcomes." *Cognitive Science Society*, 2009.
Herzog, Harold. "Forty-Two Thousand and One Dalmatians: Fads, Social Contagion, and Dog Breed Popularity." *Society and Animals*, 2006.
Humane Society of the United States. "101 Puppy Mills: A Sampling of Problem Puppy Mills in the United States." May 2014.
———. "Pets by the Numbers." January 30, 2014.
Humane Trends. "Number of Animals Killed in the Shelter System." August 15, 2011.

International Companion Animal Management Coalition. "Humane Dog Population Management Guidance." Undated, retrieved March 8, 2015.

International Federation for Animal Health Europe. "Companion Animals."
Undated, retrieved March 11, 2015.

Marketing Society Awards for Excellence. "Pedigree: Making the Brand a
Dog's Best Friend." Undated, retrieved September 6, 2014.

McDonalds. "What Makes McDonalds?" December 23, 2013.

Natoli, Eugenia, Simona Cafazzo, Roberto Bonanni, and Paola Valsecchi. "The
No-Kill Policy on Free-Ranging Dogs in Italy Revisited on the Basis of
21 Years of Implementation." 2012.

Office for National Statistics. "Population and Household Estimates for the
United Kingdom." March 2011.

Office of Missouri Governor Jay Nixon. "Gov. Nixon Issues Statement on
Missouri Solution." April 27, 2011.

Pet Advertising Advisory Group. "What to Do If You've Bought an Ill Pet."
Undated, retrieved September 11, 2014.

PetSmart Charities. "Pet Adoption and Spay/Neuter: Understanding Public
Perceptions by the Numbers." November 27, 2012.

Rhode Island Veterinary Medical Association. "RI DEM, Department of Health
and RIVMA Urge Rhode Islanders to Utilize Best Management Practices
When Adopting a Pet." Undated, retrieved August 24, 2014.

Rooney, Nicola, and David Sargan. "Pedigree Dog Breeding in the UK: A
Major Welfare Concern?" Royal Society for the Prevention of Cruelty
to Animals, 2009.

Royal Society for the Prevention of Cruelty to Animals. "Guide to Choosing
Cage-Free Eggs." Undated, retrieved September 17, 2014.

———. "The Puppy Trade in Europe." 2008.

Savino, Stephanie K. "Puppy Lemon Laws: Think Twice Before Buying that
Doggy in the Window." *Penn State Law Review*, fall 2009.

Statista. "Leading Pet Specialty Chains in North America in 2014, Based on
Number of Stores." Undated, retrieved November 19, 2015.

———. "Market Share of the Leading Brands for Dry Dog Food in the
United States in 2013, Based on Sales." Undated, retrieved September
6, 2014.

Statistic Brain. "Animal Shelter Statistics." July 13, 2014.

United States Department of Agriculture. "USDA Restores Important Check
and Balance on Retail Pet Sales to Ensure Health, Humane Treatment."
September 10, 2013.

United States Department of Treasury, Internal Revenue Service. Form 990,
American Society for the Prevention of Cruelty to Animals, 2013.

———. Form 990, Humane Society of the United States.

———. Form 990, North Shore Animal League America Inc.

United States District Court, Arizona. "Jodell Martinelli, Stephanie Booth, Melia Perry, Abbigail King, Nicole Kersanty, and Ruth Ross, on Behalf of Themselves and All Others Similarly Situated, vs. Petland Inc. and the Hunte Corporation, ABS Corps 1-100; and John Does 1-100." March 16, 2009.

United States District Court, Eastern District of Virginia. "United States of America v. Michael Vick, aka Ookie," Summary of the Facts, August 24, 2007.

Watt PetFood Industry. "2012 Top Petfood Companies." December 5, 2011.

ADVOCACY ARTICLES AND MARKETING PAMPHLETS

AKC Gazette, Secretary's Page, January 2013.

American Kennel Club. 2013 Annual Report.

———. "New York Bill Will Impose Mandatory Microchipping and Enrollment in State Registry." *AKC News*, February 5, 2007.

———. "Purebred Alternative Listing/Indefinite Listing Privilege." Undated, retrieved August 20, 2014.

American Society for the Prevention of Cruelty to Animals. 2013 Annual Report.

———. "Groundbreaking Bill Extends Federal Protections to Pets of Domestic Violence Victims." August 18, 2014.

Animal Legal Defense Fund. "Animal Law Courses." Undated, retrieved August 23, 2014.

Animal Welfare Institute. "The South Korean Dog Meat Trade." Undated, retrieved August 20, 2014.

Arms, Mike. "We Can Make a Difference." WhatWouldMikeSay.com, July 7, 2011.

Balzar, John. "A Brave Voice Against Puppy Mills." *All Animals Magazine*, November 12, 2009.

Canidae Natural Pet Food Company. "The Highest-Paid Animal Actors." May 23, 2013.

Canine Semen Bank of Columbus. "About Frozen Semen." CanineSemenBank. com, 2009.

Cryocel.com. "Advantages of Using Frozen Semen." Undated, retrieved August 12, 2014.

———. "International Regulations." Undated, retrieved August 12, 2014.

DogJudges.com. "Leininger, Mrs. Betty Regina." Undated, retrieved March 13, 2015.

Fédération Cynologique Internationale. "International Breeding Rules of the FCI." November 2014.

GermanShepherds.com. "History of the Breed." June 1, 2008.

Harrison, Jemima. "The Discredited Breeder Scheme, a Kennel Club Disgrace." PedigreeDogsExposed.blogspot.com, December 17, 2013.

Hughes, Bob. "Auction! Auction!" *Kennel Spotlight,* April–May 2012.

Hughes, Jim. "Gypsy." *Kennel Spotlight,* February–March 2013.

———. "I Hate Retirement!!" *Kennel Spotlight,* October–November 2013.

Humane Society of the United States. 2013 Annual Report.

———. "Clark, Ros-Lehtinen Bill Protects Domestic Violence Victims and Pets." humanesociety.org, March 5, 2015.

———. "A Horrible Hundred: Selected Puppy Mills in the United States." May 2013.

———. "Iowa Gov. Culver Signs Bill to Combat Puppy Mills." March 9, 2010.

———. "Progress for Egg-Laying Hens." July 7, 2014.

———. "Puppy Mills: Frequently Asked Questions." August 30, 2012.

HumaneWatch. "HSUS Lawsuit Against Petland: Dismissed in Large Part (the Second Time)." 2010.

———. "The 'Missouri Solution' Wins." April 30, 2011.

Jim Crow Dogs. "Rhode Island Has Passed Emergency Regulations." April 28, 2012.

Kavin, Kim. "The Good, the Bad, and the Biters." *Boston Globe Magazine,* May 12, 2013.

The Kennel Club. "History of the Kennel Club." Undated, retrieved March 13, 2015.

Korea Animal Rights Advocates. "Current Situation of Korea's Dog Meat Industry." Undated, retrieved August 20, 2014.

Lichtenberg, Debora. "Westminster Allows Mutts—Sort of, but Is It Just a Distraction?" *PetsAdviser,* January 22, 2014.

Mahaney, Patrick. "All-American Dogs at the 2014 Westminster Kennel Club Dog Show." *Positively,* undated, retrieved September 6, 2014.

"Maneka Claims Cabinet Post for Animals." *Animal People,* October 1998.

Mars, Inc. "Pedigree Brand Launches the Pedigree Feeding Project to Help More Dogs Find Loving Homes." October 2012.

Mountain, Michael. "The Westminster Freak Show." Earth in Transition, February 10, 2013.

Ng, Vincent. "Fear-Based Marketing: Is It a Matter of Life or Death?" MCNG Marketing, January 9, 2013.

Oxford-Lafayette Humane Society. "Animal Overpopulation." Undated, retrieved March 14, 2015.

People for the Ethical Treatment of Animals. 2014 Financial Statement.

Pet Industry Joint Advisory Council. "PIJAC Appoints Edwin Sayres as President and CEO." August 25, 2014.

PetSmart Charities. "Saving Lives One Trip at a Time." Undated, retrieved September 3, 2014.

Polsky, Richard M. "The San Francisco Dog Mauling." sfdogmauling.com, undated, retrieved March 8, 2015.

The Puppy Mill Project. "AMW Hunte Corporation." Undated, retrieved September 2, 2014.

Reiboldt, Bill. "Capitol Report by Bill Reiboldt." *Kennel Spotlight*, April/May 2012.

———. "Condemning California Egg Regulations." billreiboldt.com, March 3, 2015.

RSPCA Australia. "End Puppy Farming—The Way Forward." November 2010.

Schneider-Louter, Annigje. "History of the First Lhasa Apso Kennel in the Netherlands." el-minjas.com, August 9, 2013.

Sheller, Mary Ann. "Freezing Future Friends (or How to Make a Pupcicle)." Undated, retrieved August 10, 2014.

United States Border Collie Club. "A Short History of the Border Collie and the AKC." bordercollie.org, undated, retrieved March 8, 2015.

Westminster Kennel Club. "Border Collie Wins First Westminster Agility Championship." Undated, retrieved September 6, 2014.

———. "Westminster Facts and Figures." Undated, retrieved March 13, 2015.

Winograd, Nathan. "Who Is Nathan Winograd? The Middle Years." nathanwinograd.com, February 15, 2013.

Wise, Steven M. "Update on the Sandra Orangutan Case in Argentina." nonhumanrightsproject.org, March 6, 2015.

World Dog Show. "Interview with Mieke Cooijmans, Breeder of Banana Joe V Tani Kazari." March 20, 2014.

Yankee Shelties. "Retail Rescue Raises Its Ugly Head Again." yankee-shelties. com, undated, retrieved March 8, 2015.

TELEVISION SHOWS, RADIO PROGRAMS, AND FILM DOCUMENTARIES

Beardsley, Eleanor. "In France, the (Abandoned) Dog Days of Summer." National Public Radio, July 11, 2012.

Charles, Dan. "What the Rise of Cage-Free Eggs Means for Chickens." National Public Radio, June 27, 2013.

CNBC and USA Network. "Westminster Kennel Club Dog Show, 2014."

———. "Westminster Kennel Club Dog Show, 2015."

Passionate Productions. *Pedigree Dogs Exposed*, 2008.

———. *Pedigree Dogs Exposed: Three Years On*, 2012.

SOURCES

INTRODUCTION

xiii   "The American sector is the most saturated, with about half the households owning a dog": Humane Society of the United States, "Pets by the Numbers."

xiii   "Continental Europe and the United Kingdom are still growing as markets, with about a quarter of the households owning a dog": Office of National Statistics; Coren, "How Many Dogs Are There in the World?"

xiii   "some thirty million pet dogs are brought home around the world every year": ibid.; Humane Society of the United States, "Pets by the Numbers"; International Federation for Animal Health Europe; American Pet Products Association, "2013–2014 APPA National Pet Owners Survey"; Bradley and King.

xiii   "millions more pups would be needed annually to satisfy consumer demand": Pacelle, p. 306.

xiv   "somewhere in the vicinity of $11 billion each year": This estimate is based on sources including, but not limited to, American Pet Products Association, "2011–12 National Pet Owners Survey"; American Pet Products Association, "2013–2014 APPA National Pet Owners Survey"; Euromonitor International; the Royal Society for the Prevention of Cruelty to Animals; the European Pet Food Industry; price research on independent dog-sale websites worldwide, such as petfinder.com and puppyfind.com.

xiv   "about the same value as the global IKEA brand": Vranica and Hansegard.

xiv   "brought in on gaming revenues in 2013": Stutz.

xiv   "to buy Tim Hortons": Kedmey.

xiv   "smuggling operations everywhere from Missouri to Mexico to Poland": Mott; interview with Julie Sanders.

xiv   "scope of multinational corporate control over the meat supply": Leonard.

xv   "was selling as many as ninety thousand puppies a year": interview with Ryan Boyle of the Hunte Corporation.

xv   "auctioned a single dog for $12,600": Southwest Auction Service marketing materials.

xv   "$6 million facility": interview with Jerry Rosenthal of Monmouth County
        Society for the Prevention of Cruelty to Animals.

CHAPTER ONE: SETTING THE BASE PRICE
4   "brought in $514,371": Southwest Auction Service marketing materials.
4   "English Bulldog who went for $12,600": ibid.
8   "living in conditions that did not meet federal standards": United States
        Department of Agriculture, Animal Plant Health Inspection Service (APHIS)
        records search.
9   "largest, most successful USDA-licensed dog auction in the United States": ibid.
9   "Jim Hughes was a middling college student": Jim Hughes, "I Hate
        Retirement!!"
10   "Jim, meanwhile, was doing everything": ibid.
11   "airing on television in 1948": westminsterkennelclub.org, "Westminster Facts
        and Figures."
11   PetSmart and Petco have more locations than Petland: Statista, "Leading Pet
        Specialty Chains."
12   "Jim bought a half million dogs": Jim Hughes, "Gypsy."
12   "Southwest Missouri is still considered the epicenter": Better Business Bureau.
12   "in the early 2000s": interview with Bob Hughes.
12   "Bob worked for DoBoTri": interview with Bob Hughes.
13   "Chadd was offering one of his Bull Terriers": advertisement in *Kennel
        Spotlight*, October/November 2013.
13   "brought in nearly a quarter million dollars": Bob Hughes.
14   "nearly one out of three dogs in the auction that day did": Southwest Auction
        Service auction-day pamphlet.
16   "gave birth to six puppies just four days later": interview with Jane Rosenthal.
23   "just over $110,000": original reporting at the October 5, 2013, auction.

CHAPTER TWO: LUXURY PACKAGING
25   "only thirty-five breeds appeared (and a portion of proceeds were donated)":
        westminsterkennelclub.org, "Facts and Figures."
26   "describes himself as having spent thirty-five years": CNBC and USA
        Network, Westminster Kennel Club Dog Show, 2015.
26   "included 127 from beyond America's borders": westminsterkennelclub.org.
27   "known for bringing his private Gulfstream jet": Josh Dean, "How to Win the
        Westminster Dog Show."
28   "Michael LaFave, a breeder himself": Westminster Kennel Club Dog Show
        marketing materials.
30   "which dates from 1877": westminsterkennelclub.org, "Facts and Figures."
32   "she'd had great success after breeding Peter's daughters": McDonald.
32–33   "conceived from frozen semen in 1981": Canine Semen Bank of Columbus.
33   "has a preinsemination application it asks breeders to use": Cryocel.com,
        "International Regulations."
33   "allows some national kennel clubs to permit insemination": Fédération
        Cynologique Internationale.
33   "purebred dog getting herpes": Cryocel.com, "Advantages of using frozen semen."
33   "had been accidentally thawed": Huffington Post.
33   "widely reported as more than $300,000": ibid.; McDonald; Carroll.
34   "by claiming they could have made $5,000": ibid.

109   "multiyear refund guarantee against genetic health problems": original interview with Michael Stolkey.

109–111 Story of Andrew Hunte: original interview with Greg Brown.

112   "a two-hundred-seat chapel is on site": original reporting during a tour with Michael Stolkey and Greg Brown.

CHAPTER SEVEN: MARKETING THE MESSAGE

116   "eighty-sixth competition win" and the story of Banana Joe: CNN; Sandomir; World Dog Show.

116   "wasn't allowed to spend a single day": *Sun Chronicle*.

118   "precisely seven Affenpinscher puppies were for sale": Mayo.

118   "International Canine Semen Bank": Palma.

119   "'America's Dog' was going to the Netherlands": ibid.

119   "He isn't really what we call a player": ibid.

119   "high mortality rate at birth": Cohen.

119   "inside the home of Jude Daley": ibid.

120–121 Story of Shiloh: original interview with Pati Dane.

120   "from about eight thousand puppies a year to nearly forty-three thousand": Herzog.

121   "Dalmatian rescuers were already seeing the spotted puppies": original interview with Pati Dane.

121   "Humane Society of Boulder, Colorado, saw a 310 percent spike in Dalmatian drop-offs. The Humane Society of Tampa Bay in Florida said its increase was 762 percent": Williams.

121   "British Dalmatian Welfare, for one, reported a sharp increase": *Country Life*.

124   "One Chihuahua rescuer in New Jersey": Couloumbis.

124   "second only to the cartoon dad Homer Simpson": BBC News.

124–125 Story of Moose: Golden; Shrieves; Warrick.

126–127 Story of Rin Tin Tin: Orlean; Venning; Canidae Natural Pet Food Company; germanshepherds.com.

128   "to the Guggenheim Museum in Manhattan": Trebay.

128   "Yakee If Only": Lieber.

128   "their skulls are what veterinarians call brachycephalic": Mountain; Advocates for Animals.

128   "Brachycephalic dog breeds include": The Daily Puppy, undated.

131   "Burn the witch!": Radio Times.

131   "the fallout from her documentary was swift and severe": Cuddy.

132   "apparently been common practice to get the look": Passionate Productions, *Pedigree Dogs Exposed: Three Years On*.

133   "Imperial College London study": Calboli et al.

134   "former Crufts host Ben Fogle": Thomas.

134–135 "record 4.6 million people reportedly tuned in to watch Crufts in 2014": DogWorld.

135   "Westminster Kennel Club issued more than seven hundred press credentials": westminsterkennelclub.org.

135   "About twenty thousand dogs were registered to compete in the 2014 FCI World Dog Show": worlddogshow2014.fi.

135   "Tricky Ricky's father, Banana Joe": Mieke Cooijmans Facebook post, August 12, 2014.

149   "One longtime purebred seller from a conservative region": original reporting in Southwest Missouri.

CHAPTER NINE: THE UPSTART COMPETITOR

153   "Reiboldt is as much of a homegrown local": billreiboldt.com autobiography, retrieved August 22, 2014.
154   "Proposition B, the Puppy Mill Cruelty Prevention Act": Ballotpedia.
154   "they would have preferred something more neutral": Yokley.
155   "trend in syntax that, by 2010, extended far beyond Missouri's borders": Humane Society of the United States, "Iowa Gov. Culver Signs Bill to Combat Puppy Mills."; RSPCA Australia.
155   "He said the group spent $4.85 million campaigning for Proposition B:" Reiboldt, "Capital Report by Bill Reiboldt."
155   "Other sources put the figure closer to $2 million": HumaneWatch, "The 'Missouri Solution' Wins."
156   "Not only is HSUS seeking to limit our state's legislative process": Reiboldt, "Capitol Report by Bill Reiboldt."
156   "The governor ultimately issued a statement": Office of Missouri Governor Jay Nixon.
156   "removed the fifty-dog limit along with specifics for exercise and rest": Hartmann.
157   "describes itself as the nation's leading advocate for legislation to regulate puppy mills": Humane Society of the United States, "Puppy Mills: Frequently Asked Questions."
157   "HSUS received more than $130 million in contributions, grants, and bequests, right behind the $140 million or so that the nearly 150-year-old ASPCA reported": 2013 Annual Reports, HSUS and ASPCA.
158   "the AKC had consolidated total revenues of $64.6 million": 2013 Annual Report, American Kennel Club.
158   "cripple and then destroy all animal agriculture": Reiboldt, April–May 2012.
159–161 Story of Tracy Cotopolis: original interview.
160   "Rescue Waggin' has transported more than seventy thousand dogs since 2004": PetSmart Charities, "Saving Lives One Trip at a Time."
160   "some five million unique page views a month": Quantcast, September 1, 2014.
163   "Parvo is highly contagious, swiftly debilitating, and expensive to treat": WebMD.
164   "trying to standardize the way small-scale rescues operate": Rhode Island Veterinary Medical Association.
164   "working to institute regulations for temperament testing in Massachusetts": Kavin, 2013.
164   "at least fifteen people had to undergo precautionary rabies shots": Midura.
165   "It's ridiculous. It's discriminatory": Rodrigues.
165   "barbarians are at the gate": Jim Crow Dogs.
167   "kill rates are as high as 95 percent unless the nonprofit rescue groups step in": Kavin, "The Good, the Bad, and the Biters."
167   "The leading cause of death for healthy dogs in the United States": Winograd, p. 2.
167–168 Biography of Nathan Winograd: nathanwinograd.com.
168   "the cities of Delhi, Chennai, and Jaipur": Animal People.
168   "Italy banned the killing": Natoli et al.

168   "Spain's first to ban killing": Mead.
169   "killing has been reduced from hundreds of animals a year to fewer than ten":
       Clegg.
169–171 Tour of and statistics about Monmouth County Society for the Prevention of
       Cruelty to Animals: original reporting and interview with Jerry Rosenthal.
173–174 Tour of Homeward Bound Adoption Center: original reporting.

CHAPTER TEN: REPACKAGING AND REBRANDING
176   "it sprang from the brain of Jake Barrow": McGlensey.
176–177 Description of Human Walking Program: original reporting with Jake Barrow
       and Martha Coro.
179   "Dietrich Bangert to design its multimillion-dollar facility": Art Das
       Kunstmagazin.
179   "The Berlin shelter holds about 1,400 animals": Beton.
179   "about the size of the largest Target retail store": Hilario.
180   Description of Territorio de Zaguates unique breeds campaign: Ads of the World.
181–183 Story of Mike Arms: whatwouldmikesay.com; original interview with Arms.
182   "same concept as bringing any product to the public": Mathewson.
183   "had annual income of more than $36 million and its president earned nearly
       $350,000": United States Department of Treasury, North Shore Animal
       League America Inc., Form 990.
183   "about the same as the one given to Wayne Pacelle": United States Department
       of Treasury, Humane Society of the United States, Form 990.
183   "less than half of the $713,166 in annual salary and other compensation":
       United States Department of Treasury, American Society for the Prevention of
       Cruelty to Animals, Form 990.
183   "Sayres left the rescue segment of the dog business to become president and
       CEO": Pet Industry Joint Advisory Council.
184   "proceed to pillage and profit": Yankee Shelties.
184   "management salaries and benefits totaled $373,420": Considine and Considine.
187–188 Story of first Westminster Kennel Club Dog Show Masters Agility Champion-
       ship: Dockterman; Grier; Clyde Hughes; Susman; westminsterkennelclub.org,
       2014; Lichtenberg; Mahaney.
189   "dog snobbery and elitism": Lichtenberg.
189   "Westminster spokespeople had a decidedly different attitude": Nir.
189   "Pedigree's parent company ranks number one among all pet food companies":
       Watt Petfood Industry; Statista, "Market Share."
190   "starting the Pedigree Feeding Program": Mars, Inc.
190   "Brand trust went up six points": Marketing Society Awards for Excellence.

CHAPTER ELEVEN: LEMONS VERSUS STEALS
192–195 Story of Cassidy: original interview with Kathy Cain.
196   "a $2.5 million ongoing lawsuit brought against the facility in 2014": Hartley; Vo.
196–201 Story of Westminster Veterinary Group and WAGS: original interviews with
       Tia Greenberg, Michelle Russillo, and Cortney Dorney.
201–203 Story of Senior Dogs Project: original interview with Teri Goodman.
203–206 Story of Peace of Mind: original interview with Cari Broecker.
206   "covered under the Sale of Goods Act": Pet Advertising Advisory Group.
207   "the laws began to appear in the early 1990s": Savino; American Veterinary
       Medical Association.

207   "outpouring of reader mail was so overwhelming": Colker.
208   "like turning in a lemon automobile for a gleaming new model": Grogan.
210   "a Pennsylvania family adopted a mixed-breed puppy at about ten weeks old":
       This story is taken from the author's experience as the foster mom for the
       puppy in question.

CHAPTER TWELVE: THE GENESIS AND THE FUTURE
214–216 Story of Kate Neiswender: original interview with Kate Neiswender.
216   "stems from the Law of the Twelve Tables": Grimm, p. 135.
216   "Byzantine emperor Justinian I sponsored": original interview with Kate
       Neiswender.
218   "including Charles Darwin": Grimm, p. 64.
218   "more than a hundred exist in the United States, along with similar curricula":
       Animal Legal Defense Fund.
218   "China, as an example, is undergoing this transformation": original interview
       with David Favre.
219   "being the family dog, who is often already treated like a human child":
       Antenucci and Li.
219   "American Veterinary Medical Association is against the concept": Grimm, p. 223.
220   "Adam Karp in the Pacific Northwest": Judd.
220   "Massachusetts-based attorney Steven M. Wise": nonhumanrightsproject.org.
221   "Gary L. Francione": Unferth.
221   "living property": original interview with David Favre.
222   "about seventy thousand Beagles alone are used in US laboratories": Rhyne.
223   "details were gruesome": Gorant.
223   "longtime fans selling their season tickets in disgust": Briquelet.
223–226 Story of Rebecca Huss: original interview with Huss.
227   "Twenty-seven states do today": Humane Society of the United States,"Clark,
       Ros-Lehtinen Bill Protects Domestic Violence Victims and Pets."

CHAPTER THIRTEEN: SMART SHOPPING
235   "equal in status to children": Coren.
235   "More Young Women Choosing Dogs over Motherhood": Antenucci and Li.
236   "to study trends in AKC dog registrations between 1946 and 2001": Herzog.
236   "The nickname long tail comes from the shape of the graph": Anderson.
237   "We do it when picking baby names": Gureckis and Goldstone.
237   "We do it when deciding whether or not to take up the habit of smoking":
       Christakis and Fowler.
237   "shifts in preferences for some types of dogs show the boom-bust patterns":
       Herzog.
238   "pixie dust phenomenon": Lindstrom, p. 154.
239   "Listerine's marketing team coined the scary-sounding term": MCNG Marketing.
240   "more and more research is proving this notion false": Khuly.
241   "perceived justification symbols": Lindstrom, p. 51.
241   "children who can recognize logos by eighteen months old": Boston College
       Chronicle.
242   "part of the cognitive process actually shuts down": Science Daily, "Financial
       Advice Causes Off-Loading in the Brain."
251   "toddler-level": Science Daily, "Dogs' Intelligence on Par with Two-Year-Old
       Human, Canine Researcher Says."

INDEX

ABOUT THE AUTHOR

K im Kavin is an award-winning writer, editor, photographer, and website developer with a degree from the University of Missouri School of Journalism. Her 2012 book, *Little Boy Blue: A Puppy's Rescue from Death Row and His Owner's Journey for Truth*, helped pressure a taxpayer-funded animal shelter to end the use of its gas chamber. ForeWord Reviews named *Little Boy Blue* the best pet book in the United States, and the book earned the Merial Human-Animal Bond Award from the Dog Writers Association of America. Kim lives in western New Jersey with her mutts, Blue and Ginger. Learn more at DogMerchants.com.